THE
DIRECT
MARKETER'S
WORKBOOK

THE DIRECT MARKETER'S WORKBOOK

Herman Holtz

John Wiley & Sons
New York   Chichester   Brisbane   Toronto   Singapore

Library of Congress Cataloging-in-Publication Data
Holtz, Herman.
    The direct marketer's workbook.

    Includes index.
    1. Direct marketing.   I. Title.
HF5415.126.H65   1986   658.8'4   86-13340
ISBN 0-471-83066-6
ISBN 0-471-85032-2 (pbk.)

Printed in the United States of America

10 9 8 7 6 5 4 3 2

PREFACE

MARKETING AND ITS DIRECT RELATIONSHIP TO SUCCESS

Probably no business or career activity is as closely related to the success of both organizations and individuals in organizations as is marketing. If the organization fails to manage its marketing successfully superlative management in all other departments will avail the organization and the individuals little in the way of success. Ergo, to that extent at least, helping you to success is a major goal of this book. And a large part of that help requires that this book furnish answers to many questions. For example, just what *is* marketing and, especially, what is direct marketing? Is it really concerned only with sales and customers? What tools and other resources do you need? Where can you find them? Where else can you get help— suppliers and support services, for example—when you need it?

In these pages you will find the answers to these and many other related questions to help you create and manage direct-marketing campaigns, organizations, and staffs to help carry out the campaigns.

WHAT IS MARKETING?

We tend to use the term *marketing* interchangeably with the term *sales* and think of it as an activity of profit-making ventures. But it is not only businesses—for-profit organizations, that is—who market and must do so to even survive, let alone prosper. Most organizations, including nonprofit groups and even certain government agencies such as the U.S. Postal Service and the U.S. Federal Supply Service, now have marketing departments, whether so-called or not. Nor are the words *marketing* and *customer* always the terms used in describing the objectives of marketing—what it seeks to achieve or create—except perhaps allegorically. For example, marketing by military organizations (who often commission major advertising agencies to create campaigns for them) is called *recruiting*—attracting enlistees to the service. Marketing by associations means signing up new members, referred to euphemistically as *membership-drives.* In organizations supported by grants and/or donations, marketing means gaining grantors and donors through *fund drives.* In politics it is called *campaigning,* winning both donors and voters to causes and candidates.

Marketing is itself a major industry in the United States. Although it is an integral and internal function of most organizations (most have at least one individual and larger organizations an entire department charged with the function), all require at least some assistance and services from suppliers, and many "contract out" for all or nearly all their marketing needs. There are, therefore, many thousands of enterprises based solely on the provision of marketing supplies and services, supporting the marketing efforts of others, and often taking over the entire function for others. This includes many consultants, service firms, manufacturers, and suppliers who market to marketers. Marketing organizations make extensive use of computers, computer software, printing, mailing and commercial advertising; sundry services, equipment, and manufacturing of items used as premiums; and supplies and services connected directly and indirectly with all of those. And there are also a number of periodicals—from simple newsletters to expensive, slick magazines—dedicated to marketing.

WHY DIRECT MARKETING?

Direct marketing (also referred to as *direct-response marketing*) is as old as commercial enterprise itself. The earliest peddler who sold on a street corner, from a cart, or by knocking on doors was marketing directly—actively and aggressively pursuing customers and closing sales directly. (Of course, in that sense beggars are also direct marketers, whether they sell pencils or simply solicit handouts.)

There is more than one reason for turning to direct marketing, as compared with the indirect methods of marketing through multilayered networks of distribution channels and outlets. One compelling reason is that certain types of goods and services are extraordinarily difficult to sell by other means because they require a "hard sell," demonstration, lengthy and detailed explanations, or other such special methods. Another is that in some cases the field is unusually competitive and for that reason requires the more aggressive marketing mode. And a third reason is that in many cases the marketer simply prefers to use direct-marketing methods, believing them to be more effective, more efficient, or more desirable for another reason.

Examples can be found everywhere—as in-store demonstrations, on late-night TV, at fairs and conventions, in door-to-door selling, at seminars and lectures, via telephone calls, and in many other ways in which the seller solicits sales through direct contacts with prospects, even through the mail. In fact, although it is easy enough to draw a line between marketing in general and direct marketing, in the latter there are different schools of marketing, and the distinctions tend to become somewhat blurred here.

MAIL ORDER, DIRECT MAIL, AND DIRECT MARKETING

Although we use the term *direct marketing* we are usually referring to *direct mail*. That is because direct mail dominates the direct-marketing scene; direct marketing is the general term, and direct mail or mail order is by far the major subset of that term. (Some marketers distinguish the two from each other by identifying *mail order* as a method that makes the solicitations via advertising in "mail order" sections of periodicals, whereas *direct mail* makes the solicitations by mailing catalogs and other literature to the prospects.)

A typical issue of *DM NEWS*, a popular trade paper (tabloid) that uses the subtitle "The Newspaper of Direct Marketing," demonstrates that rather quickly. Virtually every news item, feature article, and advertisement of a typical 76-page issue concerns direct mail activities and/or suppliers of support services to direct-mail marketers. Coverage of "telemarketing" (direct marketing via telephone calls) and other variants of direct marketing are few and scattered, evidence again of the dominant role of direct mail in direct marketing.

In light of all this you may expect to find the bulk of information and services for direct marketers to be concerned with direct mail and mail order. Which brings us to the topic of why this book is offered and what it is expected to do for you.

One major objective of this book is to persuade you to avoid "reinventing the wheel"—spending time, money, and energy designing that which has already been designed and is available— which so many of us do when we fail to become aware of and use what is already at hand. This book is to offer help in avoiding that futile act of reinvention by providing a complete collection of basic tools and directory of resources already available to use in planning and carrying out direct marketing campaigns of all kinds. In these pages you will find the distilled wisdom of a great many experienced direct marketers presented as ideas, examples, samples, worksheets, forms, planning guides, and lists of sources and resources. Here you will find at least the definitive nucleus of almost every kind of tool you will need to plan, implement, and carry out your direct marketing campaigns, from ideas for writing effective copy to worksheets to help you analyze your marketing problem and synthesize a strategy and campaign idea. Whether your need is to find sources for unusual premiums, to seek out suppliers of rare and unusual mailing lists, to find unusual locations for trade shows, to develop new and different campaign ideas, or to do any of the many things required of you every day, you will find help in these pages. In each case you are free to borrow the ideas and information whole or adapt them to your own needs and purposes.

Finally, although it is addressed primarily to professionals in direct marketing and not intended as a how-to book or primer on the subject, this book will be especially valuable to the reader not yet well experienced in this field: While it offers an assortment of basic specific tools and techniques that otherwise require many years to acquire through experience and accretion, it also offers relevant explanations and rationales of each of these.

HERMAN HOLTZ

Silver Spring, Maryland
September 1986

CONTENTS

1

THE WORLD OF
DIRECT MARKETING
AN ORIENTATION

A brief appreciation of and realistic look at this special
world of creative marketers.

WHY DIRECT MARKETING?

Direct marketers usually choose to market directly for any or all of three reasons:

> The goods or services they handle can be sold effectively (or most effectively) only by direct marketing.
>
> The marketer believes the goods or services can be sold effectively (or most effectively) only by direct marketing.
>
> The marketer simply prefers to market directly for rational and/or emotional reasons.

Each of these premises merits some examination and discussion:

It is true that many items can be sold far more effectively by direct marketing than by any other method and, in some cases, can be sold effectively only by direct marketing. For example, although some stores do manage to sell vacuum cleaners in their retail establishments, traditionally vacuum cleaners are sold primarily by door-to-door salespeople.

On the other hand, other major appliances such as washing machines are almost always marketed through normal retail channels.

Many enterprises began with direct marketing through necessity — because they lacked the means to market in any other way. Becoming successful, they are understandably reluctant to abandon what has been a successful method. And so they continue to market in the same manner, although perhaps with some concessions to more modern methods of marketing. For example, whereas the Fuller Brush Company formerly used small product brochures and urged "high pressure" methods on their dealer-salesmen, today they publish a multicolored catalog and use much "softer" selling methods.

A FEW FOR-INSTANCES

Some outstanding examples of such direct marketing include, in addition to Fuller Brush products, Avon cosmetics, Mary Kay cosmetics, Amway household products, Tupperware, and Fingerhut. In fact, once you could be assured that as soon as you bought a new automobile you would be getting Fingerhut literature offering you plastic seat covers at a bargain price. But with the introduction of vinyl for automobile seats, the need for protective seat covers declined and Fingerhut diversified into a large and highly successful direct-mail operation. (Unlike the others named here, all of whom are manufacturers of the products they sell, Fingerhut is a sales distributor of a variety of products manufactured by others, and one distinguishing characteristic of Fingerhut is the inclusion of listed and surprise gifts with every order.)

SOMETIMES CIRCUMSTANCE COMPELS THE DECISION

In some cases, a new item creates its own market success almost immediately because the public easily perceives the benefit and embraces the item. The TV set is a good example. Despite the initial high price of a TV receiver, the public embraced the item immediately, as it did the videocassette recorder-player (VCR) later, and many other items. On, the other hand, some items such as teflon-coated cooking utensils and the heavy cast aluminum pots and pans—"club aluminum"—did not receive that instant warm welcome because the public at large did not automatically perceive some great benefit in owning the items, although they did later become market successes, if not spectacular victories of marketing.

One circumstance that has had decisive effects on some of the older methods is the economic situation in general, as it has been developing over the postwar decades and as it affects the attitudes and actions of job-holders. There are two factors involved here: (1) In recent years it has become increasingly difficult to find salespeople who are willing to accept jobs requiring the difficult door-to-door selling; (2) with steadily increasing numbers of women returning to work in business and industry, fewer and fewer adults are at home to answer knocks on the door during daytime hours, making the door-to-door solicitation even more difficult. (Maxwell Sroge, a direct-mail expert, is quoted in the business press as estimating that no adult is home during business hours in 70 percent of the households today.)

As a result of this, Fuller Brush (owned today by Sara Lee), after 80 years of selling exclusively via door-to-door salespeople-dealers, is increasing its concentration on catalog sales and turning to direct mail to get its catalogs into the hands of consumers, at least on a test basis, at the time this is being written. (The company has shown no growth in the past seven years, despite increasing commissions to salespeople and diversifying the product line. But, ironically, it has begun to show growth as a result of sales increases in Mexico because 60,000 Mexican representatives are selling door-to-door, in contrast to the several thousand women now selling Fuller Brush products door-to-door in the United States.) The business press has recently announced that the company has been mailing 48-page catalogs and 8-page pamphlets to homes in both metropolitan and rural areas, especially in those areas where there are relatively few door-to-door salespeople, in a year-long test to see how viable the direct-mail approach is as a replacement for the traditional door-to-door "Fuller Brush man."

Fuller Brush is not the only firm to feel the effects of change in what working people will and will not accept as jobs today, and the resultant effects on their marketing. Avon Products, maker of cosmetics sold door-to-door for many years, has also turned to greater concentration on its catalog-direct-mail operations, which have produced a substantial part of their total earnings in recent years. Obviously, if these two veteran success models have found a need to change, others must have also experienced the same problems and found the same need to consider and embrace new approaches to direct marketing.

THE NATURE OF THE ITEM MAY DICTATE THE MARKETING METHOD

Items that fall into this category of not being automatically embraced by the public are often introduced through aggressive direct marketing campaigns such as in-store demonstrations and "party plan" sales in people's private homes. Many items are forever after sold in this manner, some of them with only marginal success unless marketed quite aggressively. Other products achieve wide acceptance eventually and became staples, sold successfully through conventional marketing channels. And still others achieve a kind of temporary success, but eventually disappear from the market. However, at least some of the latter class are "one-time" promotions, not expected to become staples, as in the case of special record and tape cassette albums promoted on TV and radio.

In-store demonstrations and party-plan sales are, of course, only two of the direct-marketing methods. Depending on various considerations, many items are also sold via radio, TV, trade shows, convention exhibits, direct mail, telephone solicitation, door-knocking, and/or combinations of these. The latest wrinkle in direct-marketing media, still in its infancy, is the electronic bulletin board, which requires a computer, modem, and telephone connection to display the sales message on the respondent's computer screen.

SOMETIMES IT IS A MATTER OF INTELLECTUAL CONVICTION

Of course, many marketers simply believe that direct marketing is by far the most effective way to market anything. Marketers who offer discounted prices—which also has a profound psychological effect, as well as price-appeal per se—simply believe that there is a great advantage in "eliminating the middleman" (the brokers and/or the wholesale distributors) so that they can offer these discounts. In fact, even when an item can be sold either by direct marketing or one of its alternatives, it can usually be sold more effectively by direct marketing because despite the high costs of advertising and mass mailing, the cost of sales overall in direct marketing is usually lower. There is no need for expensive retail locations, thus all the costs of fixtures and labor are reduced and even eliminated, which sharply reduces front-end and depreciation costs.

THERE ARE SPECIAL INDUCEMENTS

But there is also the advantage of the almost unlimited geographic dimensions of the possible marketplace when direct marketing approaches are used. You can expand a typical retail operation only by increasing your advertising and/or adding retail outlets. The first alternative is a highly speculative effort, since its success depends on attracting more prospects to visit your retail location. The second alternative is a costly method, of course. Direct marketing is not so bound, since the marketer goes to the prospects in person, by mail, by telephone, by computer/telephone (although this is still in infancy) and/or by radio and TV. Some direct marketers use all the methods, and some of the methods and media are actually hybrids and combinations.

The individual's choice is not necessarily a rational one. Some individuals simply believe that direct marketing is by far the most effective and efficient way to market. Others are psychologically and emotionally drawn to it because they enjoy selling directly to the ultimate consumer or buyer. In fact, such individuals will often deliberately seek out items that are most suitable for direct marketing methods. These are usually dynamic, self-confident, aggressive individuals who would be constitutionally unable to sit passively in a retail location waiting for customers to visit. (In older days many such individuals could be found positioned in front of retail locations as sidewalk "drummers," addressing passersby and shepherding them inside to poke about and take advantage of the many bargains.)

DIRECT MARKETING VERSUS DIRECT MAIL

Despite all the alternative methods for pursuing and addressing prospects, direct mail is the most popular and most widely used method and medium for direct marketing (also called "direct-response marketing"), and obviously dominates the thinking and methodology of all direct marketing. A study of direct-marketing literature in both the editorial coverage of the trade literature and the advertising reveals this orientation quite plainly.

The fact is that except for face-to-face direct marketing, as in the case of in-store demonstrations and trade fairs or exhibit halls, most direct marketing utilizes the mail in one way or another—to solicit sales, to receive orders, to prospect and develop sales leads, and sometimes even for fulfillment—shipping the order—although many orders are also shipped by United Parcel Service and other parcel delivery services, in preference to postal services, which are now considerably less satisfactory than they once were.

THE THREE STEPS OF ALL MARKETING

All marketing requires three functional steps:

Prospecting. Getting leads.
Following Up. Making presentations.
Closing. Asking for the orders.

In some cases, especially in the typical retailing situation, all these steps may appear to be carried out spontaneously in one brief exchange, as a prospect approaches, is sold, and places the order. Of course, that is not really the case, as we shall see in a moment.

On the other hand, in a great many cases, where the nature of the venture is such that it is obviously not a "one-call business," distinctly separate steps are required for at least the first function of prospecting for leads and the subsequent functions of following up and closing the orders. In many of these cases, mail or other direct marketing may be used for one of the steps, if not for all. Mail, telephone, and trade-show or exhibit booths are often used for prospecting, with the leads followed up in person, for example. But let's go back to that first, retail situation, and see if all the steps are as spontaneous as they appear to be.

PROSPECTING IN THE TYPICAL RETAIL SITUATION

Retailers must prospect, as anyone else must. And prospecting here means somehow inducing potential buyers to come to and enter the establishment so that the marketer can make the sales presentation. To accomplish this prospecting as a preliminary to the development of sales, the retail marketer can resort to many measures. Some are addressed directly to the objective of bringing prospects to the retail establishment, while others are aimed at creating a greater awareness of the existence of the establishment, as an indirect means of developing prospects and sales leads:

Advertising

In the media—newspapers, magazines, radio, public and cable TV.

Via special methods such as billboards and posters on buses, subways, taxicabs, and elsewhere.

Via direct mail and related methods such as distributing bills and posters to homes and under windshield wipers in large parking lots.

Special Measures

Special promotions such as booths in fairs and trade shows.

Publicity such as news releases and special events (e.g., contests, street shows, prizes to students, and other special promotions).

Charge cards issued to prospects. (One department store issues special, on-the-spot charge cards for $400 each Christmas season.)

Prizes awarded to outstanding members of the community.

Active participation in community affairs and local civic groups.

FOLLOWING UP AND MAKING PRESENTATIONS

Unfortunately, it is not possible to staff each counter with professional salespeople, so the retailer who operates an establishment requiring a number of salespeople must compromise. However, it is possible to "make presentations" in a sense, if not literally, by arranging good displays, providing motivating sales specials and signs announcing them, and otherwise making the "sales presentation" somewhat independent of an actual verbal delivery. (Unfortunately, this is one of the major weaknesses of the typical retail situation in the large establishment.)

CLOSING—ASKING FOR THE ORDER

Closing is an absolute necessity in positive sales technique, and is probably one of the greatest weaknesses of too many salespeople, especially in the typical large retail establishment. Relatively few in-store salespeople make even a serious effort to close.

This is probably due far more to the lack of training as sales professionals or dedication to the profession than to any other cause; most retail-store clerks are simply unaware that they must close—ask the customer for the order—to consummate the sale. As a result, closing is left to the customers—they are expected to make the decisions to buy on their own initiative— with the inevitable result that a great many retail sales are lost, despite all the advertising, special sales, and other typical retail marketing devices.

This is one of the major distinctions of direct marketing: When it lives up to its basic rationale, it approaches all aspects of the marketing process, and perhaps closing more than any other phase, in an organized and aggressive manner. Even in direct-mail and other approaches where the seller does not meet the customer face to face, various closing techniques are employed, many of them accepted today as standard necessities in direct marketing—tools of the trade.

A COMPLETE SET OF TOOLS

That summarizes one aspect of what this entire book is about and what it offers—the tools of the trade. The philosophy underlying this book is that it is neither necessary nor wise to go on reinventing the wheel every day. There exist many methods and devices that have become virtual standards of direct marketing. Many, perhaps most, may be adopted directly, adapted to most of your own needs, or used as models to guide rapid and sure-footed development of your own methods and devices where that is the most practical course. This book, therefore, offers tools—largely models and examples—with tutorials to help you understand each, to evaluate the array in each case and select the model most suitable to your need, and to adapt and tailor your selection to (or develop a new one for) your needs for each marketing campaign. These include offerings for all phases and aspects of direct marketing, from the basic preliminaries of the campaign to the aids and devices for closing when you are not face-to-face with the customer and so cannot personally ask for the order.

But even that does not express the entire idea of this book. While it is a tool kit, it is also a planning guide. In these pages, you will find aids to conceiving and planning direct-marketing campaigns such as deciding what the offer is to be and to whom the offer is to be made, guidelines for writing copy and checklists to help you detect and avoid the errors that we are all prone to make, methods and tools for carrying on the continuous testing—monitoring, recording, and evaluating results—that characterizes the most successful campaigns, and lists of available resources—consultants, suppliers, and sundry relevant and useful services.

HOW TO USE THIS TOOL KIT

The most basic idea underlying this book is this: Direct marketing is not a random or improvised effort. It is also not dependent for its success on inspiration, genius, or the happy accident of good fortune. Despite the fact that such blessings are sometimes responsible for an outstanding direct-marketing success, such success is far more commonly due to systematic and organized systems, based perhaps partially in art, but relying for the most part on well-known principles, practices, methods, and materials that have become virtual standards, at least as models.

At the same time, we must be aware that direct marketing is not a static discipline, but is constantly growing and changing in step with changing conditions (some of which have been pointed out earlier). The direct marketer relying on intuition or chance for success, using yesterday's marketing tools, or even using modern marketing tools without adapting them to his or her own needs and/or *the needs of each given marketing campaign* runs a rather high risk of disaster.

In keeping with this philosophy, I have tried to bring you in these pages the newest and latest ideas and methods of direct marketing. But even so, it is not my intention that you should use any of these (not even the newest and brightest ideas) without change, for only rarely will any given model or example be exactly right for you. Quite the contrary, the idea is to read the tutorials carefully, select the model or example that is closest to your own need, and then adapt that model or build a new one tailored to your own need.

Even if you are a professional and experienced direct marketer, perfectly capable of developing your own materials from scratch, you will then find this book serving you in at least these ways:

You can save a great deal of your time by using the ready-made models and tools offered here.

You may also save a great deal of your time by using this book to enable a secretary or assistant to carry out many duties you would otherwise be forced to attend to personally.

You can use these models to develop standard models and methods of your own.

You can use this book as a training aid, to help develop your less-experienced staff people into expert direct marketers.

You can automate all or parts of your direct-marketing functions by establishing many of the models in computer files (on disks), as suggested in tutorials, which, of course, greatly speeds up their retrieval, modification, and adaptation, and also makes it easier to use less-experienced staff to support the effort.

Finally, no matter how expert you are, there is the distinct possibility that you may either find a new and profitable idea or two in these pages or something in these pages may be an inspiration catalyzing a new idea of your own.

On the other hand, if you are new or relatively new to direct marketing, you can use this to "get on board" rather quickly, for with the tools and aids offered here, if you read the tutorials carefully, you can function effectively as a direct marketer and learn far more quickly and on a less costly basis than you could by trial and error—that is, by that which we call "experience."

2

FIRST STEPS
DECIDE WHAT THE OFFER IS TO BE

The first step in deciding what the offer is to be is to have a
realistic view of what an offer is. Surprisingly few
entrepreneurs have thought the matter through.

WE ARE ALL IN THE SERVICE BUSINESS

It's understandable that most of us tend to define our offers in terms of what we are selling, rather than in terms of what the customer is buying. That is because we know what we are selling, but we rarely take the time or go to the trouble of discovering what the customer is buying—that is, what we really are selling. One of the major objectives of this chapter is to help you determine what your offers are or ought to be—that is, what your customers are buying or, in more significant terms, how your customers *perceive* what they get when they buy from you.

The critical factor in determining this is service, for we are all in the service business, no matter what we sell. As one observer has put it, customers don't buy quarter-inch drills; they buy quarter-inch holes. When you sell the customer a quarter-inch drill, you sell a service—the ability to make quarter-inch holes.

Citing some right and wrong advertising appeals will help illustrate this principle more comprehensively.

YOU NEED CLARITY, NOT CUTENESS

An advertisement in a current computer periodical bears the headline "When you're top banana for PCs, you're ripe for Apples[R]." Reading the text of the advertisement reveals that it is copy that is devoted almost entirely to elaborate and self-congratulatory lauding of a word processing program that can be run on at least two Apple computer models.

It is not entirely clear what the main point is here. Certainly the copy goes on at length about the merits of the product, presumably the argument for buying the product, and invites the prospect to call, write, or visit a dealer for more information.

What's wrong with this? Several things:

1. The headline is cryptic, evidently written to be clever and get attention, perhaps generate admiration for the oh-so-clever copywriter. (Why are advertising copywriters so addicted to puns as evidence of their cleverness?) But all it actually implies is some vague connection with the Apple computers. It certainly does not constitute an offer of any kind. It can hardly be regarded as an offer unless it is specific, and this headline copy certainly is not that.

2. Nowhere in the copy is any specific offer made, except as a prospect might infer it from the self-congratulations expressed in every line. The copy is about the advertiser—what the advertiser wants—when it should be about the prospect—what the prospect wants and what the advertiser promises to deliver.

3. Nowhere does the copy offer, specifically or even indirectly, to do something for the prospect—to give the reader more than the general and vague claims of quality as a reason to buy the product.

4. Even as constituted, the copy is rambling over the landscape: It has no focus and thus cannot help but confuse readers. Even under this analysis (which no casual reader is likely to make) the meaning is unclear.

In sharp contrast, the highly successful SideKick$^{(R)}$ program is advertised on the next page of the publication with the headlined promise to "clear your desk in 30 minutes and increase your productivity by 50%." That is an offer. It promises the prospect two specific and distinct benefits, and it is focused sharply. The body copy then follows up to explain how the program achieves the promised results, listing all the "goodies" (favorable features and functions) of the program.

That actually sums up the difference—the most important difference, in any case—between copy that works the way it ought to and copy that may or may not work, but certainly does not work as well as it could and should.

This has nothing to do with the quality of the product. The first product referred to here may or may not be of the highest quality. Advertising cannot establish or prove quality, of course; it can only present an appeal and explain the offer—and provide enough evidence to make a plausible case for quality. Even without that evidence, an appealing offer may induce a prospect to try the product. But it is hardly likely that any prospect will take you up on an offer when it is difficult if not impossible to comprehend what the offer is.

It is not only print advertising in the media that often falls down on the job because the writer has failed to first define the offer. Direct-mail copy offends as often. A brochure from the publisher of a well known directory of services to marketers makes the same mistake in writing a brochure. The front panel of the brochure promises to tell the reader how to get almost 23 feet of mailing-list facts into a 2-inch package, referring to the directory, of course. Here the idea went awry. The focus was on the wrong idea. The advertiser appears to be bragging about his own cleverness and marvelous achievement, when he means to stress how much the prospect gets for his money when buying the 2-inch-thick directory. He obviously means to promise the reader almost 23 feet of mailing lists facts in the directory, but the copy fails to make the promise clear. The remaining copy does make the meaning clear, and it is excellent copy, copy that ought to work. But at least some prospects are likely to not even open the brochure unless they first understand what the promised benefit is and are persuaded by the promise of some benefit to open the brochure.

AN OFFER IS A PROMISE

The offer is, then, not what you propose to sell to the prospect, but what you promise to do for the prospect. For the moment—while you are defining your offer—never mind the vehicle or the means by which you will achieve the promised result (benefit); that's a secondary issue. That is part of the proof or evidence to convince the prospect that you will make good on your promise, but first you must establish the promise. You must give the prospect a reason to be interested. To do that you must understand that everyone responds to every proposal, consciously or subconsciously, with "What's in it for me?" That is the question your headline must answer: What is in it for the prospect?

EVERY VALID OFFER IS A PROPOSAL

Note the use of the word "proposal" here. We often use that word to refer to a written offer—usually a *custom*-written offer—that may range in size from a simple letter to one or more thick bound volumes. However, the word was used here in a more general sense, in the sense that every advertising or sales document is a proposal. It says, in effect, "this is what I will do for you if you buy what I wish to sell." It is a proposal to make a trade: benefits for dollars. It must thus be an act of persuasion.

DON'T COUNT ON REASON

We humans try to be rational and logical, and we like to believe that we are. However, we are not entirely so; we are motivated far more by

emotional drives and impulses than by rational ones. Among our emotional drives are the needs to love and be loved, to be secure, to be warm,
to be well fed, to feel a sense of worth, to be respected by others, to enjoy
self-esteem, and a variety of other such realizations, all of which might
logically be characterized as aspects of our human need for a sense of
security. In fact, it is easily possible to explain all human drives as elements of the need to feel secure, both physically and emotionally or
psychologically. Our drives can also be explained as manifestations of
our universal insecurity, for no one is totally secure in our world. An
understanding of this is a prerequisite to developing a definition of
proper offers to make to prospects. But to pursue this further, it is necessary to think about and understand the more basic subject of wants and
needs.

WANTS AND NEEDS

In today's language a want is a desire, although the word originally referred to a lack of something and is still used, to some extent, to mean
that. A need, however, is an essential requirement of some sort, a lack
(want, in its more classical sense) of something that must be supplied.
So, for practical purposes, the two terms are almost interchangeable—a
want is a need. But even without respect to how the words are used in
our society today, whether a customer wants or needs something depends entirely on the customer's perception. The customer who owns
150 pairs of shoes may decide to buy still another pair, and only the customer can decide whether that is a want or a need. So whatever a customer decides to buy or can be persuaded to buy is a need.

But there are two kinds of need, at least in the philosophy of many
marketers. There is the felt need, that need the prospect identifies without prompting by anyone. The prospect who has decided that he or she
needs new shoes walks into a shoe emporium with the intention of buying. But not everyone who buys new shoes feels the need before they
are prompted by advertising. Much advertising and sales effort is designed to create a need by convincing prospects that they need new
shoes. However, the offer is not shoes, but what shoes will do for the
customer—provide greater comfort, make the wearer more stylish, enhance the wearer's personal appearance and prestige, require less care
to maintain, or otherwise benefit the customer in some coin that has far
more emotional reward than it has rational justification.

CREATING NEEDS

Creating needs is the objective of by far the largest proportion of all marketing effort. And, understandably, the intensity of the marketing effort is in some proportion to the difficulty of creating the need—of persuading prospects that they need whatever it is that the promotion is designed to sell.

The difference in difficulty is primarily the difference in the prospects' own recognition of the benefit. In some cases, the public recognizes the benefit at once, almost automatically, and embraces the product or service with little marketing effort required. Home TV, videocassette recorders, xerographic office copying machines, home air conditioning, personal computers, and many other products and services met such swift acceptance. Other products and services have had a rockier road to success and required intensive marketing to achieve whatever success they managed to reach, if at all. (Of course, many new products and services become casualties because they fail to convince prospects that they satisfy a need or provide worthwhile benefits, and that may be because the product or service is not truly valuable, or it may be simply that it has not been sold effectively.)

DO NEW DEVELOPMENTS CREATE NEW NEEDS?

In one sense, the mere creation of a new product or service creates a new need. There could have been no need for TV, individual retirement accounts, or hair sprays when those products and services did not exist. The creation of their existence produced the new need. But that is a viewpoint that depends heavily on how we define needs. If we examine the question more closely, we find it possible to discern other views, to arrive, in fact, at a concept of universal and immutable needs, needs that we can regard as basic needs. Once we consider that there are such needs, immutable and basic, we can hypothesize that there is no such thing as a new or created need, that needs never change: What new developments create are not new needs, but better ways to satisfy old and classic needs.

DO NEEDS EVER CHANGE?

This proves to be a most useful viewpoint in understanding and defining needs and through them offers. If we agree that basic needs do not change, we can organize needs into useful hierarchies. For example, we have always needed diversion, entertainment, for our spare time. The Romans staged spectacular, if bloody, diversions. All cultures have developed their own theater, including our own popular movies, plays, and musicals. But in more modern times, home entertainment has become a major focus of new development, and we have eagerly embraced radio, TV, and videocassette players, as better ways of satisfying the need for entertainment at our convenience. (Naturally, older, less convenient, and more costly forms of entertainment have declined in proportion to the growing popularity of the newer forms.)

If you embark on the quest for defining offers by deciding that there are no new needs, but only better ways of satisfying old and classic needs, you have discovered the basic mechanism for identifying and defining the offers you ought to make: deciding what basic need is best satisfied by the product or service you wish to sell, and how that product or service satisfies the need in a better way.

You could probably reduce the list of truly basic needs to a number small enough to count on your fingers. However, for practical purposes it is necessary to be able to express each basic need in a variety of ways. Physical comfort, for example, is a basic need, but there are such factors as the range of temperature in the human comfort zone. So you must promise prospects warmth when you sell heating systems, and cool comfort when you sell fans or air conditioning. But physical comfort is a factor also in selling furniture of most kinds—beds, chairs, lounges, and other such items. It is a factor in selling automobiles, too, and in selling a great many other things used for personal and business purposes and functions.

It is therefore necessary to appeal to the prospects' basic needs in a variety of ways and through use of a variety of terms. Worksheet 1 is an exercise to help you condition yourself to begin thinking in such terms. Work through this exercise as a first step.

While this worksheet is an exercise to start your brain cells working on the problem of identifying the wants and needs of prospects, it is by no means a complete list. You will be able to think up many more terms to help prospects perceive the needs and wants you offer to satisfy. It is a list that is essentially generic, so that each of these terms embraces an entire family of more specific terms that would be subsets.

There are three steps in the process of deciding what your offer (promise) is to be. You must identify/decide the following:

The basic need to which you can/shall appeal (e.g., comfort)

The specific aspect of the need (e.g., warmth)

How your offer better satisfies the need (e.g., pure wool lining)

RATIONAL VERSUS EMOTIONAL IMPACT

In most cases, the appeal relies heavily on words and their impact. Even in the visual medium, TV, the bulk of the presentation usually rests on

---

INSTRUCTIONS: Check items your product or service does or can address. Add your own candidates in the blank spaces, as necessary. (Some items may apply in more than one major category, too.)

PERSONAL NEEDS

[ ] Physical comfort	[ ] Entertainment	[ ] Convenience
[ ] Financial security	[ ] Love [ ] Pride	[ ] Self-worth
[ ] Protection of family	[ ] Accomplishment	[ ] Ego gratification
[ ] Career achievement	[ ] Freedom from fear	[ ] Prestige
[ ] _____	[ ] _____	[ ] _____

BUSINESS NEEDS

[ ] Sales success	[ ] Business image	[ ] General business success
[ ] Support services	[ ] Problem solving	[ ] Special skills
[ ] Sense of support	[ ] Security	[ ] Position among peers
[ ] _____	[ ] _____	[ ] _____

OTHER

[ ] _____	[ ] _____	[ ] _____
[ ] _____	[ ] _____	[ ] _____

NOTES: _____

_____

_____

Worksheet 1. Identifying some basic needs

the effectiveness of the words used. The choice of words, therefore, makes a difference in the results achieved.

That is because words have both denotative and connotative impact—both rational and emotional content. "Physical comfort" is almost entirely a rational idea, with little emotional content. "Heat" is also almost devoid of emotional content in most of its usages. "Warmth," however, has some emotional content, which can be either favorable or unfavorable, depending on how and in what context or under what circumstances it is used. A promise to keep you warm in the winter is an appealing promise, but would have far greater impact when delivered to prospects in frigid weather rather than in hot weather.

The point is that you should select words for their emotional content in explaining your offer. For example, if you were selling a winter garment, in rationalization—the proof or evidence portion of your sales argument—you might discuss the effectiveness of the garment in preserving body heat. But in making your basic offer, you would want to promise *warmth*, rather than heat, insulation, or other rational and unemotional terms. The kinds of words used to stimulate the prospect's imagination and help the prospect actually *feel* what you want him or her to feel would include such emotion-laden terms as *warm, cozy,* and *snug.*

There is one other effect you must strive for in choosing the terms to use in expressing offers. You want to help the prospect visualize the benefit, as well as feel it. So you must try to choose those terms that paint images. Compare, for example, these descriptions of a product:

Genuine wool
Warm, soft lamb's wool

Obviously, the second descriptor has far greater emotional impact, while it also tends to paint an image, rather than convey a rational idea. The kinds of adjectives that help create that emotional impact and paint the image are such words as *soft, cuddly, warm.* Bear in mind, however, that you must keep your audience (prospects) in mind, too, when you choose your words. *Soft* and *warm* work for both men and women, but *cuddly* works for women only because there are also masculine and feminine words.

Worksheet 2 is offered to give you some practice in applying this idea. Try to find the best word—best in terms of emotional/image-making content—among the three choices offered in each case. But don't stop there. Try to think up even better choices and enter them into the blank spaces provided for that specific purpose. This will help you exercise

---
INSTRUCTIONS: Each capitalized word in the left-hand column expresses an
idea you want to stress in your offer. Check the alternative that you would
choose to use in your offer. If you can think of a better alternative, write
it in one of the spaces provided below.

TERM: ALTERNATIVES:

COLD   [ ] Icy   [ ] Frosty   [ ] Frozen

HOT   [ ] Steaming   [ ] Hearty   [ ] Searing

SAFE   [ ] Snug   [ ] Secure   [ ] Under lock and key

STRONG   [ ] Unbreakable   [ ] Rugged   [ ] Durable

CHEAP   [ ] Inexpensive   [ ] Economical   [ ] Cost-saving

CONVENIENT   [ ] Easy to use   [ ] Near at hand   [ ] Effortless

RELIABLE   [ ] Foolproof   [ ] Unfailing   [ ] Dependable

MODERN   [ ] Up to date   [ ] Latest design   [ ] State of the art

FAST   [ ] High speed   [ ] In minutes   [ ] Like lightning

PRESTIGIOUS   [ ] Be a champion [ ] Distinguished   [ ] Mark of leaders

QUALITY   [ ] Built to last [ ] Respected name [ ] Genuine

GOOD TASTE   [ ] Fashionable   [ ] The latest   [ ] European

                            ALTERNATIVES

   TERM: ALTERNATIVE: TERM: ALTERNATIVE:

_____   _____   _____   _____

_____   _____   _____   _____

_____   _____   _____   _____

_____   _____   _____   _____

Worksheet 2. Finding the words

your brain cells in finding the best words to express your offer. This is, of course, only an exercise.

THE BASIC EMOTIONAL APPEAL

There are certain basic emotional needs we have. Most of us have the need to love someone and to be loved by someone. We need to have our egos gratified—to be recognized as worthy individuals by others and to believe that we have done worthy things, achieved worthy deeds. Those emotional needs are needs for emotional or psychological security, but we need also to feel secure financially, materially. That is why I observed earlier that probably all our emotional needs can be reduced to a basic need for security, which definitely includes appeals to ego. You will probably never go wrong in formulating your offers if you bear in mind at all times the human need for security. But you must find the many specific and concrete terms in which to express these appeals.

ONLY ONE BASIC SELLING PROBLEM

If you are introducing a new idea with your product or service, you have the basic selling problem of persuading prospects to accept the new and different way of satisfying a basic need, which is not always an easy task. However, if you are introducing a new product or service that is not a new idea, but is in competition with others already offered (and, presumably, already established), your marketing problem is slightly different. You do not have to persuade prospects to believe that they can satisfy their needs in a different way than that to which they are accustomed, but that your conventional solution is better than that of your competitors.

In either case, your marketing problem is the same in, at least, the need to satisfy the prospect that yours is a better way of satisfying the need. The need in both cases is the need to prove that yours is a better way, whether better than older, established ways, or better than the products/services offered by competitors. Prospects will usually buy better ways, but the burden of proof is on you, of course.

WHAT IS "BETTER"?

Defining "better" is one problem. But the definition is not one that you can make; it is one the prospect must make, for it is only the prospect's perception that matters. "Better" is whatever the prospect agrees is better, and it is not an absolute. "Better" is a variable, and it depends on several other variables:

The prospect
The need
The circumstances

One of the most basic and common mistakes the beginner in business makes is trying to establish universal appeal for whatever he or she is selling. The hope is to maximize the number of prospective customers by appealing to all. Unfortunately, it's a serious mistake; it rarely works. Marketing today requires focus. You must identify your target and zero in on that target. Our sophisticated business/industrial establishment offers a bewildering array of products and services today. But that same sophistication of our system has produced an equally bewildering array of marketing targets, so that matching offerings with prospects is an integral part of marketing success today. The advertising industry tends to refer to this as *segmentation*, but that word simply means that you must identify the proper prospects for your offerings, to avoid the classic (and apocryphal) blunder of trying to sell refrigerators to Eskimos.

The need is linked to the prospect, but is not necessarily a factor of the prospect, for a given prospect may have different needs, under different circumstances. (In fact, many Eskimos in modern Alaska do buy refrigerators to install in their modern houses.) Needs change because circumstances change. And so "better" changes also. However, it is essential to remember that "better" is linked entirely to what the prospect perceives as better: The prospect may perceive something as better without your help. (That is, what is referred to as a "felt need.") In other cases, you must somehow convince the prospect that what you offer is, indeed, better. It is that act of persuasion that constitutes selling. You can always hope that the prospect automatically perceives the advantages of what you offer, but you can never be sure that such will be the case. So you must operate on the assumption that you must always make a sales effort, under all circumstances—that is, you must always work at pointing out why or in what way your offer is a better way to satisfy the need.

Not everyone agrees on what better means in any given application. It may mean more convenient, cheaper, easier to use, easier to learn, longer lasting, more prestigious, or almost anything else. The words you use may also affect the prospect's reaction; a single wrong word can destroy a sales effort, if the word is offensive to the prospect. (In one case, American Indians were reviewing a training program over which they had rights of approval, and they objected to the use of the word "forage" in describing Indian activities in earlier times because they thought it demeaning, believing that the term should be applied only to activities of animals and not those of humans.)

That refers to something called *connotation* of the word, the meaning or shade of meaning—nuance—the word suggests. Connotation often reflects individual sensitivities, and a given word may suggest an entirely different meaning to one person than it does to another person, with subsequent differences in the response evoked by the word.

Of course, there is rarely anything that most of us, let alone all of us, will agree is better. We cannot hope to convince everyone that what we offer is better, but we do have to try to determine what a majority of prospects will perceive as better. Think, for example, why more people patronize one supermarket than another in your own neighborhood. Does one have a greater selection of items than another? Is it more convenient to shop in? Does it have better parking facilities? Is it in a more popular shopping center? Does it do more advertising, run more sales, generate more publicity, attract a special class of shoppers, or have a special reputation?

This calls for introspection; you must truly *think* about it intensively. The purpose of Worksheet 3 is to encourage and stimulate such introspection, to induce you to dig down deeply in your thinking about this and practice trying to view "better" from the prospects' viewpoints, rather than from your own. However, there are really no answers that are right or wrong in an absolute sense, and you must recognize this also. For example, if you are trying to induce travelers to stay at the motel you are advertising, the terms to use in your appeal can vary, according to what kinds of sales you are targeting—tourists, travelers, business meetings, social events, conventions, business executives, vacationers, or other. That may depend on the nature of the establishment (what it is best equipped to attract and accomodate)—a roadside one-night stop, a lodging in or near a resort, a luxury high-rise motel, or other type of hostelry. So your answers must be based on your own premises and interpretations as to the nature or characteristics of what you are trying to sell. But it is both the idea and the best words in which to express the idea that you seek here, for the words are the chief instrument by which you try to shape the prospect's thoughts and impressions. The idea can work only if it is communicated effectively to the prospect.

ITEMS OFFERED   "BETTER" FEATURE/CHARACTERISTIC

SUPERMARKET   _____

PERSONAL COMPUTER   _____

COSMETICS   _____

CLOTHING   _____

MOTEL   _____

FURNITURE   _____

JEWELRY   _____

HOUSEHOLD ITEMS   _____

BOOKS   _____

TRAINING PROGRAMS   _____

                          TERMS TO CHOOSE FROM

close in	convenient	wide selection	easy parking
inexpensive	luxurious	fashionable	money saving
easy to use	labor saving	easy to learn	offers security
durable	trouble free	future career	new ideas
be attractive	prestigious	others will envy	in good taste
quality items	guaranteed	dependable	a secure future
up to date	better design	economical	attention getting
sexy	greater earnings	comfortable	reputable

Worksheet 3. Searching for the better-way image

OFFER-PROSPECT RELATIONSHIP

Inevitably, a direct or even cause-and-effect relationship exists between the offer you make and the prospects to whom you make it. The two must be matched, and that is a final factor to consider in designing your offers. In most cases (although there are exceptions), you begin the analysis with something to sell already decided upon and perhaps some general idea of who the prospects are to whom you plan to sell it. However, you must make offers that are suitable to the prospects, and in many cases the same offer is not suitable to all prospects, although you plan to sell the same item to all. For example, if you are in the resume-writing business, probably the most effective offer you can make to a student is to help the student find temporary or part-time employment. However, if the student is about to graduate or is a recent graduate, the offer he or she most wants is one that will help him or her win an entry-level job in his or her chosen career. For other prospects, those already employed but not satisfied with their employment, the most attractive offer is one of help in finding a better job. And for someone who is unfortunate enough to be unemployed—between jobs—the offer of help in finding any "decent" job is likely to be well received.

Of course, a general offer of help in developing a good, job-winning resume is an attractive one and will win a certain amount of response. However, offers that "strike a nerve" by revealing an understanding of, and the promise of help in solving, an individual's specific problem get far more attention and far better response.

It is by far the most desirable practice, therefore, to construct offers that are sharply focused on well-defined market segments. This means that hard work—"your homework," in the popular vernacular—is required. You must study the market to identify the various segments, define them properly, and determine how to reach each of them, and develop the proper offer for each.

Although not the ultimate in segmenting your market (the segmentation process and the focusing of the offers can be carried much further), here is an example of market segmentation: One young woman in Washington, DC runs a highly successful resume business that specializes in writing resumes for law students, reaching many prospects through advertising in journals read by those students. The Washington, DC area happens to lead the world in number of lawyers per capita, as well as in having a large number of colleges and universities turning out lawyers steadily. This makes Washington a prime location for resumes directed to law students and recent graduates, and

INSTRUCTIONS: Write in on the line following each listed offer the number(s)
of the kinds of prospects you think most suitable for the offer. However, do
add your own definitions of prospects (market segments) in the blanks
provided, and write those in, where suitable.

OFFERS

Learn computer programming   _____

Cosmetics to make you attractive to men   _____

Make a great deal of money in real estate   _____

Enjoy greater control with a personal computer   _____

Have your own spare-time business   _____

Be the life of the party   _____

Protect your loved ones   _____

Enjoy a fun second-career venture   _____

PROSPECTS

1. Small business owner	11. _____
2. Housewife	12. _____
3. Student	13. _____
4. Teacher	14. _____
5. Laborer	15. _____
6. Executive	16. _____
7. Home owner	17. _____
8. Accountant	18. _____
9. Opportunity seeker	19. _____
10. Retired individual	20. _____

Worksheet 4. Matching offers with prospects

INSTRUCTIONS: Write in two market segments/prospects of your own choice for each item and summarize an offer for each. Space is provided for making any notes you wish to record.

ITEM TO SELL:	SEGMENT/PROSPECT:	OFFER:
BUSINESS CARDS	_____	_____
		_____
	_____	_____
		_____
RAINWEAR	_____	_____
		_____
	_____	_____
		_____
AIR TRAVEL	_____	_____
		_____
	_____	_____
VCR	_____	_____
		_____
	_____	_____
		_____
LUXURY CAR	_____	_____
		_____
	_____	_____
		_____

Worksheet 5. Selecting segments and writing offers

the young woman referred to here is wise to exploit this natural asset of the locale.

To encourage you in practicing the introspection necessary to define your markets and segment them properly, another exercise, Worksheet 4, is provided. The objective in this exercise is twofold: (1) to induce you to think hard about offers and prospects and match the two, recognizing that there are usually many prospects (much segmentation possible) for most offers; and (2) to induce you to think about and develop some prospect (segmentation) ideas of your own.

DEVELOPING OFFERS

Worksheet 5 is virtually the opposite, and addresses a major objective of this entire chapter: designing offers. In this exercise you will be given a list of items/services to sell and asked to identify prospects and offers for each item—to segment the market and define each segment indirectly via the relevant offer. Each offer is to be focused on your own chosen market segment or prospect (which is the same thing), as you perceive your best options for the item, and identifying or formulating an offer, based on a need/motivator, as you believe a customer would perceive it. You must choose two segments for each item and develop an offer appropriate to each segment.

3

NEEDS AND MOTIVATORS

Semanticists point out that "the word is not the thing," but it is words that motivate or fail to motivate buyers —that carry the promise of benefits or need fulfillment. Pictures make their contribution, but it is words on which most of the burden for selling falls, on which our sales success depends.

NEEDS AND THEIR MULTIPLE DEFINITIONS

Carried to its logical conclusion, the argument for basic and immutable needs can be reduced to identification of a very small number of needs, probably chief of which is the need for security or the sense of security. However, to base all marketing effort on the promise of security per se would be self-defeating for several reasons:

1. Security itself has at least two basic aspects, for there is the need for physical security—protection from physical danger, food, warmth, clothing, and related considerations—and the need for emotional security—love, prestige, self-regard, and other elements of emotional health.

2. Each individual perceives a basic need such as security according to his or her own value system—a steady job, a loving family, money in the bank, sound investments, respected position, or any of a multitude of other things.

3. Not everyone would agree on what his or her most basic needs are. In fact, many would deny any sense of insecurity, although it is a certainty that no one feels completely secure. Probably not everyone interprets the meaning of insecurity in the same way. In any case, it is a relative term at best, rather than an absolute one.

4. The hierarchy or relative importance of one's needs varies widely from one individual to another, so that Jones may be willing to spend a bit extra for convenience, while Smith might be willing to go to quite a bit of trouble—sacrifice convenience—to save a little money.

5. One's individual hierarchy of needs may vary for different kinds of purchases or for different circumstances. For example, Jones may feel differently about convenience versus economy when it comes to a restaurant meal than when it comes to shopping for an automobile. But Smith's views on convenience versus economy may be geared to his income, and may change considerably when he begins to earn a bit more money and can better afford to indulge himself—spend more to gain greater convenience.

6. Finally, recognize that the word "need" is used here in a highly flexible sense to represent whatever a prospect feels as a desire such as saving money. Bear in mind, for example, that many of the wealthiest people, people who do not have the absolute *need* to save money in the sense of actually not having the money to

buy and pay for just about anything they might want, have a different attitude toward money than do many of us who are less well endowed with liquid assets; they have a strong *desire* to save money. To them, that is a need, and they feel that need as strongly as do those who truly really cannot afford to indulge their whims and casual wishes. Again, as in other cases, it is the customer's perception that represents the truth for practical purposes of marketing.

TESTING THE MARKET AND THE OFFER

Obviously, then, because the human animal is an almost infinitely variable sample, it is impossible to establish absolute rules about needs or motivators on either an absolute scale or on any scale of needs versus demographics or needs versus any other parameter. We do know that certain words—offers—are strong motivators. "Free," "new," and "sale," for example, are offers— words—with an appeal that appears to never wear out. But we can only generalize about needs and drives, and we must rely on tests, in addition to instincts, to set guidelines for ourselves for specific cases and applications. Thus the belief held by most direct-marketing experts that testing is a must for avoiding disaster, as well as for finding winning formulas. Bitter experience has taught many of us to trust nothing else as completely as timely and specific testing, tests that meet three general criteria or constraints, all of which appear to be absolutely essential preconditions. (These are offered here primarily as principles. Later we will explore each of these— how to realize what the principle calls for—in much greater depth and detail.)

1. The tests, certainly at least the initial or main tests, should be of *important* factors such as the basic appeal of the offer, rather than of some relatively trivial point such as the color of the ink or the size of the headlines. (There is little point in testing anything else if the offer itself fails to capture the interest of addressees.)
2. Test only one thing at a time and make all other factors as nearly identical as possible, or you will be unable to gauge accurately what makes a difference, if any, in the results achieved by the test mailing.
3. Tests should be conducted for each campaign—the current one, that is, not a previous one. Yesterday's truths are rarely reliable

in marketing. Conditions change constantly for a variety of reasons. It is essential to test continuously so as to discover today's truths. However, if you have a continuous (ongoing) marketing campaign and do not make major changes in the campaign, you may not have to make tests specifically, after you have made the original ones, before rolling out: In such circumstances, you should be monitoring results and compiling records that reflect and correlate the significant parameters on a regular basis. This is itself an ongoing test. (Suggested forms for doing this will be offered later.)

Demographic data is useful and a great many marketers rely heavily on it, but it is not an absolute by any means. The only reliable method of coming even close to an absolute indication of market conditions—of truths and untruths about a given market at a given time—lies in testing the specific offer in the specific market at that specific time, observing the criteria listed here.

There is ample evidence for this view, if any is needed. One is the example of the TV network chains and the producers who serve them with new programs every year. These executives are definitely in the marketing business, vying for their percentage of TV viewers—"market share," as they call it—and they rely heavily on demographic data. They use the term "skew" to identify and describe what they believe to be the bulk of their audience, as when they report that their market for a given program "skews young," for example. This is one consideration that affects their decisions as to which programs to introduce each year and how to schedule them. They are evidently confident that they know what kind of program appeals to each skew—type of viewer—despite the heavy evidence of their mistakes each year, and they have never devised a test mechanism less costly than trying out new programs each season. That their methodology is only marginally successful is attested to by the heavy casualty rate of new programs every year. Those that perish after a few airings—sometimes after even a single airing—are testimony to failures of market prediction and testimony to the fact that marketing is much more art than science. (More pointedly, it reveals the fallacy of dogmatic bias and the need to find reliable ways to test before rolling out.) However, whereas networks make major investments to test their marketing estimates, with proper methods it is usually possible to test markets and materials for direct-marketing campaigns at relatively little expense.

A FEW ILLUSTRATIVE MODELS

To bring some sort of order to this and create workable and useful tools for both copywriting and testing, we must identify at least a tentative set of basic needs and lists of terms—words and promises—that are commonly used as offers and appear to be effective. In organizing an intelligent direct marketing campaign, then, you should choose whatever promises appear to be best suited to your needs and you then test them to find out if your estimates were reliable and/or if you chose the best possible options for your copy.

The following lists, offered as worksheets, are by no means complete or exhaustive; in the relative infinity of products, services, ideas, and words, it would be virtually impossible to create lists even approaching completeness. They are, rather, just a few representative samples. Use these as models. Add your own entries to the lists, and create other such worksheets, suitable to your own special needs. Each model worksheet included here addresses a given basic type or class of product or service, suggests one or more basic motivators and/or bases for offers (promises), and lists some of the terms (word choices) that appear to be effective in this use. And because the listings are only representative, space is left in each worksheet for you to add your own entries. In fact, to gain some facility with this, it's a good idea to try your hand at adding items to each of these models, even if they are for totally different products or services than those of direct interest to you. Becoming skilled in motivational analysis and appeal synthesis takes practice, as do most things, and you can only benefit from the time spent experimenting with these models.

Bear in mind that these models are not presented as perfect examples. You may very well be able to improve greatly on them, and you are encouraged to do so.

Recognize, too, that in many cases a term or item may fit into several categories. For example, many people are motivated by pride or vanity (physical appearance) in buying diets and vitamins, but others are motivated by a sense of insecurity, perhaps the fear that being overweight is a threat to their careers or even a threat to their general health and physical well being.

Here again we find confirmation of the idea that whether most of us are willing to admit it or not, we all have some conscious or unconscious striving to gain greater security. And we need not philosophize here on what we believe to be true security, but only on what prospects *perceive* as their security or lack of it, what will or will not contribute materially to their achievement of greater security, and how that influences their buying decisions. However, that notion of security and insecurity or the drive for security is often expressed in inverse terms such as guilt, freedom from guilt, and even vanity, prestige, and self-image. Catering to one's self to pump up one's self-image is a form of compensation for insecurity or feelings of inadequacy, a most common concern. You'll see this reflected frequently in these models.

Products: Locks, bolts, bars, weapons, alarms, fences

Basic Need: Physical security, safety for self, family, and possessions

---

Motivators: Fear, insecurity

Offers:(words/promises):
  Protect yourself/loved ones/property/possessions
  Keep your home/car/business safe
  Be safe in your own home
  It's your duty
  Better safe than sorry
  You owe it to your loved ones

□

Products/Services: Insurance, investments, savings accounts

Basic Need: Security

Motivator: Fear, insecurity, guilt/freedom from guilt

Offers (words, promises):
Protect your home/possessions/family/loved ones/children
Provide for your/your children's/your family's future
Have an easy mind/sleep well at night
Better safe than sorry
It's your duty/responsibility
You're in good hands

___

___

___

☐

Products/Services: Medical services, checkups, weight control, diets, vitamins, health foods, exercise equipment, health spas

___

Basic Need: Security, ego gratification, self-image, vanity

___

Motivators: Fear, insecurity, guilt/freedom from guilt, vanity

___

Offers (words, promises):
Keep fit; you owe it to your family/country
The Surgeon General of the U.S. says . . .
Add years to your life
Feel like a million
Have/keep that trim figure
Look years younger

___

___

___

☐

Products/Services: Career training, computer training

Basic Need: Security, self-image, vanity, guilt

Motivators: Gain, fear

Offers (words, promises):
    Secure your future
    Have a better future
    Make more money
    Get a better job
    Advance on the job
    Be up-to-date
    Be ready for the future
    Your future is up to you

Products/Services: Money-making/start your own business plans

Basic Need: Self-image, security, guilt/freedom from guilt

Motivators: Gain, money, ego gratification

Offers (words, promises):
    Be independent
    Have a money-making business of your own

Complete guidance assures success
Build your own future
Your future is in your own hands

Products/Services: Automobiles, low-end cost

Basic Need: Security, self-image

Motivators: Fear, gain

Offers (words, promises):
  Economical but reliable transportation
  Money-saving practicality
  The choice of sensible people
  Built to last
  The only bargain in cars today

Products/Services: Automobiles, middle and high-end of cost

Basic Need: Self-image, ego, prestige

Motivators: Mark of success, keeping up with the Joneses, status symbols

Offers (words, promises):
   Out in front!
   Steady as Gibraltar
   The mark of quality

☐

Products/Services: Newspapers, news magazines, other magazines

Basic Need: Self-image, security

Motivators: Need to know, be up to date

Offers (words, promises):
   Know what's happening in the world today
   Get the whole story, not little pieces of it
   Find out what the future holds for you
   Get the facts, the story behind the story

☐

THE MODELS MAY BE MODIFIED AND ADAPTED

Even these few models can be varied—slanted—to fit many situations. In most cases, several variations or adaptations were suggested. For example, marketing of security devices such as locks and alarms may be slanted toward the protection of homes, families, businesses, vehicles, or other property. And in most cases the broad-brush appeal that tries to sell everyone is less effective than the more narrowly focused approach that appeals to specific segments of the market. Even when the products or services have equal application to more than one market segment, separate appeals, each directed to and focused on a specific segment, tend to be more effective.

Making the offer too general tends to dilute and weaken the appeal. In fact, the very act of structuring or wording the offer to broaden the appeal is itself a key factor in weakening it, as the following discussions will show. But to identify the various segments and create suitable offers for each requires a full appreciation of just what market segmentation is.

WHAT ARE MARKET SEGMENTS?

In general, the notion of market segments is a well-known one. However, the subject is a bit more complicated than is generally appreciated. Many marketers find that it is not always easy to recognize the inherent segments in a given market.

Perhaps the most basic and obvious segmentation for department stores and many other kinds of businesses is by type of merchandise. The basic structure of the department store (from which it gets its name, of course) is segmentation by product, with each department organized to sell a given type of merchandise. In today's economy perhaps a more apt example is in the marketing of computers, which now fall into four groups: mainframes (classic, big computers), minicomputers, personal or desktop computers (which includes the portable types), and home or game computers. Each is sold to a different kind of market, but the segments are not at all sharply divided. The mainframes are viable for only large organizations and the minicomputers for medium and large organizations. Personal computers, both desktop and portable, might be sold to organizations of any size and even to individuals as home computers. Game computers are not normally sold for "serious" computer purposes and so are not normally sold by computer dealers, but are sold in department stores, by radio and TV dealers, and even in toy stores, which reveals rather clearly who the buyers of such computers are. Each market may thus be segmented, but especially that for personal or desktop and portable computers.

An only slightly less obvious way to segment a market is by demographics—age, economic status, occupation, type of residence, size of family, geographic location, and other such obvious factors that differentiate customers. Many marketers do just that and go no further in their market research and analysis.

The use of such differentiations is clearly apparent in most direct marketing. Mailing lists are often rented on the basis of demographics, and you can generally select your list on the basis of demographic factors, although many marketers select mailing lists on the basis of whose lists they are renting (e.g., if you are selling fishing lures by mail, it makes good sense to rent the subscriber lists of periodicals devoted to fishing).

That is segmentation in the most basic or even primitive sense. But it is not the only way to segment your market. There are other ways. One is by features of the product or service you sell. You do this by stressing some different, specific feature in each offer. For example, to return to personal computers, although buyers will want a complete description of all the features, it is often one specific feature that induces the prospect to buy. In my own case, after careful study I decided that the system I bought was by far the best value available at the time. It did not have as large a memory as some others did, was not amenable to expansion, and lacked several features that others offered, but those were all nice-to-have-but-not necessary features for my own intended principal use (word processing) and so were features I was unwilling to pay for. Of course, if I needed my machine for accounting, I would have reacted differently.

Still another way to segment your market is by motivators. Even when the product or service is the same for each segment, different appeals or motivators are required. The physical-fitness appeal that is so popular today, for example, may be sold as an appeal to one's ego—the need to impress others by looking fit and trim, and being able to wear clothes well—as well as via fear motivation—the need to safeguard health by reducing. That will induce certain prospects to become customers. But even the fitness appeal may be too broad as a single segment. On examination, it may reveal possibilities to be divided into more than a single segment. For example, in one case, the customer is concerned primarily with impressing business associates, while in another case the customer is motivated more by desire to impress family and friends. And in still another case it may be necessary to the customer's business or professional career to look fit and trim. (The customer may be a performer, lecturer, or public figure of some kind.)

To be maximally effective as appeals, separate offers must be created, slanted to each type of prospect as reminders of their needs, for many will not translate a general appeal to be physically fit into the specific terms of their own major concerns. The offer, whether it is in the form of a print advertisement, TV commercial, sales letter, or other, must usually "strike a nerve" by being a sharp reminder of some concern the prospect may not be highly conscious of unless reminded.

You can thus manage segmentation of your market to a large extent by anticipating the many individual problems or needs and creating more than one offer, each based on an appropriate appeal.

A LIMITING FACTOR

One of the basic requirements of marketing is that the product/service must have a large enough market to be viable as a venture. A market segment must be large enough to be worth pursuing. There are many cases of marketing campaigns that captured a good share of a market that proved to be too small to support the enterprise. That is, some services and products do not succeed because there are just not enough people who have perceived a use or desire for the item. Air ionizers, for example, electronic devices which are supposed to make one feel better by ionizing the air in a room, were not very successful products because not enough prospects found the promised benefit appealing enough. The basic appeal was simply not there, and no one succeeded in finding one that would turn this device into a major winner in the marketplace. In another case, a company that built automatic machines to package chocolates sold several immediately but ultimately failed because they did not discover in advance that there were just too few candy manufacturers large enough to make use of such large and costly machines. On the other hand, some products such as Pet Rocks and hula hoops, were highly successful for a very short time—fads or crazes—but their appeal was fleeting and would not support the marketing for a long time so that only those who got into the market quickly profited. Many others entered the market when it was already declining, and suffered losses accordingly.

YOUR WORDING MAY DEFINE THE NEED

Even so-called felt needs are often felt by prospects only subconsciously, and it is up to you to make an offer that will raise the customer's consciousness. We all want to "look good," for example, but that is a rather vague term—an abstraction, really—that has different meaning for different individuals. An offer that translates that idea into more concrete terms has far greater appeal. For example, most of us who have reached that state we might refer to as "maturity" would like to look younger than we are. Thus an offer to make us "look years younger" or "take years off your appearance" (as in advertising that preparation that darkens gray hair) has more appeal than a promise to make us "look good." Similarly, we get the message more clearly when an advertiser promises to make us "feel young again" than when the promise is to make us "feel good." (Compare the promise to make you "look good" with one to make you "trim and fit.")

IMAGERY

Good copy "strikes a nerve" in various ways. One is by painting images. The business of painting images is an important one. We think in both words and images. Usually we must handle abstract ideas—concepts— with language, but concrete ideas are conveyed more effectively with images. Images are far more vivid and dramatic, and should be the goal of all wording that describes offers.

Obviously, the TV commercial has an enormous advantage in its ability to present images. But even print advertisement and direct mail can and should be as visual as possible, using words that paint images.

If you review some of the offers suggested in the models, you will find examples of offers that are rather difficult to present as images with words alone, but you will find others that can be so modified. "Protecting" yourself and family is a relatively abstract idea; certainly, it does not offer an image. On the other hand, "burglar-proof your home" and "protect your home and family from burglars" offers the image of housebreakers and are far more specific about what "protect" means for that reason. And the impact is made even greater by the added drama of invoking images of intruders.

The imagery invoked by using words to describe specific examples, rather than general or abstract ones, helps greatly in this regard. However, there are some other ways and devices that help achieve that goal of commanding full attention. There is a special consideration in this case because fear is almost invariably the principal motivator used in selling locks and alarms, as it is in selling insurance, and it is necessary to point out as precisely as possible what there is to fear. Again, it is simply not effective to leave it to the prospect to interpret general terms into specific ones. It rarely happens that way because the prospects are often giving your offer less than their full attention—so many things are vying for our attention these days—and you must do something to command that full attention.

Obviously, actual illustrations such as photographs are or should be a first choice, especially when it is necessary to furnish a precise image of the product to prove that it exists, that it is attractive, that it is as represented, or to enhance credibility generally. There are cases, however, in which a drawing is actually more suitable and can reveal more detail than a photograph can.

COMMANDING ATTENTION

You can't deliver a message to someone until you have his or her attention, of course. But in today's busy society you must compete for the prospect's attention. And it is not easy to command the prospect's full attention when making an offer, whether the offer is made via radio, TV, print in periodicals, direct mail, or even live demonstrations. Therefore, it is usually necessary to do something special to get that attention. There are numerous methods and devices for doing so, depending frequently on the item offered for sale.

One general, basic idea for getting the prospect's attention is to open with a dramatic lead. In the case of security devices, insurance, and other such items (where fear motivation is generally used), photographs are usually even more useful than are descriptive words in painting the proper images of hazard to dramatize the offer and make the danger shockingly clear. But there are also other ways to dramatize an offer. One way, in the case of security devices, is to reproduce a montage of headlines about burglaries, fires, or whatever the threat is that your product or service is designed to protect buyers against. But whatever the item or the motivator, the right place—the only place, in fact—to get attention is in the lead or headline.

LEADS AND HEADLINES

Dramatic leads are excellent attention grabbers. But there are other effective devices such as the novelty lead used to arouse intense curiosity. When one of my sales letters started with a headline announcing that the U.S. Government had paid me $6,000 to answer their mail, most respondents were intrigued enough to take the time to read it. It had the advantage of being somewhat whimsical and amusing, as well as startling, which are other characteristics that help greatly in persuading respondents to read your sales letter.

Note the dual and encompassing references to "leads or headlines," for all writing, whatever its purpose and length, needs a lead, and headlines can and should be designed to serve as leads—*are* leads, that is. Many of those who write and teach others about copy writing appear to believe that the sole purpose of a headline is to get attention. (Or so they imply in their pronouncements about the art of copy writing.) However, ideally a headline must do a little more than merely gain attention. It ought to achieve at least the following three objectives:

Get attention

Summarize the offer (or at least the main appeal)

Serve as a direct lead-in to the body copy that follows immediately

A fourth objective is also an appropriate aim when some kind of graphic device (drawing, photograph, symbol, or other) is used: In that case, the lead or headline ought to tie in with the graphic device in some direct relationship. For example, in producing and selling publications related to doing business with the federal government, I used as a logo on all letterheads and in other appropriate places an easily recognizable drawing of the Capitol dome in Washington, DC. The reader had little difficulty in grasping immediately the general nature of the publications.

I find this a great deal more useful than the popular "arty" logos that are entirely abstract and have no significance to anyone not already familiar with the organization, product, or the literature. These kinds of graphic devices are in a class with the clever copy that fails to sell the product because it is too busy being clever. Art has its place, but in marketing that place is definitely not better than second to achieving sales results.

Another attention-getter is the dramatic lead, as already introduced in the case of the copy that points out the dangers of burglaries, fires, and other disasters and hazards of civilized life. While the fear motivation is itself an attention-grabber when presented effectively, almost any truly dramatic lead will achieve the same goal. It may be seen daily in TV commercials, many of which are classic examples and successful (although some are abysmal failures).

The effects to be aimed at in creating leads (in words and/or graphic illustrations) then, include painting images clearly and, when possible, dramatically; making the motivator clear; and making the offer. However, there is another way to summarize this: A great many highly experienced marketers, many of them skilled and successful copy writers, agree that the headline is always the most important element in the copy. What they say, in effect, is that the major portion of the selling is done in and by the headline, and that if the headline fails to do its job, it is most unlikely that the body copy will save the day. Put more succinctly, if you don't sell it in the headline you won't sell it at all.

This may appear to create something of an anomaly. If it is true that most of the selling is done in the headline, why bother with body copy at all? But the body copy is necessary to firm up the interest established by the headline and build that interest into motivation to buy.

THERE IS ALWAYS A HEADLINE

Bear in mind that the word *headline* is used here interchangeably with *lead*, but a lead is not always a headline per se. If you are making a presentation to a prospective customer (whether in person, via radio and television, or in a sales letter in which you choose not to use a printed headline), your opening or introductory remarks inevitably become your "headline" because they are your lead: They must introduce your message and set the theme somehow. They must get attention and arouse enough interest to persuade the prospect to continue to listen or read. If your lead fails to do that, all is lost, and the rest of your material no longer makes a difference. Therefore, for practical purposes, you always have a headline or lead, and it must become your first objective to make it do its job of "hooking" the prospect's attention and interest.

Worksheet 6 lists 15 headlines of actual print advertisements used in direct-mail campaigns. You are asked to rate each headline for its clarity—does it furnish a true lead to the copy by giving the reader a good idea of what is being offered?—and its motivational worth—is it likely to arouse the reader's interest?

Some of these headlines have subheads or blurbs following them, which add to either clarity or motivation, or perhaps to both. However, this exercise is based on the headline alone because that is the reality:

readers are not likely to give you a second chance to capture their attention and arouse their interest.

You are, in short, competing with every other advertiser for the reader's attention (and with all the other printed information, for that matter), no matter what the others are offering. It's important always to remember that when writing leads and headlines.

A critique follows the worksheet, offering my own appraisal of these leads for your consideration, but don't read the critique until you have made your own judgments and can make comparisons.

CRITIQUE

My own judgment on the leads listed in the Worksheet 6 is offered here. Some of my decisions are rather arbitrary because many of the leads are borderline cases. They may be relatively clear, although not as clear as they ought to be, and they may have motivations, although weak ones. Yes/No choices impose that limitation. In this case, however, it serves a useful purpose because marketing and all the related arts of sales and advertising are not sciences—are inexact, in fact—so that no rules can be absolute. Again and again, efforts appear to defy all established wisdom: "bad" advertising often succeeds brilliantly, and "good" advertising frequently falls on its face completely. In the end, the only real arbiter of good and bad is success and failure. Still, we do have some standards by which to judge copy, and we must create some guidelines for writing copy and developing marketing strategies.

Most of these advertisements appeal to specific, often rather narrow, market segments; therefore the headlines may be quite clear to those in the relevant segments—those to whom the copy is addressed—while not so clear to others. I took that into account in reaching my own judgments.

With those caveats, here are my judgments:

1. Y	Y	6. N	N	11. Y	Y
2. Y	Y	7. Y	N	12. Y	N
3. N	N	8. Y	N	13. N	N
4. Y	Y	9. Y	Y	14. Y	Y
5. N	Y	10. Y	Y	15. Y	Y

```
------------------------------------------------------------------------
INSTRUCTIONS: Write Y (Yes) or N (No) for each question.
------------------------------------------------------------------------
```

	CLEAR?	MOTIVATIONAL?
1. NEW - Free Executive Summary		
Local Area Networks	_____	_____
2. The Security Game		
Dispose of Confidential Material	_____	_____
3. Let JES Do It! VPS Replaces 'Em All	_____	_____
4. Large Screen Data Projector		
Show Your Computer Information to Groups	_____	_____
5. FREE Visual Control Planning Aids	_____	_____
6. Invest in the Cellular Revolution	_____	_____
7. Investor's Daily		
America's Business Newspaper	_____	_____
8. Imprinted Golf Tees & Ball Markers	_____	_____
9. Literature Displays		
Largest Selection in the Country	_____	_____
10. Do You Need Leads? 10-25 Good		
Leads Every Day!	_____	_____
11. Cure On-Line Printing Headaches	_____	_____
12. Get Marketing Ideas Right on		
the Button!	_____	_____
13. Draw Your Line With Our Line	_____	_____
14. Shredding Isn't Security!!	_____	_____
15. Effective Business Letters For		
Every Situation	_____	_____

```
------------------------------------------------------------------------
```

Worksheet 6. Analyzing leads

To elaborate on these and explain my decisions, here is a brief discussion of each item:

1. This has a definite motivational element in both the words *New* and *Free*, two words that are generally considered to have "pulling power." The implication that a free report of some kind is offered is clear enough also. Probably anyone interested in local area networks would want to read the rest of this copy.

2. I think the first part of the headline is a throwaway; it really doesn't say anything very useful. But the remainder of the headline saves the day by making it clear that the offer is for a means of destroying confidential material that is no longer needed, and those with the relevant problem are likely to be interested, although the motivation is rather weak. This is, in fact, advertising for a paper shredder, and the copy could have been used to better advantage selling against competitive shredders—that is, offering the reader some reason to choose the advertiser's shredder over other shredders.

3. This one strikes out on both counts. The headline is not a lead at all: It is totally cryptic and gives neither a hint of what the offer is or any reason to be interested in the copy. The item is a software program—a spooler that acts as a print buffer—but there is no way of knowing that from the headline. Even beyond that the copy is full of cryptic acronyms, so that segmentation of the market is carried to a degree here that is likely to result in exceedingly few inquiries, let alone orders.

4. This lead makes the nature of what is offered (a projection device, the nature of which is shown by the photograph of a lens that fits over a computer screen) clear and includes a motivator—something useful the reader can do with the product. Probably a great deal could have been done to strengthen this lead. Merely reading the copy that follows the headline suggests what would probably have been much stronger appeals.

5. This headline is unclear. Just what the "visual control" means is itself so unclear that the more concrete "planning aids" is of no help. (The advertiser refers to wall charts, graphs, and other such devices.) The word *Free* is motivational, and that is all that qualifies a Yes in the second column on this one.

6. This is a double strikeout, as far as I am concerned. I am not sure how many readers will even recognize that the headline refers to cellular telephones, let alone just what the word "invest" demands that they do. Note, too, that this is not even an offer, since it is phrased as a command to the reader, with not even a hint of why it would be in the reader's interest. (In fact, later reference to a prospectus reveals that this is a stock offering.)

7. This headline makes it clear that it refers to a periodical for investors, but the reader would have to get as far as the blurb below the headline to find out what the advertiser is claiming as a benefit to the reader. That message (a claim of an abundant supply of exclusive and important information) should have been in the headline, to do a job of motivating the reader.

8. This is truly an example of a ho-hum headline. In fact, this is more of a catalog sheet or specification sheet than it is an advertisement, for it makes absolutely no effort to sell. It merely provides an order form and all necessary ordering information. It might garner a few orders from any reader who wants to use the items as advertising giveaways, but it won't slow down anyone else's reading.

9. This is not a powerful headline, but it qualifies on both counts, even if it does so by a bare margin. It is reasonably clear in what is being offered—fixtures for displaying literature—and has a motivator: the claim of the largest selection in the country.

10. This one qualifies easily because it is by nature a powerful appeal. Every reader who is a marketer of any kind must answer "yes" to the question in the headline. And it is difficult for such a reader to resist reading on, after seeing a promise of 10 to 25 good leads every day. (The item is a computerized telemarketing device.)

11. This is easily a Yes/Yes rating. It is an offer to solve a problem almost every computer user is familiar with, and the headline motivates by offering a solution to a common problem, and is reasonably clear about what the problem is. Ironically, this is the same advertiser, offering the same item as in number 3, but what a difference in headlines!

12. The writer of this copy is suffering from terminal cuteness. The product is a badge-making machine, and the headline is a feeble

effort to be clever with a pun. The offer is clear enough—it's a marketing aid—but the motivator in the headline is nonexistent.

13. This is another example of cuteness blocking out good sense, not to mention good copy writing. The device offered is a plotter, and while the headline suggests something to do with drawing, just what that is remains pretty fuzzy. Unfortunately this writer, like others, could not resist offering a pun instead of a motivator, thereby administering the coup de grace to the headline.

14. This is a good headline. It is clearly implied that an alternative to paper shredding is being offered, and fear motivation is used well here. The device is a machine that is more than a shredder and can destroy other materials than paper, also compacting and bagging the waste product. (Compare this with item 2.)

15. This one qualifies for Yes in both categories, but is far from a powerful headline. It's a handbook produced by a leading publisher, and the body copy offers information that could have been used to create a far more motivating headline.

4

CREATING THE DIRECT-MAIL OFFER

Some handy planning tools with a list of dos and don'ts and relevant discussions of the key items.

CHECKLISTS

Several checklists are provided in this chapter in the form of worksheets and planning guides. But first there is a discussion of key considerations in making up a direct-mail offer, with a number of important "dos and don'ts" included. The lists and worksheets are useful in several ways.

1. They are planning tools, reminding you of the key items you must consider, and offering you a convenient way to record the decisions you make.
2. They constitute a convenient set of specifications, which you can then use as reminders of your decisions and to verify that you have implemented each decision.
3. You can use them to hand over specifications to suppliers and/or those on your staff to implement for you.

Before getting to the lists, however, review these key considerations and dos and don'ts.

Know Who Your Target Is

Decide who your buyer is. It is not everybody, and you must have a clear picture of that buyer.

Choose a Strategy

Decide exactly what is most likely to persuade that buyer—fear or greed—and how you will invoke that motivation.

Decide What Your Offer Is

Your *offer* is not what you propose to sell, but what you propose to *do* for the prospect. Choose your main promise, and make that promise crystal clear.

Focus on the Main Promise

Start with impact—the chief benefit promised, whether it involves fear or gain—by focusing sharply on it in your opening message. Don't dilute your opener by promising everything at once.

Tell Your Story in the Headline

Always use a high-impact headline, and be sure that the headline clearly summarizes the offer and the chief reason for buying—the strategy. The copy following it must reinforce, not explain, the message in the headline.

Add a Reasonable Number of Benefits

Add other benefits in the copy, but make it a reasonable number. They help persuade the prospect, but overdoing it by promising too much leads to confusion and skepticism instead of motivation.

Quantify

Find the means to state promises—benefits—in terms of quantities, for greater impact and credibility. Turn your facts into pounds, feet, numbers of people, miles, or other units of measure.

Prove Your Case

Provide the evidence to make your promises credible. Use logic, testimonials, photographs, official reports, charts and graphs, or other backup evidence.

Use More Than One Piece

Include at least a sales letter and brochure or broadside to tell the story. "The more you tell, the more you sell" is a general truth. Tell your story in as many ways as possible, with as many promotional pieces as possible.

Tell the Whole Story

In each promotional piece, retell the story *completely*, with different language and different perspectives for each.

Overwrite, Then Boil it Down

Keep your copy lean—as tight as possible, without leaving information out—by writing as much as necessary to tell everything, and then going back to boil out all unnecessary language.

Make it All Good News

Avoid anything unpleasant. Break price into palatable units such as "only $29.50 per month" and "less than 2 cents a page." If the item requires skill to use—a personal computer, for example—offer "simple instructions," "school children learn the basics in minutes," and other such reassurances. If it's something with potential hazard—a kitchen appliance, for example—stress safety features such as automatic shutoffs.

Make Copy Easy to Read and Dramatic

Keep sentences and paragraphs short, and use white space generously. Use high contrast colors—black or dark colors on white or yellow paper. Use underlines, boldface type, two colors, circling items, marginal notes, and other devices that make copy appear easy to read and also dramatize important points. Don't use these *in place of* motivating copy. What you promise and how you prove your case are the prime factors; *nothing* substitutes for them.

Use Charts and Graphs

Claims and reports are more easily understood, and more believable when they are presented as (or with the aid of) graphic devices—plots, charts, exploded views, matrices, and others.

Offer Free Gifts

Useful free gifts—cameras, radios, pens, and others—are highly motivating. Choose gifts that are appropriate for your anticipated buyers, and feature them prominently. But don't base your strategy or main appeal on the gifts. Your strategy is based on your *offer*—the main promise and the proof. The gifts should be a bonus extra.

Offer Discounts

Probably nothing, not even gifts or the word *free* is as alluring as is the lure of a bargain—discounts, special prices, and special offers. Test after test verifies this.

Close Frequently

Just as in face-to-face selling, you must ask for the order repeatedly. Remind your reader frequently of your offer and make it clear that he or she must take action—respond to your urging—to gain the advantages of your offer. Ask frequently for the order by advising and reminding the prospect of the action to be taken—"fill out the enclosed order form," "call the toll-free number," "come in for a free, personal demonstration," and similar closes.

Make Sales Letters Informal and Friendly

Use typed (not typeset) copy in sales letters, with ragged right margins (even if you use a word processor to compose the letter). Mark up the copy with a bold, felt tip marking pen to create underlines, circled items, marginal notes.

Make it Easy for the Prospect to Order

Arrange to accept credit-card orders, in writing or by telephone. Enclose easy-to-use order forms, forms that require only name, address, credit-card number, and checkoffs. Supply postage-paid response envelopes and toll-free telephone numbers.

Eliminate Risk

Offer guarantees, trial periods, delayed billings or payments, or other measures to eliminate risk and display total confidence in what you offer. But don't overdo this or it begins to sound defensive.

Use a Postscript in the Letter

A prominent "P.S." gets attention and makes the letter more informal and personalized. Many direct-mail professionals make it a standing rule to use a P.S. in their sales letters.

Don't Be a Comic

Humor has its place, but is dangerous in direct-mail copy. It distracts the prospect, when you want to focus the prospect's attention. In many cases, attempted humor offends some people, a distinct hazard. If it is not truly humorous, in the reader's opinion, it totally destroys the copy. It's safer, much safer, to shun humor completely.

Don't Be Clever

Bad copy is created every day by clever copywriters, people who believe that irrelevant puns, acronyms, and other clever gimmicks sell. They don't. Worse, they are often used *in place of* the right copy, the copy that *would* sell, and so are destructive. Forget cleverness and keep your eye on the ball—what you offer and why the prospect ought to buy.

Tell the Prospect the Price

You can't close an order, in most cases, without revealing the price. Make it as palatable as possible, but do tell it.

Test, Test, Test

Nothing is quite as reliable as actual results. Every mailing, large or small, should be a test mailing, and can be made so by establishing and keeping records that are designed to help you interpret results and put the information to good use in future campaigns.

A General Checklist

Worksheet 7 is a general checklist. It is also a suggested form for planning and specifying major characteristics and elements of your direct-mail package. But it is general, and you will have to get down to more detail, using other forms and lists supplied here for many of the items. However, this checklist will serve you well as a preliminary planning tool and reminder of some key considerations. Refer to it repeatedly as you build your direct-mail package, to ensure that you have not allowed anything to slip between the cracks.

Each item has two boxes, one on the left and another on the right. Use the box on the left to decide what items you plan to incorporate or utilize in your offer. Use the one on the right to to verify that you have done so.

You can also use this form as a guide for others. Check off the left-hand boxes as your specifications, and have them check the right-hand boxes as they complete each task.

INSTRUCTIONS: Check left-hand boxes to remind yourself (or others working on
your campaign planning) of items to consider. Check right-hand boxes for
items as you implement your planning and/or to have others certify such
implementation and compliance.

[ ] KNOW WHO YOUR TARGET IS	[ ]	[ ] MAKE COPY EASY TO READ	
[ ] CHOOSE A STRATEGY	[ ]	AND DRAMATIC	[ ]
[ ] DECIDE WHAT YOUR OFFER IS	[ ]	[ ] USE CHARTS AND GRAPHS	[ ]
[ ] FOCUS ON THE MAIN PROMISE	[ ]	[ ] OFFER FREE GIFTS	[ ]
[ ] TELL YOUR STORY IN THE		[ ] OFFER DISCOUNTS	[ ]
HEADLINE	[ ]	[ ] CLOSE FREQUENTLY	[ ]
[ ] ADD A REASONABLE NUMBER OF		[ ] MAKE SALES LETTERS	
BENEFITS	[ ]	INFORMAL AND FRIENDLY	[ ]
[ ] QUANTIFY	[ ]	[ ] MAKE IT EASY FOR THE	
[ ] PROVE YOUR CASE	[ ]	PROSPECT TO ORDER	[ ]
[ ] USE MORE THAN ONE PIECE	[ ]	[ ] ELIMINATE RISK	[ ]
[ ] TELL THE WHOLE STORY	[ ]	[ ] USE A POSTSCRIPT IN LETTER	[ ]
[ ] OVERWRITE, THEN BOIL		[ ] DON'T BE A COMIC	[ ]
IT DOWN	[ ]	[ ] DON'T BE CLEVER	[ ]
[ ] MAKE IT ALL GOOD NEWS	[ ]	[ ] TELL THE PROSPECT THE PRICE	[ ]
		[ ] TEST, TEST, TEST	[ ]

Worksheet 7. General checklist

Second Checklist

This second checklist (Worksheet 8) is a more detailed and specific planning tool, and is also useful to guide others in assembling a direct-mail package. This checklist concerns decisions or specifications regarding items to be included in direct-mail packages.

Note that options are available in some of the items, so that you can specify your decisions and wants in much greater detail than in the first checklist.

INSTRUCTIONS: Check left-hand boxes to remind yourself (or others working on
your campaign planning) of items to consider. Check right-hand boxes for
items as you implement your planning and/or to have others certify such
implementation and compliance.

[ ] Sales letter   [ ]   [ ] Order Form

[ ] Brochure   [ ] Separate item   [ ]

   [ ] 3 x 9   [ ]   [ ] Clip or tear off   [ ]

   [ ] 8-1/2 x 11   [ ]   [ ] Special Items

   [ ] _____   [ ]   [ ] Plastic "credit" card [ ]

[ ] Broadside   [ ]   [ ] Novelty item   [ ]

[ ] Return envelope   [ ] Discount coupon   [ ]

   [ ] Plain   [ ]   [ ] _____   [ ]

   [ ] Postage paid   [ ]   [ ] Envelope copy   [ ]

NOTES: _____

_____

_____

Worksheet 8. Planning elements of direct-mail package*

Third Checklist

Identifying your target—your intended buyer—precisely is important
in many ways, especially in deciding what mailing lists and/or other
media to use, what to offer, and otherwise planning and assembling
your campaign. (E.g., you would not use spots on the late, late show to
reach teenagers, nor would you use fear motivation in appealing to children.) The third checklist (Worksheet 9) is intended to help you think
this matter through and sketch in some identifiers of your target population. Because so many variables are possible, write-in blanks are provided, along with space to make special notes.

---

*This plan can easily be adapted to the design of an offer to be made via another medium,
such as TV or print advertising.

INSTRUCTIONS: Check left-hand boxes to remind yourself (or others working on your campaign planning) of items to consider. Check right-hand boxes for items as you implement your planning and/or to have others certify such implementation and compliance.

GENDER:

[ ] Male   [ ]   [ ] Female   [ ]

AGE GROUPS:

[ ] Children   [ ]   [ ] Teenagers   [ ]

[ ] Young adults   [ ]   [ ] Mature/middle-aged adults   [ ]

[ ] Senior citizens   [ ]   [ ] _____   [ ]

OCCUPATION(S):

[ ] Students   [ ]   [ ] Housewives   [ ]

[ ] Blue collar   [ ]   [ ] White collar   [ ]

[ ] Craft workers   [ ]   [ ] Professionals   [ ]

[ ] _____   [ ]   [ ] _____   [ ]

MISCELLANEOUS:

[ ] Home owners   [ ]   [ ] Apartment dwellers   [ ]

[ ] City residents   [ ]   [ ] Suburbanites   [ ]

[ ] Rural residents   [ ]   [ ] _____   [ ]

[ ] _____   [ ]   [ ] _____   [ ]

NOTES: _____

_____

_____

Worksheet 9. Defining the target population

Fourth Checklist

Strategy is critical to sales and marketing success. At the same time, a checklist for devising a sales or marketing strategy is difficult to provide, except in general terms because strategic possibilities are usually so numerous and varied. However, it is possible to offer some ideas and suggestions for at least the basis of strategies—basic motivators, for

---
INSTRUCTIONS: Check left-hand boxes to remind yourself (or others working on your campaign planning) of items to consider. Check right-hand boxes for items as you implement your planning and/or to have others certify such implementation and compliance.

MAIN MOTIVATOR

FEAR: GAIN:

[ ] Embarrassment   [ ]   [ ] Making money   [ ]

[ ] Health   [ ]   [ ] Getting an education   [ ]

[ ] Accident   [ ]   [ ] Learning a secure trade   [ ]

[ ] Failure   [ ]   [ ] Being popular   [ ]

[ ] Disaster   [ ]   [ ] Being more attractive   [ ]

[ ] _____   [ ]   [ ] _____   [ ]

[ ] _____   [ ]   [ ] _____   [ ]

NOTES: _____

_____

_____

Worksheet 10. Planning basis of strategy

example—to start thought on the subject. Worksheet 9 does that, and provides spaces for writing in ideas as well. Incorporated inevitably in your ideas for this worksheet and checklist are other considerations— your offer, the main promise, and the chief feature to be included in your headline.

Fifth Checklist

No matter how appealing your offer, you must prove to your prospect that you can and will make good on your promise. Worksheet 11 offers some ideas for items that prospects will usually accept as such proof.

Sixth Checklist

Worksheet 12 offers ideas for extra motivators, items intended to help close hesitant prospects. Of course, the extra motivators should be

INSTRUCTIONS: Check left-hand boxes to remind yourself (or others working on your campaign planning) of items to consider. Check right-hand boxes for items as you implement your planning and/or to have others certify such implementation and compliance.

[ ] Logic--rational argument   [ ]   [ ] Charts, graphs   [ ]

[ ] Testimonials   [ ]   [ ] _____   [ ]

[ ] Photographs   [ ]   [ ] _____   [ ]

[ ] Official documents   [ ]   [ ] _____   [ ]

[ ] Citations from documents   [ ]   [ ] _____   [ ]

NOTES: _____

_____

_____

Worksheet 11. Planning proofs of offer

INSTRUCTIONS: Check left-hand boxes to remind yourself (or others working on your campaign planning) of items to consider. Check right-hand boxes for items as you implement your planning and/or to have others certify such implementation and compliance.

GIFT ITEMS:

[ ] Luggage   [ ]   [ ] Digital clocks   [ ]

[ ] Calculators   [ ]   [ ] Subscriptions   [ ]

[ ] Books   [ ]   [ ] Purses   [ ]

[ ] _____   [ ]   [ ] _____   [ ]

DISCOUNTS:

[ ] Package prices   [ ]   [ ] For prompt ordering   [ ]

[ ] Coupon enclosed   [ ]   [ ] _____   [ ]

NOTES: _____

_____

_____

Worksheet 12. Ideas for gifts and discounts

```
-----------------------------------------------------------------------
INSTRUCTIONS: Check left-hand boxes to remind yourself (or others working on
your campaign planning) of items to consider. Check right-hand boxes for
items as you implement your planning and/or to have others certify such
implementation and compliance.
-----------------------------------------------------------------------
```

MAKING IT EASY FOR THE CUSTOMER TO ORDER:

[ ] Separate order form [ ]	[ ] Credit card ordering	[ ]
[ ] Toll-free telephone [ ]	[ ] Postage-paid postcard	[ ]
[ ] Prepared order (customer	[ ] Self-stick customer	
need only sign and mail [ ]	return-address labels	[ ]
[ ] _____ [ ]	[ ] _____	[ ]

REVEALING THE PRICE:

[ ] Break it into weekly	[ ] Unitize it on some other	
or daily rate [ ]	basis	[ ]
[ ] Accept payment schedule [ ]	[ ] List several payment plans	[ ]
[ ] _____ [ ]	[ ] _____	[ ]

ELIMINATING RISK:

[ ] Money-back guarantee [ ]	[ ] Guarantee of results	[ ]
[ ] Free trial period [ ]	[ ] Delayed/deferred payment	[ ]
[ ] _____ [ ]	[ ] _____	[ ]

```
-----------------------------------------------------------------------
```

Worksheet 13. Miscellaneous considerations

appropriate to whatever it is you are selling. For example, correspondence schools selling technical courses often gave the student-enrollee a handsome slide rule as a gift. Today, those schools would offer a free calculator, since pocket calculators have made slide rules obsolete.

Seventh (Miscellaneous) Checklist

There are a number of miscellaneous items to consider such as ways to make it easy for the customer to order and ways to break the price to the customer as gently and as diplomatically as possible. Many of these subjects do not merit a worksheet or checklist of their own, but some can be combined in one miscellaneous checklist, as in Worksheet 13.

5

TESTING
DIRECT-MAIL
OFFERS

Without testing you are only guessing, a risky procedure that
may even spell disaster.

THE ABSOLUTE NECESSITY OF TESTING

Even after years of experience, sometimes selling the same item or kind of item for many years, we still find ourselves surprised by the results of our campaigns. We soon discover that what worked very well last year, or even last month, may not work now. The one predictable event is change, and what the marketer needs most to know is what the changes will be.

A large percentage of organizations that make an effort to expand their marketing by turning to direct mail never test at all. They develop direct-mail packages based on intuition and roll out expensive direct-mail campaigns that rarely achieve more than a tiny fraction of the results they should.

There are exceptions. Occasionally such a hunch-based program works. But the true expert, the professional direct mailer, soon learns to turn to testing as the only reliable guide in direct marketing.

WHAT TO TEST?

Even those pundits who recognize the need for and urge testing when preparing a direct marketing campaign appear sometimes to be confused about what testing really is. Testing is not a campaign to discover the prospects' preferences for color of inks and paper, or the prospects' willingness to go to the trouble of finding an envelope and stamp with which to mail their orders. In fact, the main purpose of testing is simply to ask the prospect what he or she wants! If we accept the premise that you cannot sell a prospect anything that he or she does not truly want— *or cannot be induced to want*—marketing becomes a proposition of finding out what the prospect does want or can be persuaded to want. Obviously, no one but the prospect can really tell you what he or she wants; everyone else is simply guessing.

WHAT IS A "WANT"?

True want is an emotional need, not the physical item you offer. The prospect never really wants a home exerciser, per se; what he or she really wants is to be slim and trim, feel good, look good, be healthy, add years to life expectancy, wear clothes well, fit into a smaller size, be attractive to the opposite sex, be envied or admired by others, and/or otherwise avoid disasters and gain satisfactions. The real question is this: What kind of promise (and proof) will persuade the prospect to give up some of his or her cash? For most people who might be persuaded to invest in your home exerciser, the promise of satisfying one or more of those wants is most important and most likely to induce an order. Which offer (promise) should you feature most prominently? Not all equally, for that is a shotgun approach that dilutes the entire package, and generates doubt as to your sincerity. The package demands that you focus on some single, powerful motivator to rivet the prospect's attention. Other motivators must be subordinated to the primary one to be properly effective.

There is no reliable way to actually *ask* the prospects to choose the most motivating promise. In fact, the prospects should not be aware that they are the subjects of a test. You should send out two or more test mailings, each exactly the same as the others, except for the headline and lead. In each of the mailings, a different offer—promise—is featured, and the results of each are recorded most carefully.

The offer is the first thing to test, and it is what you promise to do for the prospect, the specific benefit you pledge, not the product you wish to sell and the terms of your sale— cash, time payments, bonuses, discount, free trial, and so forth.

In short, if I promise that I will help you lose 15 pounds in 30 days, *that* is my offer. If I ask you to send me $39.95 for my patent exerciser, agree to a 30-day free trial with a money-back guarantee, that is my proposition.

None of this should be interpreted to mean that other factors and elements such as response devices, bonus add-ons, and special inducements should not be tested. Such elements can help fence-sitting prospects decide to buy, help you close more than a few doubtfuls. And even where the differences in response are fractions of a percentage point, in large mailings or sales of "big tag" (costly) items, that fraction of a point can mean many thousands of dollars added income. Ergo, those matters are not unimportant, but can become important only when enough prospects respond with orders to make the entire program viable.

WHAT IS THE ANSWER YOU SEEK?

There are three possible outcomes of your initial mailings:

One of your test mailings may demonstrate that one offer not only produces a highly satisfactory response—volume of orders— but is also overwhelmingly superior to the others. In that case, you usually opt to roll out with that offer.

Sometimes two or more offers pull satisfying responses, and do not show one offer significantly greater in pulling power than the others. In that case you might try either combining the most effective offers somehow or you might do consecutive mailings to the same list, alternating the offers. (There is a cumulative effect in a great many cases, where follow-up mailings, even of identical material, pull better responses than predecessor mailings have, and this is often by far the most effective way to maximize the results of mailing to a given list of prospects.)

It is possible that none of your offers will pull an adequate response. In that case, you must decide whether to develop other offers and test further, seek other mailing lists, or drop the whole idea and seek something else to sell.

THE NORMAL AND TYPICAL SEQUENCE

Presumably, before you reach the go/no-go decision stage you will have verified the suitability of your mailing lists by split testing the lists you have selected for your initial tests. Although many stress the lists as the first item to be tested, I consider it the second item to be tested. In my own experience the early sequence should be generally along this line:

1. Frame the offer
2. Choose what appears to be a suitable list
3. Split test the offer
4. Choose the better result
5. Split test it again or split test the mailing list
6. Continue with other tests and/or roll out

There is at least one other important thing to test: price. But here the aim is not necessarily to determine which price will bring the greatest number of orders but which price will bring the greatest profitability and how price affects response. And here, as in all testing, results are often surprising. Lower prices do not always produce greater response; sometimes the opposite is true.

ITEMS TO TEST

The fact that the offer, mailing lists, and price are the most important items to test does not mean that all other factors are trivial. Not at all. The persuasiveness of the copy is important. The relative effectiveness of the offered proofs— testimonials versus rationales, for example—is important. Response devices and other elements are important, too, although in a subordinate sense, as discussed already. Even such factors as color inks, the use of response envelopes, involvement devices, and even, in some cases (such as when you are trying to develop an overall sense of class and quality as a necessary selling atmosphere) the quality or apparent quality of the paper may be important. And so may even some of the more minor items referred to earlier. But only subject to certain qualifications.

At the risk of belaboring the point (but a surprising number of marketers tend to forget this point), these other things cannot become important until after you have tested your offers to verify that at least one of your offers works well, and to find the one that works best. If no one is interested in your basic offer and/or proposition, why waste time on anything else?

There is at least one other factor: Some of these other considerations can mean as little as 0.1 or 0.01 percent difference. That difference is not significant in dollars-and-cents terms if you are mailing only a few thousand pieces, but it can represent a great many dollars in the practical sense of overall cost and profitability if you are mailing out several hundred thousand pieces.

Among the many items that you might wish to test are the following:

Business response envelopes ("BREs")
Headlines versus no headlines (in sales letters)
Long versus short headlines
White versus colored papers
Black ink versus colored ink
1-color versus 2-color printing
2-color versus 4-color printing
Small brochures versus large brochures
1-page versus multipage sales letters
Discounts

Guarantees

Premiums

Bonus

Free trial offers

Long copy versus short copy

All text versus text with graphics

Solid text versus lots of white space

DO RESPONSE RATES HAVE MEANING?

Among the wisdom offered you in this field, opinions on response rates—how many orders per 1000 direct-mail pieces your mailout must produce—are evident in great abundance. Many will confidently assure you that you must get a 3-, 4- or 5-percent rate of response to be successful. That is, they say you must get four or five orders for each 100 pieces of mail you send out to have a successful campaign.

That idea does not stand up at all to rational analysis. If you are trying to sell a $5 or $10 item by mail you need a great deal better response rate than 4 or 5 percent to turn a profit. (And it is risky to undertake a mail-order proposition that would require such relatively large response rates to be successful.) At the same time, if you are selling a big-tag item by mail—perhaps $300 or even more—you are most unlikely to get anything approaching that rate of response. In fact you usually can do quite well with such rates as one-half-to one-percent response when the item is a costly one, and especially when it is one that by its nature offers a generous gross-profit margin. Many campaigns succeed on the basis of a response rate considerably less than 1 percent. It is rate of return—net dollars realized versus investment dollars risked (known generally as ROI, for return on investment)—that counts here.

Even this is not an unvarying truth, however, for in many cases the primary objective of the mailing is that of creating new customers such as in the case of catalog sales campaigns. This, then, is more important than immediate profits on the mailout. That is, it is the long-term ROI, rather than the short-term ROI, that is important. In that case, maximizing the rate of response, rather than dollars received, can become a primary objective. Still, price can affect the rate of response, too, and not always predictably. Ordinary logic suggests that the lower the price, the greater the response rate. But that is not always true. In many cases, raising the price increases the response! That is because when the prospect has nothing else by which to judge the quality of what you wish to sell or the validity of the promise (offer) you make, he or she tends to judge by the price. Therefore, prospects will often mistrust what appears to be a bargain price, assuming that the product or service cannot be very good at that price. The only way to learn what the prospect thinks is the right price is to test more than one price.

A CHECKLIST FOR TESTING

There are some basic rules to observe in devising tests. The checklist following sets forth the chief ones.

Test Only Important Items. The two most important items are the offer itself—your promise of what you will *do* for customers—and the price. (Again, there may be exceptions, but these are usually the most important items.)

Test Significant Differences. The differences between the items tested must be great enough to be significant. Not "good health" versus "better health," but "good health" versus "poor health," and not $9.95 versus $8.95, but $9.95 versus $5.95 or $15.95.

Test Only One Thing at a Time. It is essential that you make alternative offerings identical except for the single item being tested. Otherwise, you have no way of knowing for sure what was responsible for the difference in results. Even the mailing lists used should be as nearly like each other as possible. A common method for achieving this is to split a single mailing list into as many randomly selected portions as needed to furnish a list for each offer to be tested.

Keep Careful Records. The degree of detail in your records will have a great deal to do with how useful the tests are to you. You need to keep records that furnish a complete database and tell you what to do next. You need to be able to relate the results to causative factors if the tests are to be of practical value.

Test Continuously. Many experts in direct marketing test only representative samples when beginning a campaign, and then base the entire campaign on those initial tests. You might, in this philosophy, test a few thousand of a projected mailing to 100,000 names, and then roll out the full mailing when you have satisfied yourself that you have tested a representative sample and know where you are going. This is a sound enough practice, in theory, and avoids the expense of compiling statistics for the entire mailing. My own conviction is that this is a false economy, and that it is far better to record results and study them continuously throughout the campaign. This enables you to detect changes in response—a not uncommon occurrence, especially in large or long-term campaigns—while there is yet time to react to them by making suitable changes. The data has some value as history, but has a great deal more value as real-time feedback.

Study the Records. An amazingly large number of direct marketing executives invest the time and money to design good tests and have the data assiduously recorded—and then rarely if ever look at the data. Of course, the best designed and most exhaustive and tests do you no good if you do not analyze the results and act on what they tell you.

KEYING MAILOUTS

In most cases you will have no way of knowing which offers pull the best results unless you key or code the mailing in some way that enables you to tell which offer produced which result. (An exception would be price tests, since the customer will enclose payment or charge number and order form will also include price data, so that the price is itself the key.) Among the popular and easy methods people use to key their mailings are these:

Department Number. The respondent is advised to address offers to a "Department" number such as A1, A2, and so forth with the number varying, of course, for each test mailing. (Or for each mailout, if you agree that testing should be continuous throughout the campaign.)

Company Name. You can make slight variations in the company name to key the mailings, such as "A. Green Company," "A. Green & Company," "A. B. Green Company," and so forth. This is somewhat unreliable, however, because you are dependent on the respondent copying the name faithfully, something they do not always do. And even if you use the name variants on your order form you will not get total compliance because there will always be some people who order without using the form you provide.

Address. Some mailers rent more than one post-office box, and some can be reached by using more than one street address. This enables them to key mail by using a different return address for each mailout.

Address Suffix. Many people use the device of adding a symbol such as "A" or "X" to their post office box number, office suite, or street number. In my early days in mail order I was assured that this would not cause any problems, but I found mail carriers often confused by this device, so I do not recommend it without some reservations.

Drawer Number. The post office will deposit your mail in the box or drawer you have rented whether addressed as POB, Box, Drawer, Dwr, or by some other designation. (The larger post office boxes are literally drawers, rather than boxes, in most modern post offices.) Many people use this device—varying the prefix to the box number— to key their mailouts.

FORMS FOR RECORDING DATA

Figure 1 is a suggested basic form for recording results of mailings. This is a form for making the daily recordings of orders as received. The orders should be sorted by keys and the daily total for each key entered as indicated by the form.

Figure 2 is a somewhat more elaborate form, and is designed to collect the results of each mailing—each offer and/or other test, that is, so that you can finally compare the results and decide which one to roll out on. However, the form is designed to be somewhat universal, so that you can, if you wish, ignore Figure 1 and use the form of Figure 2 for both daily recording and compilation of results by key. In either case, you should eventually have separate records totaling results for each key, so that you can get totals for each after the mailouts are completed and you have gotten back all the results. (Usually, orders will dribble in slowly for some time after the last mailout, but at some point you will have gotten most of the response and must cut off recording so that you can evaluate results and draw conclusions.)

If you use both forms, you will not need some of the columns in Figure 2 such as the two leftmost. You may find the form of Figure 3 more useful and more appropriate, in that case, since it provides columns for more extensive analysis of results than does Figure 2.

Day and Date_____

Key	No. Orders	Sales ($)
Totals:		

Figure 1. Form for recording daily orders

Key:_____   Day and Date_____

Day, Date	Key	Mailing Date	No. Pcs	Cost	No. Orders	Sales ($)
	Totals:					

Figure 2. Form for collecting (or recording) daily orders

Key: _____ No. Pcs Mailed: _____ Date _____ Cost: $_____

No. Orders	Response %	Sales ($)	Fulfil.Cost	ROI %	Gross Profit

Figure 3. Alternate form for analysis of results

Key: _____   Date Mailed: _____   Cost: $_____

Date	No. Calls	No. Cards/Ltrs	Notes
Totals:			Cost per Inquiry: $ _____

Figure 4. Data form for evaluating responses of inquiry mailout

Key: _____   Date Of Mailing: _____   Cost Per Lead: _____

Date	No. Sales	Sales Total ($)	Remarks
Totals:			Cost Per Sale: $ _____

Figure 5. Data form for evaluating final results of inquiry mailout

These forms are designed to help you count orders, dollars, and ROI. However, there are occasions when you are seeking something other than orders and dollars—when you are seeking inquiries, in fact, perhaps even seeking to give away an item as a means for collecting a mailing list or a set of sales leads. In such case you want to determine how effective your campaign is in terms of drawing inquiries—building a mailing list or pulling leads.

Figure 4 suggests a format for collecting data relevant to that objective. Cost per inquiry is a pertinent measure, of course, and Figure 5 suggests a format for collecting the important follow-up data to determine how well the entire effort paid out in terms of final orders (if the original mailout was to collect a mailing list) or closes (if the original effort was to collect leads for direct follow-up).

6

TESTING MEDIA OFFERS

Testing offers made via media advertising is in some ways
even more important than testing direct-mail offers.

SOME BASIC DIFFERENCES AND SIMILARITIES

Campaigns to be conducted via print media—periodicals—and broadcast media—radio and TV—should be tested just as direct-mail campaigns are. However, there are some differences in the problems to be overcome and the methods to be used.

In testing campaigns conducted via direct-mail, you can usually (1) test on a relatively small scale—a few thousand pieces—and (2) start observing and recording results within days after the mailout, with the results generally on the order of 90 percent complete within a few weeks at most. Those are among the major advantages of testing via direct mail. In the case of other media used for direct marketing campaigns—periodicals, that is—with the possible exception of advertising in daily newspapers and via local radio and TV, the situation is somewhat different: It is rare that you can get your offer presented in a monthly magazine in less than 60 to 120 days after placing your insertion order. That makes testing and evaluation of campaigns carried out via print advertising in periodicals an entirely different proposition. It is, in fact, rather difficult to make a small-scale and/or inexpensive test via the print media, and even more difficult to do it in a short time. The lead time required for getting copy run in a periodical means a delay of 60 days or more, and that means that a single test cycle can take several months to carry out and can cost a great deal of money, as well. In direct mail, you can make small representative mailings and get reliable data from them, indicative of the total target population, if they are properly conducted, in a few weeks at most. This is a major consideration in testing. It is difficult, even impossible, to do the same thing in testing via the print media.

On the other hand there is one important parallel: In direct mail you are testing the appeal of your basic offer, your copy, and the list or lists you are using. This latter test, evaluating the suitability of the mailing lists for your offer, is quite important, and many marketers appear to think it the most important element of the campaign. In using print media, the counterpart of the mailing list is the medium, and the form in Figure 6 indicates the kind of data you normally wish to gather in these tests, based on print advertising. Figure 7 offers a similar form for recording the results of radio/TV commercials. These are forms for recording the orders received each day, but the same forms may be used for a monthly and/or end-of-campaign recapitulation of total results from each advertisement or commercial and each periodical/insertion and/or station.

Day and Date _____

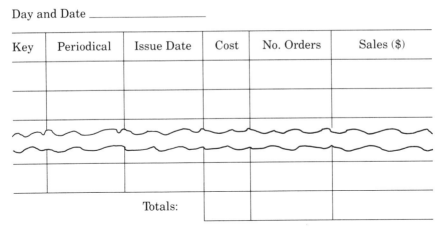

Key	Periodical	Issue Date	Cost	No. Orders	Sales ($)
	Totals:				

Figure 6. Form for recording results of print advertising

With such suitable records maintained and analyzed you can quickly determine a number of factors, including at least the following:

The relative appeal of each offer and/or advertisement

The relative effectiveness of each medium— periodical versus periodical, station versus station, and periodicals versus stations

The seasonal effects, if any

The ROI for each medium

Of course, you can cross-correlate these factors, as your database grows. But you will also want to make some direct comparisons of the various media in terms of costs and effectiveness, beyond that of the first figure. Figures 8 and 9 offer formats for these records and evaluations.

As in the case of direct mail campaigns, it is possible that you may conduct a campaign for the purpose of eliciting inquiries—gathering names and addresses or sales leads for follow-up via mail or other means, that is. The response rate is no less a concern, but it has another meaning, since its value is different—not immediately ascertainable in dollars and cents.

Day and Date:_____

Station	Date(s) Time(s)	Cost ($)	No. Orders	Cost/Order	Profit (Loss)
Totals:					

Figure 7. Form for recording results from radio/television commercials

In such case, you will want to compare the media for relative effectiveness and cost per inquiry. And ultimately you will want also to know what the eventual cost and effectiveness of the media are in terms of final sales resulting from the campaign. Figures 8 and 9 offer formats for doing this. (These factors will be considered and discussed more fully in the next chapter.) Other than these differences, the overall significance of testing direct-marketing campaigns before making major com-

Day and Date _____

Key	Periodical	Issue Date	Cost	No. Orders	Sales ($)
	Totals:				

Figure 8. Form for comparing periodicals

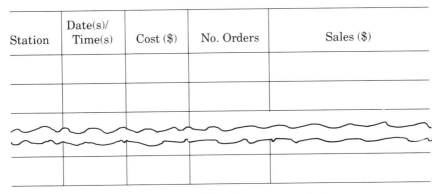

Station	Date(s)/ Time(s)	Cost ($)	No. Orders	Sales ($)

Figure 9. A suggested form for comparing stations

mitments is the same for all media, and the discussions in the next chapter will make this idea even more clear.

You can also test to compare the effectiveness of all three main media—direct mail, print, and broadcast. The form of Figure 10 serves the purpose by comparing the media in several terms: Actual number of orders produced, cost per order, and profit or loss on each use of the medium. For most cases, the cost per order (i.e., advertising cost per order or cost of getting the sale) is likely to be the most significant figure. However, as in all cases of testing, the results can be analyzed and interpreted sensibly only if the offer and copy are the same in each case.

Date: _____

Medium	Date(s)	Cost ($)	No. Orders	Cost/Order	Profit (Loss)

Figure 10. Comparing results from different media

7

PLANNING AND PROJECTIONS

Disasters happen all by themselves. Victories usually result
only from careful analysis and planning.

THE COST OF DOING BUSINESS VIA DIRECT MAIL

All marketing is expensive, and direct mail is often the most expensive, in terms of the cost of getting each order. (Many direct-mail specialists warn that it can cost as much as one-half the selling price to get the order, and even then many direct-mail campaigns fail.) Certainly, it is not a venture to be undertaken lightly, without advance analysis and planning—cost and profit projections. We have already discussed testing at some length, and made the point that the most important objective of testing is to determine what it is that the customer really wishes (or is willing) to buy. But there are other aspects to testing, for successful major dm campaigns do not often spring suddenly from the brow of inspiration. They are usually developed laboriously from a basic idea through a series of analyses and projections—premises, in fact—and these premises are the basis for the tests, are in a sense what it is that is being tested. This enables a major direct-mail campaign to be mounted in a series of steps designed to introduce as much scientific method and certainty into the process as possible and thus reduce the risks as much as possible.

This is done through a logical series of steps: First, the basic idea for the campaign—what is to be sold and to whom, with some general idea (often intuitive or based on observing market trends) of its probability of success. Next, an analysis or series of analyses and projections, based necessarily on hypotheses, to develop some figures and projections of probable results. And finally tests such as those already described must be conducted to validate or refute those hypotheses and estimates before making the major investment, so that you may drop the idea and withdraw at any point in these processes. The analytical methods and models offered in this chapter may precede test mailings, but they may also follow such mailings and be based on results ascertained in and by those tests. Study of the analytical methods and the very idea of order margin shows clearly why this is true.

ORDER MARGIN

As Shell Alpert, a long-time acknowledged expert in the field (and head of his own consulting firm, Shell Alpert Direct Marketing, Inc.) has observed in one of his many articles, you know how much a mailing costs you to send out, but you can only guess—even with an educated guess—how many responses it will bring, and wrong guesses in direct mail can be quite costly. He offers valuable guidance in making those preliminary analyses and estimates, and I am indebted to him for much of what appears in this chapter.

The key to success is a factor called *order margin* (OM). The definition of the term is simply that it is the maximum amount you can spend to get the order—the *selling expense*—without actually losing money on the order. If, for example, the cost to you of the item you are selling, plus all the related costs—shipping, handling, and overhead—is $25 and you sell it for $60, you have a $35 OM. Your profit is the difference between what it actually costs you to get the order and that $35. Your profits, if any, must come out of that OM. On the other hand, something we might call the *risk factor* in the campaign is in inverse proportion to the size of the OM. Therefore, keep in mind the importance of the OM— of its magnitude, that is—and the necessity for making it large enough to keep the risk factor to an acceptable level.

The OM tells you what response you must get to make your campaign viable. It enables you to know precisely what response rate (number of orders received per 1000 pieces of mail, per 1000 readers, per 1000 listeners or viewers, etc.) you require. If, for example, you made a 5000-piece test mailing at a cost of $2,000—$400 per 1000 pieces mailed—you would need a minimum of 1.6 percent response—16 orders per 1000 pieces mailed—to break even and recover your costs. Of course, you would require a better than 1.6 percent response rate to turn a profit on the campaign.

That can be somewhat misleading, however, for this reason: The unit costs of many things go down with increases in volume.

It's a reasonably straightforward calculation to reach an estimate of the OM for a campaign aimed at getting orders as a direct result of the campaign. You need to estimate all the costs of satisfying the order— item cost, fulfillment, labor, overhead, and any other direct and indirect costs.

This idea is illustrated in Figure 11, designed to illustrate the process and furnish a model for your use in making these analyses and presentations. (This is a simplified model, inspired by a somewhat more sophisticated copyrighted instrument of Shell Alpert Direct Marketing, the Order Margin Analysis form.)

This analysis is based on the establishment of several— three, in this case—hypothetical cost/OM models, because many different hypotheses are possible. One is that of variations in costs, according to size of mailing and/or magnitude of campaign overall. Many costs of the campaign will vary—come down, actually—with volume. But the model may also

ORDER MARGIN CALCULATIONS

UNIT COSTS	HYPOTHESES			ACTUAL
	#1	#2	#3	

COSTS & CREDITS:

Item offered	$_____	$_____	$_____	$_____
Premiums	_____	_____	_____	_____
Fulfillment labor	_____	_____	_____	_____
Other fulfillment costs	_____	_____	_____	_____
Royalties, commissions	_____	_____	_____	_____
Returns & refunds	_____	_____	_____	_____
Credit checks	_____	_____	_____	_____
Credit card costs	_____	_____	_____	_____
Resale value of returns	_____	_____	_____	_____
New customer names, value	_____	_____	_____	_____
Est. bounceback sales	_____	_____	_____	_____
Misc. overhead costs	_____	_____	_____	_____
_____	_____	_____	_____	_____
_____	_____	_____	_____	_____
_____	_____	_____	_____	_____
_____	_____	_____	_____	_____
TOTAL COSTS & CREDITS:	$_____	$_____	$_____	$_____

INCOME:

Selling price	$_____	$_____	$_____	$_____
Other charges	_____	_____	_____	_____
TOTAL RECEIPTS:	$_____	$_____	$_____	$_____
LESS COSTS (= OM):	$_____	$_____	$_____	$_____

Figure 11. Form for finding order margin calculations

consider costs of rolling out a direct-mail campaign versus a radio, TV, print-media, or other campaign, and may also be used to compare the latter with each other. Ergo, the several hypotheses may be predicated on alternative media, as well as on alternatives within a medium.

This makes the form extremely versatile because this analysis and projection can be used profitably to follow or to precede a given test mailing or series of test mailings—that is, you can use it to make early estimates, but you can also use it again after making some early tests to review and evaluate results, as well as to plan the rollout, to plan follow-up tests, or for other applications.

Of course it is impossible to anticipate all the costs you might experience in any given campaign, so several blanks are provided for unanticipated items.

Note that the order margin is not made up entirely of costs per se, but may be enlarged by "credits," or assets with cash value accruing to the campaign. For example, when you rent a mailing list you pay for a one-time use only of all the names on that list. However, the names of any who buy from you become your customers. They are your names, to be added to your own customer lists (a preferred and especially valuable mailing list, of course). Each of those new names represents an additional profit, both in its rental value and in its contribution to your premier—customer—house lists.

Other assets are bounceback sales—additional sales you make to customers through the inclusion of more sales literature enclosed with the merchandise you ship. (And still another asset, difficult to place a value on at this point but still a distinct asset, is the future business you can do with a satisfied customer—the expansion of your customer base, that is.)

The "resale value of returns" is entered as an asset because return of merchandise and refunds of purchase prices are not total losses or totally chargeable as cost items, since you do return the merchandise to stock, so the cost is only that of handling the order and shipping charges, unless there are significant costs associated with returning items to stock, or the returned item cannot be sold as new, as in some cases. In that case, credit the item at whatever you think is its salvage value.

The basic assumption in all of this is that the selling price is fixed, and the campaign thus depends on factors that are referenced to that fixed price. This may be true on some cases, but is certainly not true for all. There are cases where you have some flexibility in establishing a

Great North American Widget Corp.

Consumer Solo-Mailing Campaign
Two-for-One Widget Offer

(Approx. Net Quantity, 100,000 [100M]; Scheduled Drop Date, 2/30/83)

WORKING BUDGET
Prepared by Frank N. Stine, Nov. 31, 1982

A. CREATIVE
1. Preliminary roughs and dummies .... $ 200.00
2. Copy, including revises 2,750.00
3. Tight comp. layouts 550.00
4. Contingency reserve 350.00
                                              TOTAL $ 3,850.00   (6.3%

B. ART & PREPARATION
1. Mechanical art & preparation .... $ 900.00
2. Typography, including AAs 1,200.00
3. Repros, position prints, reading copies, etc. 175.00
4. Line illustrations (7) 210.00
5. Photography 800.00
6. Model fees 350.00
7. Color separations (2) 900.00
8. Colorkey proofs 300.00
9. Stripped-in print films 360.00
10. Contingency reserve 1,000.00
                                              TOTAL $ 6,195.00   (10.2%

C. PRINTING PRODUCTION
1. 4-pg. litho let., 8-1/2" x 11", 2 colors* (105M @ $21/M) $ 2,205.00
2. 16-pg. booklet, 5-1/2" x 8-1/2", 4 colors* (105M @ $63.60/M) 6,678.00
3. Reply card, 3-1/2" x 5-1/2", 2 colors (105M @ $11.50/M) .   1,270.50
4. BRE, #7-3/4, one color (105M @ $10.70/M) 1,123.50
5. Outer env., 6" x 9", 2 color, cello wind. (105M @ $43.23/M) 4,539.15
6. Contingency reserve 2,000.00
      *Folded   NOTE: Freight charges included   TOTAL $17,816.15   (29.3%

D. MAILING LISTS
1. Mail order respondents (tape) 70M* @ $85/M .... $ 5,950.00
2. Active magazine subs (tape) 45/M* @ $55/M 2,475.00
3. Contingency Reserve 1,000.00
           *Extras needed for merge/purge.   TOTAL $ 9,425.00   (15.5%

E. COMPUTER PROCESSING
1. Reformatting, Data Conversion, etc. .... $ 350.00
2. Merge/Purge (115M @ $9.25/M) 1,063.75
3. Code and run 4-up labels (100M @ $3.50/M) 350.00
4. Reports & directory printout 175.00
5. Contingency reserve 400.00
                                              TOTAL $ 2,338.75   (3.9%

Figure 12. Sample budget projections and estimating worksheet. Courtesy of Shell Alpert.

86

. **LETTERSHOP PRODUCTION**
  <u>1.</u> Insert, label, sort, mail, etc. (100M @ $19.85/M) ...... $ 1,985.00
  <u>2.</u> Affix bulk-rate stamps (100M @ $5/M)...................   500.00
  <u>3.</u> Audit & pull samples (100M @ $1.75/M) 175.00
  <u>4.</u> Contingency reserve 250.00
                                                     TOTAL $ 2,910.00   **(4.8%)**

. **ALLOCATED FEES**
  <u>1.</u> Ad Agency .... $ 5,000.00
  <u>2.</u> Consultant 1,200.00
  <u>3.</u> Contingency reserve 1,000.00
                                                     TOTAL $ 7,200.00   **(11.9%)**

. **POSTAGE**
  <u>1.</u> 100M @ $109/M ....TOTAL $10,900.00   **(18%)**

                                     BUDGETED GRAND TOTAL   <u>$60,634.90</u>   **(100%)**

Budgeted Total without Cont. Reserves = $54,634.90

Cost-per-M range, high/low = $606.35/M -- $546.35/M

© 1982, The Shell Alpert Direct Marketing War College

Figure 12. *Continued*

selling price and, in fact, where some of your tests are designed to determine what the optimum selling price is. In such case, you have some
flexibility, and you may wish to run an entire series of tests and calculations based on two or more different selling prices as another variable
or hypothesis.

ESTIMATING AND CALCULATING COSTS

Again I am indebted to Shell Alpert for the following example of a working budget, which presents most of the many items you must consider
when making up a budget. Note that contingency reserves are established for every class of costs except postage, in recognition of the fact
that these are estimates and thus subject to some variation. (The postal
rates have changed since this example was prepared.)

In any given case you may or may not incur all the expenses listed.
However, the form is a useful one for general purposes, and I have based
several estimating worksheets, Worksheets 14 through 17, on it.

The worksheets may be used as both checklists and estimating forms
for budget estimates, as needed, with "XXXX" entered for items that

CREATIVE EFFORT

[ ] Preliminary roughs and dummies........................... $_____

[ ] Copy, including revisions............................... _____

[ ] Layouts, rough/comprehensive........................... _____

[ ] Reserve for contingencies.............................. _____

[ ] _____............. _____

[ ] _____............. _____

[ ] _____............. _____

TOTAL............ $_____

ART AND GRAPHICS

[ ] Mechanicals.. $_____

[ ] Typography... _____

[ ] Repros, prints, etc.................................... _____

[ ] Line drawings.. _____

[ ] Photography.. _____

[ ] Model fees... _____

[ ] Color separations...................................... _____

[ ] Colorkey proofs.. _____

[ ] Stripped-in print films................................ _____

[ ] Reserve for contingencies.............................. _____

[ ] _____............. _____

[ ] _____............. _____

[ ] _____............. _____

TOTAL............ $_____

Worksheet 14. Package-development estimates

are inappropriate to your campaign. At the same time, blanks are provided for write-in items, since these worksheets are based on the premise of a direct-mail campaign, but may be adapted readily to promoting your campaign via radio/TV and/or print media by changing some of the items of cost.

PRINTING PRODUCTION

[ ] __-pg litho letter, __colors, @ $___/1000................. $_____

[ ] __-pg booklet ___x____, ____colors, @$___/1000........... _____

[ ] __-pg brochure ___x___, ____colors, @$___/1000........... _____

[ ] __Order/reply card ___x___, ___colors, @$____/1000....... _____

[ ] BRE, #___, ___colors, @$____/1000......................... _____

[ ] Outer env. ___x___, w, w/o window, ___colors, @$___/1000.. _____

[ ] Reserve for contingencies................................. _____

[ ] _____.............. _____

[ ] _____.............. _____

[ ] _____.............. _____

                                             TOTAL............ $_____

MAILING LISTS

[ ] _____lists, ____M @ $___/M......... $_____

[ ] _____lists, ____M @ $___/M......... _____

[ ] Reserve for contingencies................................. _____

[ ] _____.............. _____

[ ] _____.............. _____

[ ] _____.............. _____

                                             TOTAL............ $_____

Worksheet 15. Printing and mailing estimates

COMPUTER PROCESSING

[ ] Reformatting, data conversion, other...................... $_____

[ ] Merge/purge, ___ M @$ ___/M................................ _____

[ ] Code and run 4-up labels, ___ M @ $____/MG................. _____

[ ] Reports and directory printout............................ _____

[ ] Reserve for contingencies................................. _____

[ ] _____............. _____

[ ] _____............. _____

[ ] _____............. _____

                                    TOTAL........... $_____

LETTERSHOP PRODUCTION

[ ] Insert, label, sort, mail, ___ M @ $___/M................. $_____

[ ] Affix bulk-rate stamps, ___ M @ $___/M.................... _____

[ ] Audit and sample, ___ M @ ___$/M.......................... _____

[ ] Reserve for contingencies................................. _____

[ ] _____............. _____

                                    TOTAL: $_____

ALLOCATED FEES

[ ] Ad agency... $_____

[ ] Consultant.. _____

[ ] Reserve for contingencies................................. _____

[ ] _____............. _____

[ ] _____............. _____

                                    TOTAL........... $_____

POSTAGE

____ M @ $___/M... $_____

Worksheet 16. Estimates of fees and production costs

RECAPITULATION, ALL COSTS

Creative effort.. $_____

Art and graphics.. _____

Printing production... _____

Mailing lists... _____

Computer processing... _____

Lettershop production... _____

Allocated fees.. _____

Postage... _____

GRAND TOTAL OF BUDGET WITH RESERVES FOR CONTINGENCIES........ $_____

TOTAL BUDGET WITHOUT CONTINGENCY RESERVES.................... $_____

Cost per M, high/low: $_____/M--$_____/M

Worksheet 17. Recapitulation of budget estimates

8

COPY-PREPARATION AIDS

Part art, part method (no surprises there), but also the beneficiary of the new, bright prodigy called desktop publishing, copy preparation is undergoing some revolutionary changes.

THE CREATION OF "SELL COPY"

Modern times have brought with them the doubtful blessing of a growing trend to and demand for specialization. But no business activity
exists in a vacuum; every business must support or be supported by
many others. Ergo anyone who must manage an effort, whether as an
executive of a large organization, as factotum of a small organization,
or as an individual entrepreneur, soon finds it necessary to be a
generalist and so to be at least familiar with a wide variety of crafts
and skills peripheral to his or her major business interest and responsi-
bility. And this is most definitely true for marketing and especially for
direct marketing, which requires the practitioner to have at least a
working knowledge of a number of related fields.

   Copy preparation is one of these fields: You may or may not have to
personally prepare or oversee the preparation of your copy, but even if
you do not have a direct involvement in actual creation of copy, you certainly must be able to discuss it with those who do, and thus you need
to have a good understanding of its preparation, for copy is the very
heart of direct marketing. The "rightness" of the product or service sold,
the offer made, the mailing lists used, and the timing of the campaign
are all important, but at least as important as any of these is the quality
of the copy itself.

COPY PREPARATION AND DESKTOP PUBLISHING

Copy preparation is part art and part method. The art of creating "sell
copy" has been discussed briefly in earlier chapters and will be discussed only peripherally here. The art of copy creation is relatively
stable and changes rather slowly. In contrast, the methods of copy preparation have been changing steadily under the influence of growing and
changing technology. In this chapter, we will focus primarily on the
methods—forms, checklists, procedures, and techniques—used commonly to turn out professional copy efficiently. And of course a great
deal of copy preparation methodology has grown up over the years, but a
quite large portion of it is of relatively recent origin and great changes,
virtually revolutionary changes, are still taking place. This is the consequence of the microcomputer revolution and that which is its most recent burst of interest and activity, generally referred to as "desktop publishing." This is an outgrowth of the most popular use of desktop com-

puters, word processing. By far the majority of offices installing desktop computers do so in the interest of automating that work (typing) which formerly kept secretaries and typists busy most of the day, and the machines have been operated in business offices almost exclusively by typists, now called, euphemistically, "word processor operators."

Suddenly (and recently), however, has come the realization that word processing and the latest technological developments in the microcomputer field are the key to revolutionizing the special small-scale publications work of many offices, giving birth to this new term. Desktop publishing refers to publishing in a somewhat special sense. It refers to turning out highly specialized products, usually on a small scale such as proposals, annual reports, newsletters, brochures, catalog sheets, salesletters, specification sheets, and other such items. Of course, most of the items normally prepared for direct marketing campaigns are included in this list. However, to get a full understanding or even a working knowledge of the enormous advances which are already virtual standards in copy-preparation methods coming into use as a part of desktop publishing, it is necessary to first look at their antecedents, some of the basic forms and methods used classically as the functional base of the methodology overall.

A FEW PRINCIPLES

As a matter of basic principle, all copy, both text and artwork or illustrations, undergoes at least four major, broad phases in its development:

1. Conceptualization and planning
2. First (rough) draft
3. Revision and finalization
4. Conversion to physical product

For purposes of explanation, these are presented as though they were four discrete functions or phases. But in actuality, they are often iterative. That is, there may be (and more often than not are) an entire series of drafts before copy is finalized and made ready for conversion to the physical product (e.g., printed or manufactured), and you may also have to "go back to the drawing board"—return to the first phase—a few times before you reach that final stage. This is a pattern that is generally true for all such work—writing a manual, turning out an annual report, developing a catalog, or writing sell copy of any kind. But it is especially true in the latter case for at least two reasons: One, sell copy is usually relatively brief: a salesletter of a very few pages, a small brochure, or—as the most extreme case of brevity, usually—print advertising or script for a radio or TV commercial; and, two, because a great deal—a large investment in time and dollars—is riding on that copy.

The shorter the copy, the more difficult it is to write. In lengthy copy, such as a book or manual, there is ample time and space in which to make a point, elaborate on it, and make your meaning clear, even if the writing is not too efficient at doing so. But in brief copy, every word must count, and so each word is usually contemplated and weighed most carefully. Hence, the many drafts, reviews, and revisions before copy is finalized.

STAGE 1: CONCEPTUALIZING AND PLANNING

The initial process of conceptualizing and doing some preliminary or tentative planning was covered in earlier chapters, and a number of pertinent worksheets were offered to help you develop ideas for the several elements of the direct-mail package. However, you do need to make some preliminary estimates or judgments on the nature and length of the copy you will use before you invest time and effort in writing your first (rough) drafts. Worksheet 18 is offered as a planning form to help you record these estimates, and the worksheet includes some guidelines to help you make these estimates. However, these are early—preliminary—estimates and are by no means final decisions, but are hardly more than first benchmarks, which will almost surely be modified several times as work progresses. Use the worksheet in that philosophy, as a preliminary setting of benchmarks, perhaps in preparation for a first meeting to brainstorm the campaign, but certainly as a first step of some kind.

WRITING DRAFTS

One problem that often arises in developing copy is that of confusion as to which is the most recent draft, and that problem has been made enormously more prevalent and troublesome by the convenience of office copyers, which is responsible for a superabundance of copies of each

---

INSTRUCTIONS: Check off items you plan to use and develop preliminary estimates of word counts and sizes, where appropriate, using guidelines offered in lower portion of the worksheet. If your package will have more than one brochure, circular, or other item, use additional forms or write the additional items in on the blank lines provided for write-in items.

[ ] Salesletter ___ words, ___pp   [ ] Envelope teaser copy

[ ] Brochure ___ words, ___ x ___ inches, ___pp/panels, ___ illustrations

[ ] Broadside ___ words, ___ x ___ inches, ___ illustrations

[ ] Order form ___ x ___ inches   [ ] Circular ___ x ___ inches

[ ] _____   [ ] _____

[ ] _____   [ ] _____

GUIDELINES FOR PHYSICAL SIZES;

Salesletters may be one page, but are usually 2-4 pages, sometimes longer.

Common brochure sizes are approximately 3 x 9, 6 x 9, 8-1/2 x 11, and 9 x 12 inches.

Broadsides are usually 11 x 17 to 17 x 23 inches.

Order forms may be of any size, from postcard to full page, depending on whether they are to be self (prepaid) mailers and amount of copy to be used.

Circulars are usually of the same sizes as this suggested for brochures.

HINTS AND SUGGESTIONS FOR COPY LENGTH:

Short copy for soliciting inquiries and leads and/or where payment is not asked for.

Long copy for higher qualification of leads, orders/payment asked for and/or extensive sales arguments to be made.

Worksheet 18. Form and guides for copy planning

draft, and word processors, which make their own contribution to the excessive propagation and proliferation of copies. Too often, by the time copy is in its third or fourth stage of writing and revision, writers, editors, and/or managers are working on the wrong (other than the latest and current) draft. And sometimes there is an even worse contingency: Copy has been revised and polished for the last time and exists in final form, but there is confusion as to which is draft and which is final copy, and disasters are possible.

Using forms for drafts offers a degree of control over this. A suggested form appears as Figure 13. It includes, in addition to head data which provides such general and typical head data as date of origin, serial draft number, element (sales letter, brochure, broadside, etc.) and writer/reviewer, 24 numbered lines of copy, which enables reviewers to refer to specific lines, thus minimizing errors of reference. More important, however, is the designation of whether this is still some generation of draft or final copy, which is validated only by the signature of some approving authority. At the least, it makes clear that this is not final copy unless the appropriate box is checked and an official authorizing signature supplied.

This form is useful for copy of any length—print advertising, brochures, salesletters, or other, for example—for the basic problems of developing and finalizing copy are the same in all cases. Still, they are much more serious in the case of short copy (such as print advertisements) because editing is much more critical for short copy, as suggested earlier.

This is not foolproof, for any system can be defeated by carelessness, indifference, or failure to follow through, but it is definitely an aid to control overall if used conscientiously. Thus the form takes on a great deal of added meaning, and anyone reading the form will know or can inquire as to whether this is the current "edition" of the copy and can easily distinguish between draft and final copy. (The latter will normally be a clean typescript—a copy of the form, sans the final changes, markups, corrections, and/or comments.)

It is important, for purposes of control, that the writer or reviewer (editor, supervisor, manager, or other) sign this form whenever a new edition is generated to document changes or approvals. Accountability is an important element in control, and the signatures furnish that accountability.

In most offices today this copy will be generated by a word-processing system, based on a master-file copy of the first draft, using this form. In your own application you can choose for yourself whether to keep master copies of each draft generation or only of the most recent and current version. My recommendation is to keep a file of each generation because it is not unusual to find that an earlier draft was better than the one you are now studying. It is easy enough to keep file copies,

PROJECT TITLE:_____ ELEMENT _____

[ ] DRAFT (#___)   [ ] FINAL   PAGE #___   DATE:_____

WRITER/REVIEWER:_____ APPROVED BY:_____

1

2

3

4

5

6

7

8

9

10

11

12

13

14

15

16

17

18

19

20

21

22

23

24

Figure 13. Form for drafts

whether they are paper or computer files, until the campaign goes to the roll-out stage. Time enough then to scrap all the earlier paper as outdated and unnecessary.

Finalizing copy is far from being the final stage, of course. There are other operations and stages necessary to bring the entire campaign "up to speed"—to the next step of preparing to test or roll out. The logical next step, after final copy development and approval, is layout or design of the physical product. And that, like development of the copy, requires draft and final stages.

OTHER USES OF THE FORM

Art work—illustrations—generally go through the same stages that text does: repeated drafts and revisions until decisions are reached on final illustrations. In many cases illustrations begin with writer's sketches, which are usually pretty sketchy indeed, given that most writers are not especially blessed with professional drawing talent. But however it begins, the early sketch or word description of an illustration (words which describe an idea for a line drawing, rendering of some sort, or photograph) merits the same treatment as draft text does and can be documented on the same form (Figure 13). (The line numbers are not necessary, of course, in this usage, but it is more efficient to use this same form than to create another one.) When the job is turned over to an illustrator or photographer, suitable notations may be made on the form and copies of the drawing(s) and/or photo(s) attached.

Even that is not all, however, for there are other considerations and elements that must usually progress through draft and revision stages before final decisions are made. The decision to create a brochure and make it 3 x 9 inches or 9 x 12 inches (as called for by Worksheet 18) is only a first step in designing it, and the full design must go through several stages of development, deciding on layout of the copy, copy elements to be included (e.g., an order form or bonus certificate), colors of paper and ink, and other details. So the form of Figure 13 is useful for working through drafts and other elements of the package beyond the early decisions, including illustrations and general design particulars.

There is a psychological advantage in using a form such as this: It is characteristically much more difficult to induce most people to make the first cuts—exercise initiative—than to get them to criticize others' efforts and suggest changes as improvements. But because it suggests rather clearly that there will be several stages of draft and revision—

that what is written or designed in the first and succeeding early stages is tentative and will almost surely be changed—it helps greatly to overcome that all-too-common reluctance and so encourages initial efforts.

Again, Figure 13 is designed to be used without change for all these draft efforts—copy, illustrations, and identifying basic characteristics of various project elements.

DEVELOPING THE SALESLETTER

Layouts are a later stage in the development of copy, and are necessary in preparing brochures, broadsides, print advertisements, and several other types of copy. However, the centerpiece of a direct-mail package is normally the salesletter, which usually requires one or more drafts, but not layouts because it is simply a letter, usually on a letterhead and including only straight text—sans illustrations of any kind. (When we discuss layouts shortly, it will be evident why they are not usually necessary in developing the salesletter.)

Figure 14 illustrates a rather typical such salesletter. Note that the letter begins with a headline. (It would normally be on a letterhead—have such letterhead copy or identification of the sender—at the top or bottom of page 1, although this is not shown in the example.) In this case, the headline makes the whole offer clear in a single statement and is followed by a subhead that expands on the first statement and a blurb that summarizes the basic proposition (the promise to reduce overhead) and adds the promise of still another benefit, (increased control, in this case).

The reader can have no doubt about what the offer is: it is all explained in the headline, as it should be in any well-conceived headline.

This is a multipage letter, of which the additional pages will appear shortly. However, let us first note the other elements of this letter (see page 102).

The several promised benefits are made as prominent as possible by using headlines (which can be done in another ink color in printing) and devoting a special paragraph to each, with generous white-space separation to make them stand out. (Unlike the case of advertising in print media, you can easily afford the extra white space in a direct-mail salesletter.)

Major emphasis is on the proof or evidence, rather than on the promise, in this case. That's because it is reasonable to assume that the

CUT OVERHEAD $237/MONTH WITH THE NEW ORION WORD PROCESSOR

It's not an expense; it's an **investment!**

It pays for itself with the extra profits it creates, and yet it does more, much more, such as increasing your control of all operations.

Yes, it's true. The new Orion word processor can be yours for only $89.50 per month, and still reduce the overhead of the average small office by $237 per month, as shown by our study. (Of course, this is an average, which means that many busy offices, such as your own, save even more than this every month.

(Of course, the Orion is actually a personal computer, so you can also use it to make up payrolls, keep the books, keep track of purchase orders, do billings, manage inventory, do mass mailings, and all the other things computers do to help businesspeople increase efficiency, reduce costs, and improve profits.)

We are so eager to have you try this fantastic new system, with its fabulous price breakthrough, that we offer all the following if you order within 10 days:

FREE INSTALLATION AND TRAINING: Our representative will come out with your new Orion to install it and train someone in your office in its use as a word processor. (Later, after you decide to keep the Orion, she will be back to conduct a seminar and deliver more extensive training.)

FREE TRIAL: Use for 30 days at our cost and return it at our cost if you you are not delighted.

FREE GIFT, just for trying the Orion: Desk set—handsome mahogany and onyx stand with pen and pencil set and digital clock. Yours to keep even if you return the Orion! Value: $45.

FREE SOFTWARE: You'll get thousands of dollars worth of software FREE with the new Orion. You will probably never need to buy software for this system.

(over, please -->)

Figure 14. First page of typical salesletter

appeal of the benefit—reduction of overhead costs—may be taken for granted, and all that is necessary now to make the sale is to convince the prospect that you can and will make good on the promise. Willingness to promise a "FREE TRIAL" is one of the proofs offered.

Additional benefits such as a free gift, free installation and training, and free software are promised as additional inducements.

Additional headlines are used in follow-up pages, along with follow-up arguments that reinforce the original offer by promising such additional benefits as these:

Reduce the need for office help, cutting costs and minimizing a problem.

Speed up correspondence and mailing operations

Strengthen marketing

Increase management of many functions

Create an in-house telex system

Finally, the entire offer is summarized, with a final appeal to act promptly, and a postscript to reinforce the latter urging of prompt action to either order or come in for a free demonstration.

Among the devices used commonly in such letters is circling key elements—bonus offers and special benefits promised—in bold handwritten strokes of a marking pen and making notations with that same pen, usually printing these in another color ink such as red or bright blue.

You might note that there is no salutation in this letter, although many direct-mail specialists still use salutations. However, the modern idea is that a salutation is not a necessity for salesletters, especially when that salutation would have to be "Dear friend," or some similarly obvious insincerity. Today it has become accepted by many that you may simply forego any effort to address the reader directly in a salesletter and not suffer any undesirable consequences therefrom (i.e., that you may start a direct-mail salesletter with a headline and/or blurb and no salutation, without giving offense to the respondent. In fact, many today believe that salutations should never be used unless the letter is addressed specifically to an individual whose name is known and used in the salutation).

Whether you use a headline or not in your salesletter is your personal choice and decision, but my recommendation is to use one, and do not worry about whether it is too long. There is good evidence today that there is no such thing as a "too long" headline. It should be long enough

WHY ARE WE MAKING THIS OFFER?

We want you to discover the many other benefits of owning the new Orion. We know that even after a few days of use, you will wonder how you ever got along without this modern system for managing your office--for GETTING MORE DONE WITH FEWER PEOPLE.

This is really the bottom line: With the new Orion you can get a great many things done you couldn't do before, while you are also reducing your costs in a number of areas. A few, <u>only a few</u>, of the benefits Orion delivers are listed here:

REDUCE YOUR NEED FOR HARD-TO-FIND OFFICE HELP: With all the office chores the Orion does <u>automatically</u>, you don't need as much help, which not only reduces your costs, but relieves a major headache in most offices today.

SPEED UP (AUTOMATE) CORRESPONDENCE AND MAILING: Now you can type out letters individually, each with individual names and addresses.

ADD NEW POWER TO YOUR MARKETING: The Orion system can handle all your mailings in-house, address and type envelopes and letters--even form letters--individually, maintain your customer lists and mailing lists, make up your sales letters, newsletters, brochures, and other marketing publications, and otherwise support and strengthen your marketing.

DO YOUR INVOICING, SEND NOTICES OF OVERDUE ACCOUNTS PROMPTLY: The Orion accounting system, which comes FREE with the Orion, keeps track of your receivables and does this for you <u>automatically</u>.

MANAGE YOUR CASH FLOW, INVENTORY, PURCHASE ORDERS: The bundled accounting system also ages payables, manages inventory, makes up purchase orders, can be programmed to handle dozens of other details and <u>issue regular reports</u> on all these details.

HAVE YOUR OWN TELEX: With the communications software and built-in modem, the Orion can be used as a telex to communicate with customers, suppliers, and anyone else <u>anywhere in the world.</u> Send and receive specifications, cables, telegrams, orders, and information almost instantaneously.

Orion, then, does three important things for you:

1: Reduces costs, which, of course, increases profits.

2: Supports marketing, to increase sales.

3: Increases your in-house capability and control to lesson reliance on vendors and contractors.

                                        (over, please -->)

Figure 15. Additional pages of salesletter, sheet 1

Here is what you get, all for the low monthly price of $89.50:

The Orion personal (desktop) IBM-compatible computer with 256KB of RAM, built-in modem, four ports, two parallel and two serial.

Two 360KB DS/DD floppy disk drives. (Hard disk drive available.)

High-speed dot matrix printer with letter-quality option.

FREE software bundle that includes the following:

   Word processor
   Spelling software
   Mailmerge software
   Accounting program
   Spreadsheet program
   Inventory management program

Use the enclosed easy order form to get your Orion on a 30-day trial basis without obligation or, better yet, <u>call right now</u>, for faster processing. (Of course, you are also most welcome to visit our showroom for a personal demonstration, if you prefer.)

                       Cordially,

                       George Harvey
                       Vice President

P.S. Remember that this is a special offer that will not last long, so we must have your response within 10 days to take advantage of this low introductory price.

Figure 15. *Continued*

to deliver the message you need to deliver, however long that makes it, even two or three lines (or a headline and subheadline). If you can deliver your message in a short headline, that is highly desirable, but it is not essential. What is important is to deliver the message, and if you make that message appealing enough—help the respondent perceive his or her own interest at stake in what you promise— your message will be read with interest no matter how long it is. And the converse is true: A dull and uninteresting message will not be read no matter how short it is or how many gimmicks are used in efforts to make it more appealing.

LAYOUTS

At some point, after copy and related matters are finalized (i.e., when the form of Figure 13 for each element of the package has a check mark for FINAL) the time has come to prepare layouts. But layouts, too, are usually done in two stages: preliminary or "rough" layouts and final or "comprehensive" layouts, which are referred to generally as "roughs" and "comprehensives." These are actual designs or plans for making up or organizing and assembling all the copy elements (e.g., text, illustrations, headlines) to be made into final camera-ready copy called "mechanicals" colloquially. These will be made into printing plates through one of several photographic processes. (Hence the term "camera ready.") This, the preparation of the mechanicals, is the objective of and reason for making the layouts. They are the means for fitting together all the elements—chiefly headlines and captions, blurbs, photographs, charts, line drawings, and/or other items—to make the presentation.

Layouts are not normally necessary for copy that is all text, as most salesletters are. (Relatively few salesletters include such "other elements" as those which make layouts necessary as planning tools.) All that is necessary in developing salesletters and most other straight text pieces is rough draft and final copy, whether that is composed by typewriter, computer printer, or formal typesetting. However, when a layout is required, the forms are simple enough, and Figure 16 demonstrates the rough layout format. In fact, the figure portrays the comprehensive format too, for the chief difference, usually, is in the addition of copy in the comprehensive that identifies headlines, captions, and illustrations to be used, thus offering a rather complete idea of the final copy, as it will appear when printed. However, arrangements may be altered also, for there is the matter of copy fitting—arranging to be sure that all the copy fits the spaces planned without leftover space—to be finalized here also. This is another important objective of using layouts.

REPRODUCTION FORMS

Although salesletters and similar presentations rarely require layouts, they do have to be made up into camera-ready form. This can be simple typed (or word-processor-printed) pages on your letterhead, single- or double-spaced, as you wish, with headlines composed on the same machine. The usual aim is to make this presentation appear to be a let-

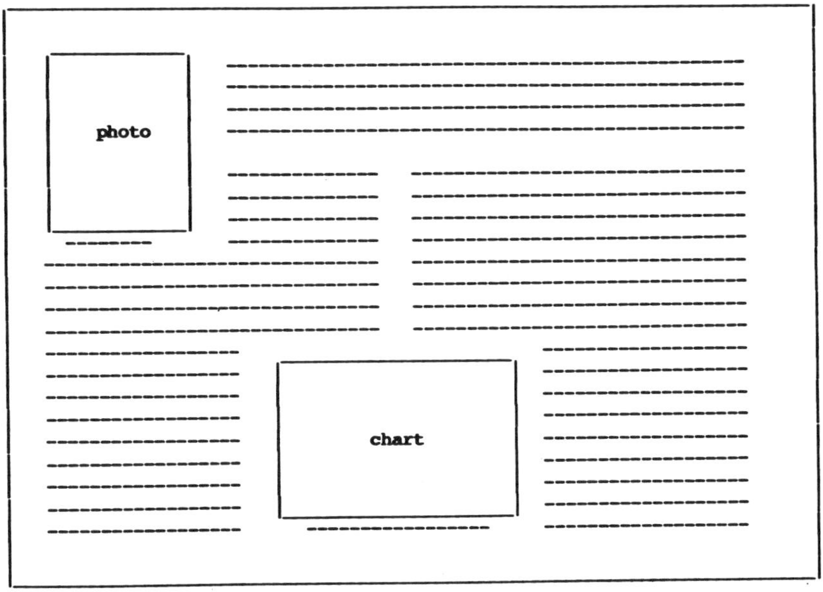

Figure 16. Typical layout in rough form

ter, indeed, and so the use of formal type, such as large headlines, is the exception, rather than the rule.

For any of several reasons many organizations prefer to use a form made up on what is called colloquially "repro" paper. (One reason is that the organization's standard letterhead is on a paper that is not white and will therefore not reproduce well.) This is white, even "super white" paper, often of special texture (e.g., clay coated and rather heavy), imprinted with guidelines in a light blue because the camera is blind to that shade, and light blue appears to be perfectly white. (The guidelines are therefore known as "nonrepro" markings.)

Figures 17 and 18 illustrate such forms. They can be used for single- or double-spaced text in single- or double-column format, with guides in nonrepro blue for page numbering and finding the middle (both vertically and horizontally) of the page as an aid to copy fitting, and a marker for the page numbers. They can also be used as forms on which to plan and lay out brochures that will be straight text.

Many organizations make such forms oversize—11 x 14 inches, instead of 8-1/2 x 11 inches—which helps make the final type of somewhat better quality as a result of being photographically reduced to normal page size, while it also conserves space.

Figure 17. Typical "repro" paper form

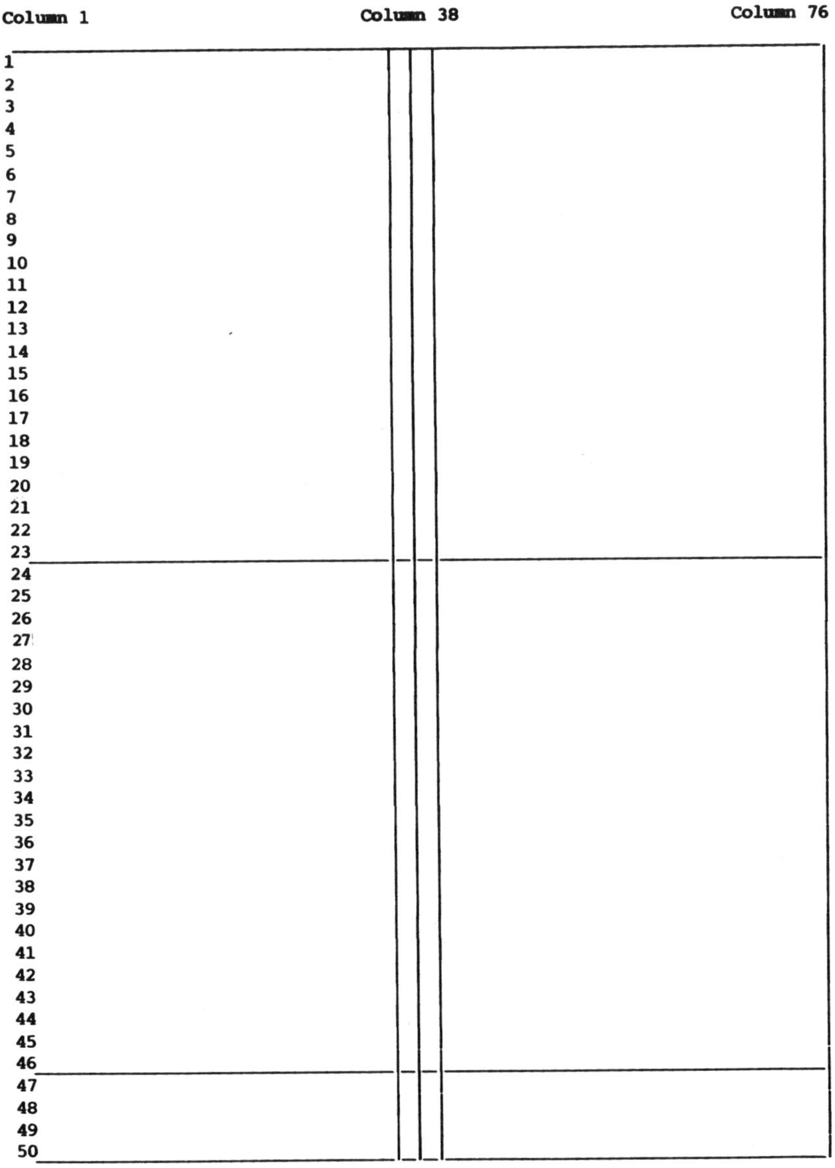
Column 1 Column 38 Column 76
1
2
3
4
5
6
7
8
9
10
11
12
13
14
15
16
17
18
19
20
21
22
23
24
25
26
27
28
29
30
31
32
33
34
35
36
37
38
39
40
41
42
43
44
45
46
47
48
49
50

Figure 18. Alternate "repro" form

ORDER FORMS

It is·generally accepted that a direct-mail package must include some means for the customer to order what is offered (i.e., to fulfill that "ask for action" item in the classic AIDA marketing acronym). That means an order form or, as some put it in more technical terms, a "response device." That term is used because the mechanism the customer is offered for placing an order is not always an order form per se, at least not an order form in the classical sense.

It is possible, of course, to send out a direct-mail package without an order form of any sort, simply instructing the customer to write or call to place an order. That almost inevitably limits the response because a great many customers will postpone ordering when they must go to some trouble to do so, and many will never get around to doing it at all. The rule is to always make it as easy as possible for the customer to order. Ergo, the assumption that a truly professional package always includes an order form.

There are several basic ways to make up an order form: Where the requirement is a simple one—where, for example, there is only one item to be ordered, the size of the purchase (in dollars) is a small one, and the buyer would normally need and buy only a single one—the form need not usually be much larger than a postcard. In such case, many marketers use the bottom one-third of a circular as an order form, with a dotted line indicating where the order form should be cut to separate it from the circular, or even as an insert in the circular (as in Figure 19). This is usually the easiest and least expensive way to include an order form. Unfortunately, it is also the way to include the least effective order form, for the reasons stated, as well as for the psychological effect of another separate item with its own sales appeal. However, the disadvantage can be overcome, as in Figure 19, by making the circular small enough and light enough to be mailed in its entirety as the order form. (In this case the circular is designed to develop sales leads—it is inquiry advertising—rather than orders.)

A compromise between the separate order form and the order form to be clipped is the circular on heavy paper or even on light card stock with the order form on the bottom third, but with perforations so that the order form can be separated easily (e.g., without the trouble of finding and using a pair of scissors).

An example of this can be found as Figure 20, a page of Rene Gnam's brochure (printed on light card stock in black and red) announcing one of his direct-marketing seminars. (Gnam is a well known consultant/ specialist in the direct-marketing field.)

Rest assured your Order Form/Envelope *will* work —in the bindery *and* in the mail.

345

We'll do the job *right*—as we do for 3/0 other trusting customers.

Ask any of our growing list of over
300 CALM CUSTOMERS

Order Form/Envelopes that <u>run right.</u> We know we won't keep customers long if our Order Form/Envelopes don't work in the bindery <u>and</u> in the mail. Ours **do** work, because we dig out all the facts before going to press, check your artwork carefully, and meet bindery specs to the last detail. The best proof is more than 300 satisfied customers who **<u>stay with us</u>** because they trust us – and no complaints from some of the country's best and busiest binderies.

High quality, on-time delivery <u>and</u> lower costs. We pay equal attention to quality and aggressive cost controls. We buy directly from the converting divisions

of six major paper mills – no job lots, no leftover specials. We constantly search out the best freight rates and consolidated shipments to save your money, and use carriers proven to deliver on time. We run efficiently seven days a week, with three shifts Monday through Friday (no charge for overtime). We're interested only in making your schedule and your bindery's schedule work.

Can we produce your job, on time? B&W runs more than a million Order Form/Envelopes a day on six web presses. Give us reasonable notice, and we can do your job – from 10,000 to 50 million – accurately and economically.

Simple to complex formats, one to all process colors, flexibility to change copy easily. We can also schedule large runs in portions to allow market testing, seasonal or price changes - at your original contract price!

Can we do everything? No: we don't do die cutting, numbering or other costly gimmickry. But we **are** equipped and experienced to produce the majority of designs/formats that work, and do the job right at an affordable price. We also believe the customer is intelligent, hardworking and busy – and treat him accordingly.

B&W PRESS

41 Pope's Lane (U.S. Route 1 North)
Danvers, MA 01923

Call Don Sanderson for answers:

(617) 593-9400 ● **(617) 774-2200**
(617) 595-4271

☐ I'M INTERESTED.
Catalog and magazine order form/envelope inserts
————— Package inserts —————

Name _____

Title _____

Company _____

Address _____ State ____ Zip _____

City _____

Telephone ( ) _____

Figure 19. Example of clip-out order form (Courtesy B&W Press, Inc.)

Figure 20. An example of a perforated (tear-off) order form (Courtesy Rene Gnam Consultation Service)

It is also possible to include an order form in a simple postcard mailing, as in Figure 21. This is one side of an 8-1/2 x 10-1/2 inch card, which is itself the entire response device. The customer can fill out and clip off the order form and find an envelope in which to mail it, or simply turn it over and put a stamp on it, for the reverse side is already addressed to the advertiser. (This is known as having your cake and eating it too!)

In these days of technological innovations many new response devices are making an appearance. One is shown partially in Figure 22. In actuality, the original of this figure is approximately 8-1/2 x 26 inches long, printed on both sides and including at one end an attached envelope, and at the other end an attached circular with photographs of the merchandise offered. The customer is invited to fill out the order form (note that this is a somewhat complex one) and mail it in the attached envelope. Special devices such as this are offered by suppliers to direct-marketing organizations.

In the first case (Figure 19) and third case (Figure 21) no payment was asked. Where it was, in the other cases, the customer was offered the convenience of credit-card purchasing and was invited to use the telephone to speed up the fulfillment process. This, accepting credit-card orders by mail and telephone, is itself a response device, and is also a relatively recent marketing innovation, reportedly first used a few years ago as a radical and bold marketing measure by Chicago's Joseph Sugarman, doing business as JS&A Associates. But what was then deemed to be revolutionary and bold became commonplace almost overnight, as others perceived the boost it gave to sales response. In fact, almost without exception offers made on radio and TV, by mail, in print, and via other methods (such as electronic bulletin boards and online databases) invite telephone orders, to be charged to the caller's credit-card.

Note that one of the advertisers identified in the figures offers a toll-free number for the further convenience of the customer, something that is becoming almost a standard practice. Accepting credit-card offers by mail and telephone and providing toll-free numbers are among the most popular inducements to order. Experience indicates rather clearly that convenience is a great motivator, and therefore wise marketers try to offer prospective customers every possible convenience.

HOW BIG SHOULD THE ORDER FORM BE?

The size of the order form dictates or should dictate the size of the response envelope (or vice versa). It, the response envelope, should be

TWO NEW 1986 ANTHOLOGIES!
Dottie Walters, C.S.P. **INVITES CHAPTERS NOW !**

NOTE

*Chapters must be 3,000 words (12 double-spaced pages) plus a 200-word
biography. Please send four black-and-white glossies.*

**YOU PAY FOR BOOKS AT WHOLESALE. MAKE 100% ON YOUR
INVESTMENT. HAVE GREAT PRODUCT TO SELL WITH YOUR
PICTURE ON FRONT AND BACK OF THE DUST JACKET!**
(Freight charges not included.)
- Hard cover anthology
- Prestige quality
- Beautiful color covers
- YOUR picture on the cover-front and back!

MAKE 100% PROFIT OR MORE ON YOUR MONEY! - Minimum
Order 250 Books.

THE GREAT

(Silver and Gold Foil, Crimson and White Dust Jacket)

SEND CHAPTER NOW - Book will be published **FALL '85.**
We invite those speakers who work in this exciting world to write a
chapter in this magnificent new book.

With an introduction by **TY BOYD, C.P.A.E.**, Famous T.V.
Communicator, Past President N.S.A, World Class
Speaker, Recipient of the N.S.A. **CAVETT** Award.

With a Foreword by **NIDO QUBEIN, C.P.A.E.**, Author of
many books, Past President N.S.A., World Class Speaker.

BOOK WILL BE IN YOUR HAND BY THIS CHRISTMAS!

Our Two 1986 Titles Will Be
SPRING 1986
THE STRESS STRATEGISTS
(Chapter Must Be In By March 1986)

FALL 1986
SECRETS OF SALES CHAMPIONS

FILL OUT AND RESERVE YOUR PLACE NOW !
ROYAL PUBLISHING ● *P.O. Box 1120, 18825 Hicrest Rd, Glendora, CA 91740*

THIS IS THE BOOK I WANT TO BE IN! ! !
- ☐ **The Communicators:** Will have my chapter in before August 1985.
- ☐ **The Stress Strategists:** Will have my chapter in before March 1986.
- ☐ **Secrets of Sales Champions:** Will have my chapter before August 1986.
- ☐ **YES!** I am working on my chapter now ! I am serious!
- ☐ **YES!** Send details on how I can purchase my books and custom dust jackets at
  wholesale prices.
  ☐ **I will need** more than the minimum 250 books. Please give me a price on #

Name _____

Address _____

City _____ State _____ Zip_____

Phone ( ) _____

Topic of chapter_____

Number of books I plan to sell each year _____

NO FEES !
*JUST BUY AT
WHOLESALE,
SELL AT RETAIL*
First Order:
250 Books Minimum
(with custom jackets)

Figure 21. An example of a self-mailer response device (Courtesy Dottie Walters)

THE KING-SIZE CO.®

TO PLACE AN ORDER
CALL (617) 580-0500

For All Other Business...
Call (617) 580-0510
Sorry, we cannot accept collect calls.

SPECIAL CHRISTMAS HOURS
Our Telephone Order staff will be on duty from 9 A.M. to 9 P.M., Eastern Time, on the following weekends:
- Saturday & Sunday November 12 & 13
- Saturday & Sunday November 19 & 20
- Saturday & Sunday November 26 & 27
- Saturday & Sunday December 3 & 4
- Saturday & Sunday December 10 & 11
- Saturday & Sunday December 17 & 18

Yes, for your convenience, our Telephone Order Staff is on duty Monday thru Friday from 9 AM to 10 PM and on Saturday from 9 AM to 4 PM, Eastern Time, to answer your questions and take your MasterCard, VISA, and American Express orders. To save your phone time, we suggest that you write out your order completely before calling.

For those customers who wish to place a Master Card, VISA or American Express order after our normally scheduled hours, on Sunday, we have installed automatic telephone answering equipment. If you fill out your order form completely before calling, ordering this way will be simple and efficient.

MONOGRAMS THAT ADD A PERSONAL TOUCH

Personalize your fashions with a handsome monogram. The KING-SIZE Co.® offers three attractive styles. Fancy Script, Old English or Full Block. Your choice will be meticulously embroidered to enhance your fashions.

Fancy Script Style

Old English Style

Full Block Style
ABCDEFGHIJKLMNOP
QRSTUVWXYZ

THE KING-SIZE CO.®

Accepts These Charge Cards.

VISA — AMERICAN EXPRESS — MasterCard

Now you can charge your KING-SIZE Co.® order to your MASTERCARD, VISA or AMERICAN EXPRESS. Simply fill in the required information at right. We'll ship your order and you will be billed on your Charge Card.

Remove peel-off label from back cover and affix here. (No glue needed.) We need the information on your label to speed your order, even if it is not your correct shipping address.

IMPORTANT SHIPPING INFORMATION
We ship cash or credit card orders via UNITED PARCEL SERVICE wherever possible. Be sure to give street address.

The CORRECT SHIPPING ADDRESS for this order is: (Do not duplicate your label. Only fill in below if different.)

Name _____
Address _____
City _____ State _____ Zip _____

If you have filled in a shipping address above, please check where we should send future catalogs.

☐ CHECK HERE If This Is Your First Order ☐ Continue to Send Catalogs to the Label Address only ☐ Start to Send Catalog to the Shipping Address only ☐ Send Catalogs to Both Addresses

IMPORTANT—WE NEED THE FOLLOWING INFORMATION TO FILL YOUR ORDER PROPERLY.

MY TELEPHONE NUMBER (area) _____
HEIGHT_____WEIGHT_____CHEST_____WAIST_____NECK_____SLEEVE_____
INSEAM_____THIGH_____SPORTCOAT SIZE_____ ☐L; ☐XL; ☐REGULAR
SHOE SIZE _____ SHOE WIDTH_____ SHOE BRAND_____

FOR OFFICE USE ONLY	QTY.	STYLE NUMBERS 1ST CHOICE	2ND CHOICE	Size	Width	Sleeve Length	INSEAMS Complete only if we are to finish bottoms	PRICE DOLLARS	CENTS

MONOGRAMMING INFORMATION

SELECT
FULL BLOCK / FANCY SCRIPT / OLD ENGLISH

				MONOGRAM PRICE
☐	☐	☐	DRESS SHIRTS ☐ POCKET ☐ CUFF	$3.00 EA.
☐	☐	☐	JACKETS	$6.50 EA.
☐	■	☐	JEANS	$6.50 EA.
☐	■	☐	JEANS (CORDUROY)	$6.50 EA.
☐	■	☐	JOGGING SHORTS	$5.00 EA.
☐	■	☐	KNIT SHIRTS	$3.00 EA.
☐	☐	☐	PAJAMAS/ROBES	$5.00 EA.
☐	☐	☐	SPORT SHIRTS ☐ POCKET ☐ CUFF	$3.00 EA.
☐	■	☐	SWEATERS/SWEATSHIRTS	$5.00 EA.
☐	■	☐	SWIM TOPS/SWIM TRUNKS	$5.00 EA.
☐	☐	☐	TOWELS	$6.50 EA.
☐	■	☐	TRAVEL BAGS	$6.50 EA.
☐	■	☐	WALK SHORTS	$5.00 EA.

NOT AVAILABLE WHERE ■ IS INDICATED

PLEASE MONOGRAM ITEM(S) MARKED (✱) ABOVE WITH THESE INITIALS...

EXAMPLE   Style Number   981✱

SORRY, NO MONOGRAMS ON C.O.D. ORDERS

ADD Pants Alteration Charge @ $2.45 per pair if we are finishing bottoms _____
ADD Monogram Charge _____
Sub Total _____
ADD 10% of Above Sub Total for Shipping, Insurance and Handling. (Do Not Add more than $3.75) _____
TOTAL Amount of Order _____
If AIR SHIPMENT Desired ADD $3.50 Additional _____
TOTAL _____

☐ PAYMENT ENCLOSED (Check or Money Order Preferred)

☐ CHARGE MY MC, VS, OR AX. (I have filled in the information below.)

☐ C.O.D. PLUS CHARGES A $25.00 deposit is required on all C.O.D. orders. Merchandise will be shipped via Parcel Post for the balance plus C.O.D. charges due. A certified check, Money Order, or cash payment upon delivery is required.

Card No. _____   4 Digit Interbank No. _____   Expiration Date Month / Year

FOR OFFICE USE ONLY		
AUTH. NO.		1

FOR OFFICE USE ONLY		
	S · S · S CO8 Z	

TEAR ORDER FORM ALONG DOTTED LINE

Figure 22. A more complex response device (Courtesy B&W Press, Inc.)

TABLE 1. Commonly Available Envelope Sizes

Envelope and Dimensions (Inches)		Remarks
Standard Business Envelopes (Usually light paper stock, most often white)		
#10	4-1/8 × 9-1/2	Standard size for most business correspondence; often supplied with window
#9	3-7/8 × 8-7/8	Fits into #10 envelope; makes good response envelope when using #10 as main carrier envelope
#6-1/4	3-1/2 × 6	This fits inside #6-3/4 envelope, is probably most commonly used response envelope
#6-3/4	3-5/8 × 6-1/2	
Typical Oversize Envelopes (Usually heavy brown Kraft paper or Tyvek, available with or without metal clasp, side or end flap, and glue or self-stick adhesive)		
3-7/8 × 7-1/2	6-1/2 × 9-1/2	9-1/2 × 12-1/2
4-5/8 × 6-3/4	7-1/2 × 10-1/2	10 × 13
5-1/2 × 11-1/2	9 × 12	10 × 15
6 × 9		

large enough to accommodate the order form. That is, if the order form is 8-1/2 inches wide (the width of a sheet of standard typewriter paper and most full-size business forms, to which standard the U.S. government and the legal profession have finally agreed) the envelope should be at least a number 9. (This is a size that fits easily into the standard number 10 business envelope.) If you compel the customer to wrestle with a sheet of paper, trying to fold it so that it fits into a small envelope (such as a number 6-1/4 or 6-3/4, a size often used as a response envelope), you are again making it less than easy for the customer. Keep this in mind when designing the order form. The dimensions of many envelopes commonly available as standard sizes are listed in

Table 1. That is, these are the sizes normally made and carried in stock by stationers and similar suppliers of such items. However, there are other sizes commonly used in direct mail and usually available without difficulty from companies specializing in envelopes and related supplies for the direct mail industry. One found quite commonly is 8-1/2 x 5-7/8, with or without a window. The significance of this size envelope is that it quite nicely accommodates standard 8-1/2 x 11-inch sheets folded once, and will thus easily accommodate almost any size order form and response envelope you are likely to wish to use. However, it has the virtue also of presenting a substantial area available for printing on the outside of the envelope—for envelope teaser copy, that is, which is used to good advantage by many direct marketers.

9

COPY WRITING

Hardly anything is what it appears to be. And that may be said for copy writing, which is something that is quite a bit more than writing per se, and therefore merits some quite extended discussion here.

WRITING VERSUS COMMUNICATION

The writing of copy is a key element in direct marketing, of course, and as direct marketers we certainly must understand the function. And yet what most of us mean by the very word "writing" itself is misleading, and we must address the subject of writing per se before studying that special branch of it known as copy writing.

Many conceive of writing as an activity that concerns and is concerned with words and words alone. But that is a literal and therefore perhaps overly simplified interpretation of the word, for the term is much broader in its practical application. The writer's job is to communicate, perhaps primarily on the basis of using language—through words—but using also whatever tools are necessary—graphics, for example—to augment the language and convey the images, concepts, ideas, and other messages that must be communicated.

That is not all of it, for communication is not a unilateral process. It is not communication at all, in fact, unless the recipient gets the same message as the message that was sent. And if words alone cannot bring that about—and that is quite often the case—any device that is necessary to ensure that the message received is the same as the message sent is a legitimate part of writing. But even that is not all: there is yet another matter to consider before we can decide what "copy writing" really is. There is the psychology of belief or belief versus understanding, and that is a separate subject, albeit a closely related one.

BELIEF VERSUS UNDERSTANDING

We considered earlier in these pages the nature of persuasion and, especially, the proposition that people tend strongly to be rational only to the extent that reason is subordinate to emotion. We will believe that which we want to believe or, at best, that which does not conflict strongly with what we prefer to believe.

Exactly the same rationale applies to understanding. We "understand" that which we prefer to believe, and we stubbornly refuse to "understand" that which we prefer not to believe. We can never understand another's political or religious rationales when they conflict with our own, for example, much less why or how they can have ever come to hold such views. So, contrary to the popular view, which is that we come to believe that which we understand, the reverse is true: first comes belief, and then comes understanding.

We can put that another way, with equal validity, but with a clearer gateway—bridge—to direct marketing and copy writing considerations: Belief—and understanding—are the result of persuasion. And persuasion is simply giving someone the opportunity to believe what he or she wants to believe and then assisting him or her in believing it by furnishing the necessary rationales—evidence or proof. When the late Joe Karbo offered to teach his prospects how to get rich in his famous and highly successful full-page ads, THE LAZY MAN'S WAY TO RICHES, his readers weren't totally naive; they were skeptical enough to require some proof that Karbo could deliver on the promise, and Karbo certainly realized that. That is why he included a confessional— that he had been stone broke, had his car repossessed, and bill collectors after him before he discovered the secrets that he now offered to share for $10 and which explained how he had gotten so wealthy and would do the same for others. And, as further evidence to back up his statements, he reproduced in his full-page copy a miniature affidavit, made and sworn to by his accountant, that the wealth he professed was real and exactly as he presented it. (That was an innovation of his own, which has been widely copied since.)

That affidavit wasn't a testimonial to the effectiveness of what Karbo offered to sell, but only to the fact of his personal wealth. But that distinction was lost on most of his readers and therefore didn't matter; the psychological effects of reading the affidavit, verifying the reality of the advertiser's claims of wealth, and the evidence that he had been truthful (at least in that respect) was enough to win the belief and understanding of the readers to the extent of well over a half-million in orders rather swiftly, and the perpetuation of the advertising and the enterprise by Karbo's successors, even to this day. Moral: Proof or evidence is whatever prospects will *accept* (believe/understand) as proof or evidence. And even that does not depend entirely on what the words *say*, but often on how the respondent interprets what the words or response device means—on the message that the respondent gets, by whatever means the writer succeeds in conveying the message.

RESPONSE AND INVOLVEMENT DEVICES

That is the rationale underlying many of the novel enclosures in major direct-mail packages, and also explains the use of the term "response device," rather than simply "order form." And sometimes the term "involvement device" is used to refer to some of those items, for reasons that will be apparent in a moment.

In the case of those magazine-subscription firms launching major lotteries of millions of dollars each year, the direct-mail packages they use represent something of an extreme in the many items and many kinds of items included, while they are cleverly designed models of the direct-marketer's art. For example, the words state, iterate, and reiterate that you do not have to order anything—subscribe to one or more magazines—to enter and win. However, the entry form to be used for those who wish to enter without ordering any magazines is a different one than the one to be used for those ordering magazines. It is a simple, black and white sheet, while the form for entering with magazine subscriptions is multi-colored, large, and commanding in many ways. It is extremely likely that most people firmly believe that use of the non-order entry (as it is labeled) form forecloses any chance of winning, no matter what the rules state (if those people have even read or understood those rules).

There are numerous brochures and broadsides, as well as several response devices, devices that compel the reader to become involved in the process by such things as tearing out stickers from various sheets and pasting them on the entry form. And in their search for these various stickers, the respondent is unavoidably compelled to at least scan the many forms describing all the wonderful prizes, the wonderful magazines, and the marvelous free gifts that come with some of the subscriptions.

PROS AND CONS OF SOME SPECIAL DEVICES

Special devices are used with more than one direct goal in mind. Many devices are aimed at getting the respondent directly involved, under the theory that involvement leads to and generates or amplifies motivation thereby. Others are aimed at building a rising structure of emotion-stirring reasons to respond by offering a laundry list of promised benefits. And still others are aimed at inducing the recipient to open the envelope, under the theory that it is usually futile or at least self-defeating to attempt to conceal that the envelope contains advertising matter. But arguments can be made both for and against some of these devices. The president of a direct-marketing agency observes, in a recent column in *DM News*, that she is herself a frequent buyer by direct mail, and she finds certain devices highly offensive to her as a direct-mail buyer. One item she mentions is that same nonorder form mentioned a few paragraphs ago, and she includes as objectionable all other devices that discriminate against respondents who respond without purchasing anything. (She obviously refers to the implied threat and the none-too-subtle blackmail that may be inferred from it.) But she also complains of false checks—discount forms that are made to resemble checks—when those forms are emplaced behind the window of an envelope so that the recipient is led to believe that the envelope contains a true check.

One of these types of devices is based on fear motivation, obviously. In the case of the sweepstakes offers, the fear that is encouraged is that unless one includes an order with his or her entry, the entry will not be considered in the competition, despite all assurances to the contrary. The other type of device, the coupon resembling a check (or, as a variant on this, a simulated credit card) is based on deception, equally objectionable.

There is a moral consideration here, but there is also a practical one. It is not possible, probably, to ascertain positively whether there is a net loss or net gain resulting from using such devices. But it is certain that there is some element of risk in using them, the risk, that is, of offending and thereby losing at least some prospects as customers. It is worth giving this some consideration in designing response devices and other items.

THE GENERAL IMPACT OF DIRECT-MAIL COPY

The consideration of sincerity and honesty in direct-mail copy applies not only to the many special devices used in dm packages, but has broad application to copy writing generally. It is necessary to consider not only the specific effect of specific items in the package, but the overall effect of the copy. The prospect may believe that you are mistaken, may disagree with you, and yet may be persuaded to buy. But if anything in the copy, whether it is some specific item in the package, a sentence in the salesletter, or anything else, comes across to the reader as obviously dishonest or deliberately misleading and insincere, it is likely that disastrous and irreparable damage has been done to the entire presentation.

Thus, although you must furnish the prospect with specifics—the specific offer, with its promise of benefits and evidence to support the promise—the overall impact of the copy is quite important and may very well become the determinant of how the respondent responds, finally, to your offer—whether he or she accepts it, that is. Inevitably, especially in lengthy copy (such as a salesletter or large brochure), an overall impression is made by the copy, and to quite a large degree the persuasiveness of the copy depends on that overall effect. If the respondent is not comfortable generally with your copy—does not believe that you are sincere or fair in your representations—he or she is not likely to have any faith in your offer, and faith is the primary basis of persuasion. You must somehow make the prospect *believe* in what you say and in your honorable intentions—integrity, if you will—if you are to succeed.

A FEW BASICS OF PERSUASIVE COPY

Despite the fact that we humans are emotion-driven, we are also intelligent. There are many things we *want* to believe, but we have become astute enough and worldly enough generally (largely through the benefits of radio, movies, and TV) to mistrust obvious hyperbole or "hype," as it has become known popularly. Simple superlatives, repeated loudly and frequently, may have once worked, but they no longer do. (They were probably never quite as effective as some thought them.) Quite the contrary, they do actual damage to credibility, arousing the reader's suspicion and, often, amused skepticism.

Effective copy therefore avoids such hyberbole by minimizing the use of adjectives generally, while maximizing the use of nouns and verbs, especially quantitative terms and in following up general statements with evidence. Effective copy consists of two elements or types of copy:

Claims—promises of benefits and statements claiming certain product or service attributes and capabilities to deliver what was promised.

Evidence—information tending to prove the validity of the claims.

And yet the matter is not that clear cut, for there are gray areas in which copy falls, although that merely serves to validate the idea that the copy must, by its very tone, *persuade* to reader to believe. The fact is that even that which is intended to serve as evidence is rarely absolute, but is evidence only if the reader accepts it as evidence. In short, there are certain psychological factors which determine quite effectively whether the average reader accepts and believes the statements—which set that tone of believability or sincerity.

BELIEVABILITY FACTORS

There are, fortunately, specific positive factors that create, increase, add to, and otherwise reinforce believability, just as there are the negative factors that militate against believability. The main principles are two: maximize the use of nouns and verbs, while minimizing the use of adjectives and adverbs—especially the superlatives—and quantify as much as possible, using the most precise figures possible in so doing. And the two principles are not unrelated to each other, as a few examples and expanded discussion will show quickly enough.

The examples that follow are all of salesletters included in thick direct-mail packages I have received, all from substantial organizations, even from supercorporations, in two cases. The point of mentioning this is simply to point out that the size and resources of the organization have little to do with the quality of the copy. In this, at least, the small organization can easily be the equal of the large one, and may very well be superior.

Vague and Rambling Copy

A salesletter from a division of a well-known corporation specializing in big-tag office equipment starts by offering to provide my secretary with a "remarkable, new professional service" on a two-month free trial. It goes on to philosophize and mumble endlessly and equally vaguely about what this marvelous new service does, and not until the middle of the first page does the letter even approach the subject of benefits to *me*, the prospect. But even then it is a vague statement about how important my secretary is to my own productivity. And after reading two single-spaced pages of close-packed text, I still have virtually no idea of what the service really is, much less what the specific benefits to me are. I have rather little confidence in any offeror who will not or cannot give me a better idea of what I am asked to buy (even on a free-trial basis!) or what it will do for me.

Admittedly, it is often more difficult to explain a service than to explain a product, especially when that service is a somewhat abstract one, as management services often are, but that does not excuse the lack of specificity and certainly does not relieve the need for it. There are ways to cope effectively with that problem, as we shall soon see.

Clear and Crisp Copy

In contrast to the first example, a salesletter in another package begins with a headline that promises an easy and inexpensive new way to create slides and transparencies. The first sentence says, "We'd like to show you how you can now make sophisticated slides and overhead transparencies ... over the *phone*, in *minutes!*"

I know immediately what is being offered. I know in terms of end-result, and I have been offered three inducements: the promise of low cost, convenience, and speedy results. This letter, unlike most but appropriately, considering its subject, includes color photographs and a headline set in formal type. Then the letter goes on, after this opening, to detail all of this with backup explanations and an offer of demonstrations and more detailed information. At another time, when I did indeed use such products frequently, I would have found the letter most persuasive and would undoubtedly then have pursued the offer immediately.

The moral here is a simple one: A large element of the credibility factor is simple clarity. You can't expect a prospect to place much credence in an offer that is not clearly explained or to be impressed by vague and rambling copy that appears to be either deliberately evasive or, at best, somewhat muddleheaded. That latter trait does not tend to breed confidence in the writer for obvious reasons.

Style Versus Content

A list broker writes, offering me a "new list" that he promises will greatly increase the response I get on my mailings. He names the list, but the name is not definitive in any way and thus gives me no real idea just what it is a list of, except that it relates to business publications of some sort. He assures me that his organization has worked hard to "identify" those he identifies as decision makers who are hard to reach (does he want a gold star?), although he gives no idea as to who these people are to whom he refers. The style of the letter is crisp, as it should be, and gets directly to the point, as it should do. But the content does not match the style. The content offers assurances, but not evidence—it demands that I accept the assurances simply because the writer uses many adjectives and *adverbs—greatly—increase—response, new and exciting list, effectively penetrate these lucrative markets,* etc. The claims are there; the evidence of validity is not. Hence the credibility is also lacking.

A Classic Salesletter

A midwest supplier of meats, specializing in steaks and selling them by direct mail, as well as by more conventional means for selling meat, uses a most classic salesletter—typewritten, with frequent underlines and handwritten marginal comments and markings in bright blue. The only formal printing is the letterhead. The salutation is "Dear Friend," a discount is offered, and the appeal is immediate and to the emotions, speaking of tender, juicy, and flavorful steaks, with rationales of the advertiser's credentials as a supplier of fine steaks to the best restaurants. The marginal comments include such items as "top quality," "magnificent *steaks—at home*," and "no-risk guarantee." The offer and the entire message are crystal clear, and I find the proposition attractive and immediately tempting.

Qualitative Versus Quantitative Claims

The factors discussed here are not peculiar to salesletters, of course, but apply also to all other copy used in advertisements, radio and TV commercials, and direct mail pieces. There is a need to be highly specific about all aspects of your offer if you are to be credible. A large and important part of that specificity lies in making the information you offer, especially in offering evidence to validate your claims, as quantitative as possible. Instead of using superlatives and making claims, use quantitative data and make objective reports. For example, don't claim "thousands" of satisfied users. Even if it's true it doesn't *appear* credible. Instead, state that you have more than 375 testimonial letters from satisfied users (or whatever number you have, of course) and don't round off the numbers by calling it "nearly 500," when it is really 465. Numbers have that quality of appearing to be factual so that you appear to be reporting objectively, rather than making loud and unjustified claims. They thus help you to be convincing and even persuasive, as long as they are not obviously rounded off numbers. ("Millions" and "hundreds of thousands" are in the same class as hyperbole. Don't use such terms if you want to be believed.)

Apply this idea as widely as possible. With a bit of ingenuity and a bit of hard work you can always develop some useful statistics such as the following examples:

Over 110,000 units (use product name) in use today.

Letters from satisfied users in all 50 States, the District of Columbia, Puerto Rico, and the Virgin Islands.

Backed by guarantees of a manufacturer in business for 73 years (since 1914).

Average length of service before maintenance required is 7.3 years.

Average weight loss reported by 37,000 users is 32.6 pounds.

Be sure that these numbers are credible, however. Remember that if the numbers are too startling—*even if accurate and true*—you have a problem making them believable, and so may find it better to understate them. Suppose, for example, that 95 percent of the purchasers of your patent diet pills reported a weight loss of 60 pounds in three weeks, that you could truthfully report this. Those would be quite unusual results and would not be easy for prospects to believe. Their typical reaction would be one of skepticism, in all probability. So unless you are prepared for a probably uphill battle and a strenuous marketing campaign to make these claims convincing, you might do well to pare the numbers a bit and thus make them more easily believable.

HOW MUCH EVIDENCE DO YOU NEED?

The weight of evidence required to back up offers—promises and claims—varies with the basic believability of the offer. As a general rule—and as inescapable logic—the more startling the claim or offer you make, the more difficult it is to prove. That is, the more extravagant your promise, the more evidence you need to back it up so that the prospect can believe it and agree to buy what you are selling.

But that is not the only factor that affects the amount of evidence you must produce. There is the risk factor also: The risk involved for the customer—e.g., the size of the price tag, the amount of time and effort the customer must invest, or other commitment the customer must make—imposes its own penalty on the amount of evidence you must produce and the persuasiveness required of your copy. You must therefore weigh the two and decide whether you can and wish to fatten up the evidence portion of your copy or cut back the offer suitably. (Logically, you would normally try to find the material to back up the most extravagant claims you can make.)

THE TWO BASIC MARKETING PROBLEMS

In every marketing problem you are face to face with either of two basic marketing problems: You are trying to sell against either instinctive buyer prejudice against change or you are selling against competition. Buyers resist change. They are reluctant to buy strange, new products and services. In fact, they perceive this as risk, and so this is really part of the risk factor. This is exemplified with increasing frequency because we experience new products with increasing frequency. Visit any supermarket or department store today, and the chances are excellent that you will find a salesperson demonstrating some new product in an effort to make this strange new product a familiar one and thus overcome the almost instinctive resistance to change. On the other hand we are often faced with selling a familiar product, but competing with a more familiar supplier of the same product or one quite similar to it—one of the same class.

The marketing problem is quite different in each case and calls for different marketing strategies and tactics. In the first case the strategy must be one that overcomes resistance to—fear of, probably—the new and strange product or service, whereas in the second case the objective is to demonstrate some advantage in buying brand X or buying the well-known product/service from supplier X.

Overcoming Resistance to Change

There are two possible ways to attack resistance to change: 1) try to persuade the prospect that the change is good, involves little or no risk, and will deliver great and new—even unprecedented—benefits. That is a challenge, but it is often met with great success. But not always: Some new products simply fail.

Unfortunately, meeting problems head-on in this fashion is not always successful: Although we know that change is inevitable and will continue, almost surely at an accelerating rate, many individuals (the ones we must sell to) are not prepared to accept that. They are fearful of the unfamiliar and need to be shielded from it in some manner. One way to do this is to demonstrate that the new product or service does not really represent as much of a change as it appears at first glance.

This is the other approach to overcoming resistance to change, and it is considerably more sophisticated and usually more effective than the head-on, take-the-bull-by-the-horns method: It requires simply explaining the new product (or service) in a familiar context. It is based on demonstrating to the prospect that there is really no great change proposed at all, but that the product or service offered is simply a new and better way to do something we have always done. For example, if you were required to sell a blender or food processor for the first time—when it was a new and strange product—you would explain to prospects that this is simply a better way to mix, chop, beat, puree, or otherwise do familiar tasks—better, rather than different. And, to a great extent, this is equally true for new brands of familiar products or services, such as yet another laundry or housecleaning product. These are often in the same category as a new kind of product or service and may be merchandised in much the same way. (More on this subject later.)

This is feasible for all new products and services because in the final analysis there are no new needs. It is the modern ways in which we satisfy our classic needs that are new, and that is probably by far the best basis for introducing new products. Radio, black and white TV, color TV, and videocassette recorders, for example, have been the progressing series of newer and better ways of providing home entertainment, and the public has made each of these types of products an almost immediate success because the buying public has had no difficulty in perceiving that truth. And the same might be said for air conditioners (both home and automobile), and many other products of relatively recent origin.

Psychologist Abraham Maslow developed what is now a brief but classic list of our most basic needs—to have someone to love and to be loved, for example. However, these basic needs were in psychologists'—clinical—terms, rather than our own everyday lay terms. We need to translate these into a list of practical manifestations that should be and usually are the basis of sales strategies. Such a list could be almost endless, as reference to almost any of the better books on advertising will demonstrate. Therefore, the following is only a partial list of those classic needs, translated into various sets of everyday terms that might serve as prompts for devising sales or copy strategies, but the list is intended to serve as a sample to provoke your own creative imagination.

Here, then, is a brief representative list:

Entertainment (generally)	Home entertainment
Convenience	Love
Someone to love	Feeling of self-worth
Recognition/respect	More money
Physical attractiveness	Popularity
Physical comfort	Emotional comfort
Escape from stress	Sense of security
Freedom from guilt	Success
Ego gratification	Pride
Achievement	Self-congratulation
Freedom from fear	Independence

These ideas and motivators—for they are both ideas and motivators—have many possible applications and many implications as well. For example, some people are motivated by low prices because they are compelled by circumstances—i.e., they are needy or are, at least for the moment, in financial straits—to find the least costly item. But others are so motivated because they are by nature frugal, and consider it wasteful to buy any but the lowest priced item. And still others are not motivated by either the need to economize or frugality, but consider it an achievement of which they can be proud (it is ego gratification) when they manage to buy something at less than the normal market price. And even that is not across the board, for the same customer who will pay more for convenience in some cases (e.g., a six-pack of beer) will sometimes go to a great deal of trouble and willingly submit to severe inconvenience in another case (such as in buying an automobile) to save a little money. (We humans are not entirely rational, of course, and you must consider that in devising sales strategies for your copy.)

Worksheet 19 is designed to provoke you into using your creative gifts and offers an opportunity to do some thinking and analysis along these lines. Because of space limitations, only a few possible needs or motivators are listed in the worksheet, but you are free to write in others of your own, as you wish. (In fact, it is to be desired that you do think up your own and write them in.) Many of the items listed are now well established as commodities, but for this purpose assume that these are new kinds of items, now being introduced to the consumer for the first time, and you must sell them. How would you analyze the product or service versus classic need? What would you use as the basis for de-

INSTRUCTIONS: Match the items in the left-hand column by writing in letters (from list provided) in the right-hand column, but feel free to write in any need/motivator definitions of your own, as you wish.

ITEM OFFERED	NEEDS SATISFIED
Audiocassette training	
Personal computer	
Laundry detergent	
Pocket calculator	
Investment newsletter	
Computer training course	
Real estate investment seminar	
Hair color restorer	
Exercise machine	
Food processor	
Kitchen gadget	
Cordless small appliance	
Rechargeable batteries	
Digital TV	
TV cable service	
Group travel plan	
Air freshener (machine)	
Spa membership	

a: Convenience	b: More money	c: Popularity	d: Success
e: Recognition	f: Achievement	g: Independence	h: Pride

Worksheet 19. Identifying needs being served

veloping a sales strategy and motivators? Remember, as you work this, that you may have to incorporate more than one motivator or need satisfier in developing your strategy.

You can and should do some kind of brainstorming in working on this. Obviously, different people buy the same item for different reasons, and you must decide which are the most common and most compelling reasons, and see whether you cannot assemble them logically in a single presentation. For example, if you are selling a personal computer of the inexpensive game type—one that uses the family TV as a monitor, for example—you might dwell on its qualities as an entertainment medium, as convenient means for cataloging household items, as a super-calculator, and other such applications. But it would be self-defeating to laud its capabilities as a medium for running sophisticated business programs, for not only would it be the wrong machine for that, but the benefit is completely inappropriate to be joined with the others mentioned here. Such mention would be likely to suggest to many that this is simply not the right machine for them and thus have a negative effect.

This is something to brainstorm with the others involved, but it is easily possible to brainstorm this all by yourself, if necessary, writing down all possible benefits/motivators/needs, and sorting them to select the main one and the several that might be grouped with and support the main use. But do so in moderation. Making too many promises dilutes the presentation and weakens it fatally. Make sure that the secondary benefits reinforce the primary one.

Selling Against Competition

Some products and services are immediate successes, perhaps because they appear at the right time and in the right place or because the buying public recognizes the value of the item and embraces it immediately. Some items never catch on, as we know, and disappear after a brief existence. But most new products and services that succeed do so only after a great deal of effort, time, and money are expended on creating a market—persuading enough members of the public that the item is a worthy one.

In the first case, overcoming customer resistance to change, you must sell against a specific (and perhaps peculiar) customer bias—fear of the unknown or new and strange item. And if what you offer is truly new and unique, you must actually "make a market" for it all alone, a most difficult proposition because it calls for pioneering or missionary efforts. (And, as widely quoted author/seminar-leader Don Dible puts it, pioneers are people who get arrows in their backs, while missionaries wind up in the stew pot!)

Thus competition is a most healthy, even needed, influence in that competition is needed to help make the market. (If you need evidence, consider the sorry state of the economies of communist countries, where competition is virtually nonexistent.) What would be difficult, if not impossible, for any of you to do alone, even if you were all large corporations, you can do together.

At the same time you do have the problem of vying with others for sales. Typically, in this, the more common case, the item you are selling is not unfamiliar to the prospects and thus does not require that they be "educated" in its usefulness, but is a case in which there are others selling the same or a similar product or service. This is selling against competition, and requires somewhat different copy to generate sales, copy to persuade prospects to order from you, rather than from someone else.

In some respects this could parallel the first case and offer the problem of selling against a kind of bias, too, such as when you must compete with someone who is so firmly entrenched as to dominate and even almost own the market—IBM in the computer market, for example, and Polaroid in the instant-picture camera market. When a company is as firmly established and commands as much customer loyalty or "brand name loyalty" as these do it takes special efforts to overcome that advantage. Even "heavy" competitors, such as Control Data Corporation or Honeywell, competing with IBM, and Kodak competing with Polaroid find the battle an uphill one.

To find success in any competitive situation, but especially against such unusually strong competition as those firmly established and well known in the market, you must somehow discover what your competitors' weaknesses are, for one thing, for you must attack where they are weak, of course, and not where they are strong.

Quite often the Achilles' heel of competitors who dominate the market is price: Those who are in a commanding position in a market often demand—and get—a higher price than most of their competitors (although the reverse is true, in some cases). There is always a segment of the market made up of those who are reluctant to pay the higher price and who are thus susceptible to offers of equivalent products or services at a lower price.

There are other approaches to the problem. In some cases strongly entrenched competitors give poor service simply because they have become complacent and excessively bureaucratic ("fat, dumb, and happy"); they have become contemptuous of their competitors and their customers. In other cases they give poor service simply because they are so successful that they are overwhelmed with sales and truly have difficulties in satisfying the demand. And in some cases the size and bureaucratic nature of a large competing seller automatically injects molasses into the delivery—fulfillment—system so that customers become unhappy at waiting a long time for response by the seller and are thus ripe for the appeal of better service. (Some merchants do well by locating a retail outlet near a large department store and accommodating the overflow and otherwise taking advantage of the traffic created by the large store nearby, for example.) But whatever the reason, such factors are problems for competitors and these problems—the "worry items" of their customers—are the opportunities for you to penetrate the market.

But even when your competitors do not enjoy an advantage of any kind over you—when you are on a par with each other—you are still vying with competitors for sales. Even when you have a unique product or service (and aside from the fact that this invokes the problem of customer resistance to the unknown) you must vie against others for the customers' dollars.

In this situation the problem of producing copy that sells successfully against competition is again one of deciding what points to attack: where competitors are vulnerable to arguments and customers susceptible to persuasion. And again it calls for brainstorming, in-group or, if necessary, as a solo exercise to decide what the major arguments are.

That is the negative side—selling against competition by seeking out and exploiting competitors' weaknesses and vulnerabilities. It is a form of fear motivation, in fact. But there is another way, a more positive way, of selling against competition by promising something special to attract sales.

THE SELLING PROPOSITION

It has been made clear earlier in these pages that to me the *offer* is what the advertiser promises to *do* for the prospect—the benefit(s) to be delivered. On the other hand, there is the matter of what I choose to refer to as *the selling proposition*. That, in my terms, consists of what I offer to sell you and the terms under which I offer to sell this—what it is, what it costs, how you may pay for it, what guarantees I offer (if any), and any other circumstances that surround or are included in this proposition, such as special features and benefits I promise to provide to my customers.

Let us suppose, for purposes of illustrating some points that must be made here, that I wish to invite you to attend a seminar I plan to deliver, and for which purpose I send you a rather elaborate brochure. The typical fee for attending a seminar is many times the cost of a book on the same subject, and often even more than the entire cost of an evening course in some local university or a complete correspondence course. Seminars are usually quite expensive, in fact. The prospect can and should therefore be expected to react to a seminar solicitation with "Why—what makes this presentation worth $200 per day?" (Not to mention one or more days of the prospect's time and, in many cases, travel, lodging, and related costs.)

Your problem is therefore how to answer that question in your solicitation. And there are several factors to consider here. A brochure and/or other literature soliciting attendance at a seminar is not likely to draw much response if it does not provide certain specific kinds of information, including at least the following:

Specifically what information will be revealed at the seminar—a detailed outline of contents.

Identification of the presenter(s), along with his/her/their technical and/or professional qualifications.

Why that information is worth the price of attendance, and/or what specific items are worth the price of attendance. (And remember that "price" includes the attendee's time, itself no small consideration, and in many cases travel and related costs.)

Unique Features and Benefits

There are many seminars offered every day. Seminars have become a major business, almost an industry itself. And they are competitive with each other. In my own case I have offered many seminars in marketing to the U.S. government and, especially, in writing proposals to government agencies in pursuit of government contracts. But I am not alone in so doing; there are others who offer similar seminars. Each has its own main reason offered for attending, the promise of some special benefit, claimed or at least implied to be unattainable elsewhere, something unique—unique, at least, in that no one else is offering it.

This unique feature, called the unique selling point or unique selling proposition by some (some even refer to it as the USP), is itself a competitive strategy. As examples, among the proposal-writing seminars, the unique selling points include these:

A proposal-writing system based on graphic presentations.

The "graduate course" in proposal writing.

Special tips, such as how to *appear* to be the low bidder.

An exclusive manual, itself a complete course, free to all attendees.

Some of these special appeals are explained in enough detail in the solicitations to verify that they are indeed unique and quite possibly as valuable as they are represented to be. Others are mere claims, which may or may not prove to be what is claimed for them. However, for promotional purposes, the important thing is not whether these are everything claimed, but whether the prospect believes that they are everything claimed. (Never forget that the customer's perception is the customer's truth, and that is the only truth that matters, as far as your marketing is concerned.)

Incidentally, that brochure that offered to deliver a "graduate" course in proposal writing also announced in that connection that it was not a course for neophytes, but only for those who were already proficient in writing proposals, and who were ready to learn the finer points of how to win. Ironically enough, this appeared to challenge those who were neophytes indeed, and thus many who showed up at the seminar sessions had to be offered basic information that the presenter had not originally planned to offer. This kind of effect delivers its own message in marketing psychology, does it not?

In selling against competition, some unique feature that promises a unique benefit is almost an essential. Beware of copy that merely tries to shout louder than competitors' copy. "Me too, but I am better than him," is not a sales argument nor a reason for buying. A unique feature must be a reason for buying, if it is to be truly effective, a reason, moreover, for buying from you, rather than from your competitors.

The late Frank Bettger, became an especially successful insurance salesman after he survived disastrously unsuccessful early efforts and learned from experience. One of his most successful techniques was arranging in advance for a medical examination for prospects he thought ripe for closing and then announcing to them his own USP: "Mr. ———, I can do something for you this morning that no one else in the world can do for you." He then followed up this attention-arresting shocker with an explanation that he could have the prospect completely covered with a major policy in less than one hour. It usually resulted in a successful close.

Victor Kiam, whose face has become a familiar sight on TV screens, as he shows his Remington shaver and makes his promises to prospective buyers, makes his own point about the USP: He agrees that it is a necessary element of the sales presentation, but points out that it must

INSTRUCTIONS: Write in one or more ideas for unique features/benefits, using but not restricting yourself to the suggestions at the bottom of the worksheet.

ITEM	UNIQUE FEATURES/BENEFITS
Your own seminar	
A printing service	
Digital watches	
Office supplies	
Computer programs	
Office copier	
Training hardware	
Vitamins	
Weight-loss pills	
Word processors	
Correspondence courses	
Office furniture	
Home improvement	
Newsletter subscriptions	
Magazine subscriptions	
Beauty supplies	
Kitchenware	

a: Exclusive manual   b: Free training   c: Prizes   d: Free gifts
e: Unusual guarantee   f: Special sale   g: Free trial   h: Rebate

Worksheet 20. Devising unique features and benefits

be suited to the market or audience. As an example, he cites a successful slogan for girdle advertisements, "Win the battle of the bulge," pointing out that it would strike out badly in Germany (because of its reminder of the final battle in Europe of World War II). And his now-familiar, "I liked it so much I bought the company," is a USP of its own.

There is also the matter of correctly identifying customer worry items and responding to them in your copy. In offering seminars on consulting (as the result of having written a highly successful book on the subject) I pursued the same philosophy as I did in writing the book: My experience had taught me that most independent consultants require help in marketing their services more than they need anything else, but others offering such books and seminars had failed to perceive this evidently. I therefore focused my seminar coverage, as I had my book, on material to satisfy this need. And of course I also focused the appeal in my seminar solicitation copy on that material and the promise to deliver effective help in marketing consulting services. The highly satisfying response verified the rightness of this decision. Attendees did indeed want guidance in marketing more than they wanted anything else.

Worksheet 20 offers you a chance to do some creative thinking along these lines. The left-hand column lists kinds of items you might be marketing. Think of some unique features or sales arguments to use in copy for selling these items. You can use the starter items that appear at the bottom of the form to stimulate your imagination, but don't confine yourself to these. Try to think up some really new and different ideas, new and different "twists" on old ideas, or, at least, new and different ways to present the ideas so that they at least appear to be fresh and different. But "unique" needs definition: Don't overlook the matter of "worry items"—what prospects are most likely to feel a great need for, especially when competitors have failed to perceive and respond to that want. That is "unique" if no one else offers it or, at least, if no one else makes a point of promising it and explaining its worth.

10

FREE ADVERTISING (PUBLICITY)

Marketing, especially direct marketing, depends directly on advertising. Publicity, when it is properly inspired and managed, is one of the most effective forms of advertising.

THAT PUBLICITY IS FREE IS INCIDENTAL

There are several basic observations about publicity that should be made at once:

Publicity is free advertising. At the minimum it makes many people aware of your existence and your enterprise. At the maximum it promotes many sales directly and has often been directly responsible for major marketing triumphs (as in the case of Robert Ringer's book, *Winning Through Intimidation* and Gary Dahl's Pet Rocks of a few years ago). But even between those extremes favorable publicity generates sales leads and paves the way for direct sales efforts in other ways.

For our purposes here publicity is defined simply as public information about you, your enterprise, and/or what you do or sell. It appears in newspapers, periodicals, on radio and TV, and in any other medium which reaches the general public, although there are some exceptions to this which we shall discuss later.

Sometimes publicity comes about spontaneously, as a byproduct of something else, but useful publicity is most often the result of your own specific efforts.

Publicity is free, at least in the sense that you do not pay directly for it (although it may sometimes cost a great deal of money to get the "free" publicity!). However, while that is an advantage, the cost or lack of cost is incidental. What is significant is that good publicity can be and often is far more effective than paid advertising. In fact, publicity has in many cases been truly priceless, producing results that could not have been achieved through paid advertising of any magnitude.

THE RELEASE AS A CHIEF MEANS

Since by its nature publicity is most frequently information in print via newspapers and other periodicals, it is not surprising that the news release (also called press release, publicity release, and simply "release") is by far the most commonly used tool of publicity or public relations (PR) specialists. And it is fair to say, too, that it is also the most commonly *mis*used tool of PR. Probably some 90 percent of all releases are promptly discarded with hardly a glance when received.

That's not a condemnation of the release as a useful tool of PR. It is simply the consequence of hasty, careless, and perhaps unenlightened release-writing practices. And it is due, in some part, to thoughtlessness in sending releases out to inappropriate destinations. Good releases, mailed to suitable recipients, are picked up and used, as intended.

WHAT MAKES THE DIFFERENCE?

Releases are sent to editors in the hope that the editors will use the release or some part of it in their publications or broadcasts (in the case of radio and TV newsrooms). There are at least three reasons for releases often being spurned by editors:

1. Some releases are pure hype, thinly disguised commercial advertising, offering no news or information of value to the editor and his or her audience.
2. Some releases are adequate enough in their content and writing, but are sent to inappropriate prospects or sent at the wrong times.
3. Some releases are scheduled by editors for use but are unfortunately shouldered aside at the last moment by more important material that competes with the release.

No editor will print unadulterated hype. Editors welcome good material — it is their job to find suitable news and other material — but it must have some value for their audience, either as news or as interesting information. You need to sell editors on using your releases by offering something the editor believes his or her audience will be interested in or entertained by. The editor knows, of course, that you are seeking some free advertising, but he or she is willing to swap the publicity for the copy, if the copy is worthy. It's up to you to make it worthy.

However, even good copy is not going to be used if it goes to the wrong editor. Business information should go to the business editors and to business publications. Feature material should go to feature editors. Material of regional interest should go to appropriate city or state desks and regional publications. Material about health should go to publications devoted to the subject, as well as to the appropriate editors of general-interest publications.

Seasonal material must go out at the right time. You can send Christmas material to a newspaper days before the holiday, but most magazines work months ahead, and plan Christmas material during the summer and early fall. Seasonal material sent at the wrong time will not be used.

There is nothing that you can do directly to combat the misfortune of having a major news story break just when an editor is planning to run your release. The news story will elbow your poor little release aside, and that's the end of it—usually. However, there is at least one thing you can do about this, which we'll discuss in a moment.

NEWSLETTER FORMATS

We have looked at the negative aspects—the hazards and the don'ts. But now let's have a look at the things you can and should do to maximize the effectiveness of your releases. But first of all, let's look at the general format, for which see the example release of Figure 23.

The release carries your organization logo—it can be your regular business letterhead—and a notice that it is a release, which can use any of several titles such as NEWS, RELEASE, NEWS RELEASE, or PRESS RELEASE.

The "contact" item is important. An editor may become interested enough to want more information, photos, interviews, or otherwise give you an opportunity to expand the story greatly. Make it easy for the editor to call the right person for this.

Not everyone recommends the use of headlines in a release. I do. It helps the editor grasp the message in the briefest of glances, if the headline is well conceived. Even better, a good headline is your main selling tool. Use it to capture attention and persuade the editor to get interested and read the release.

The dateline—place of origin and date—is classic, although not everyone uses it. Some date the release as though it were an ordinary letter. I prefer the more classic dateline.

The line "For Immediate Release" advises the editor that there is no "embargo" on the material. An embargo is a notice to the editor that the copy should not be released until whatever date is specified in the notice of embargo, which may simply read "Please do not release before (date)." This device is used, for example, when an advance copy of a speech is released to the press, so that the speech is not reported or printed in the newspapers before it is made by the speaker. This is one example of an embargoed release.

At the bottom of the first page use the word "more" if there is one or more pages to follow, and "end" or other symbol (some newspaper people like "###" to signify the end of the copy) at the bottom of the final page.

Federal Office Systems Expo

FOR IMMEDIATE RELEASE

MEDIA CONTACT:
Rosalind Price-Raymond
703-683-8500

BUCK RODGERS

DYNAMIC FORMER IBM MARKETING EXECUTIVE

TO GIVE KEYNOTE ADDRESS AT FOSE '86

Alexandria, VA, November 1, 1985 ... International Business
Machines (IBM) is synonymous with incomparable business marketing
(ibm). The man responsible for helping to make the former three
initials a world-wide success, Francis G. (Buck) Rodgers, will
share his views on methods of marketing and management excellence
at the FOSE '86 (Federal Office Systems Expo and Conference)
keynote address on Monday, April 7, 1986. FOSE '86 will be held
at the Washington, DC Convention Center.

Rodgers, former Vice President of Marketing at IBM, will explain
the management philosophy that he developed for IBM, which in turn
created one of the greatest marketing and service organizations
ever assembled.

- more -

APRIL 7-10, 1986/WASHINGTON CONVENTION CENTER, WASHINGTON, D.C.

National Trade Productions, Inc. • 2111 Eisenhower Avenue, Suite 400 • Alexandria, Virginia 22314
(703) 683-8500 • 800-638-8510

Figure 23. Example of a news release

All copy should be double-spaced, for the editor's convenience, with generous margins, and typed on one side only, using plain white paper of normal typewriter size. (Some organizations use long paper, 8-1/2 x 13 inches, for their releases, however.) The idea is to make life as easy as possible for the editor, who may be inspired to discard your release if it presents even minor problems, or to use yours in preference to another, if yours is more convenient to use.

NEWS VERSUS FEATURES

Like newspaper coverage, news releases do not always offer news. In fact, they usually fall into one of two categories: They offer news or they offer feature-type material—interesting information, such as oddities, news behind the news, human-interest tales, and other such material. Each offers advantages and disadvantages. Releases that do offer news are probably more likely to be attractive to news editors. However, there is a distinct advantage in releases that are not especially timely—that can be used at almost any time, that is. That characteristic of a release being useful at any time increases its chance of being used because the editor can save it for a "dull day," when he or she is looking for material. Moreover, if it is scheduled and then shoved aside by something more important, the editor can save it for use at a later date. (I have found some of my own releases appearing in publications months later for example and often the full benefit of a release did not materialize for many months.)

You will see many variations in others' releases, but every variation from these methods (all of which conform with what is normally considered good journalistic procedures and practices) represents an obstacle in the way of getting your releases picked up for publication.

WRITING STYLE FOR RELEASES

Writing a release properly is as important as writing advertising copy properly, and the basic rules are the same: Write the material out at length, including all the information in the first draft. Then rewrite, organizing the material for the most effective presentation. Then rewrite at least once more, editing heavily to eliminate all unnecessary verbiage. A cliche of the writing trade is that all good writing is rewriting. Most experienced professionals believe that firmly, and expect to rewrite at least once. But most rewrite again and again before they release their copy. And truly professional writers are not entirely satisfied with their copy even then, but always ponder whether they ought to do at least one more edit and rewrite.

By then the release should tell its story, get to the point as directly as possible, and then stop. And like advertising copy, it should have a lead with some opening grabber or hook that can be summarized in the headline and expanded on in the body copy, preferably in the opening sentence. That headline and/or first sentence or two may very well determine whether the editor reads further before deciding to be interested—or not to be interested—in the release.

Here, for example, are just a few ideas for creating such a lead:

A dramatic statement, perhaps a prediction of something such as "Amalgamated Foods President Predicts Shortage of Coffee Next Year" or "New Vitamin Discoveries Promise Longer Life"

Something novel such as "University Study Reveals Pet Owners Stay Married Longer" or "Government Hires Go-Go Dancers"

Something with a special appeal such as "Gross Corporation Offers Senior Citizens Special Opportunities," or "New Ways of Working Your Way Through College"

FREE NEWSLETTERS

Many direct marketers use free newsletters to promote their offerings. Some of these are quite simple, some relatively elaborate. Figure 24 illustrates the first page of one example of such a newsletter, produced every month by the Quill Corporation, a direct marketer of office and related business supplies. Currently, this is a four-page publication. Pages 1 and 2 are devoted to information and ideas, including responses to readers' queries. Page 3 is an order form (the newsletter is mailed with the company's monthly packet of brochures announcing the month's specials), and the fourth page is the back of the order form and contains information relative to shipping, exchanges, and other such details.

Not everyone who publishes a newsletter to support marketing chooses to publish every month. Many publish their free newsletter

THE QUILL® PEN PAL

A friendly newsletter just for you!   Vol. 1, No. 8 September, 1985

Dear Quill Pen Pal:

Recently, Dr. Frank Payne, of Berlin, New Hampshire wrote to thank us for caring about a "small person's small purchases." We've received similar comments from others who consider themselves "little guys."

We're glad that our concern for small businesses comes across. To us, they are what the American free enterprise system is all about.

Sure, it may be the "big guys", those Fortune 500 movers and shakers of industry, that we always read about. But ironically, they make up only 2% of American Business. The remaining 98% are small businesses with less than 100 employees!

So, Dr. Payne, and the rest of you pen pals, don't be so surprised when we give you the great buys and the "we care" kind of service that you think is reserved only for the "big guys." After all, at Quill, you are the "big guys" and you deserve the best!

Sincerely,

Marilyn Kier

Marilyn Kier, Editor

QUOTE OF THE MONTH

"If you add a little to a little and do this often, soon that little will become great."

—Hesiod

THE "EXPLODING" MARKET OF COMPUTER ACCESSORIES ADDS TO CONVENIENCE AND USEFULNESS OF COMPUTER

If your company has joined the ranks of the "automated" offices it's time to think about accessorizing for greater convenience and performance.

And there's a lot to choose from! Everyone is scrambling to grab a piece of this fast-growing market. Hundreds of new helpful accessories are hitting the market every month, it seems. And the best part is, we're getting more and more useful items at lower and lower prices. (That's our great free enterprise system at work).

Here are just a few of them in our Information Processing Catalog.

Acoustical Covers: Prevent noisy printers from distracting attention in the office.

BDT Sheet Feeders: Save you time and money. Ideal for printing on letterheads or other single sheet forms.

Diskette Safes: In the event of fire, you'll need a special "diskette" or "media" safe to guard your valuable company data. Ordinary fireproof safes will not protect the information stored on your diskettes. (See July PEN PAL.)

Dust Covers: Keep your computers clean! Dust can clog your ventilation system and cause your unit to overheat.

Head Cleaning Disks: Disk drives should be cleaned on a regular basis, approximately once every two weeks. Don't let a dirty drive destroy your disks.

Keyboard Trays, Monitor Arms and Vertical Stands: Don't let your computer rob you of valuable desk space. With these items, you can set up your system to suit your needs and keep your desk space free.

Non-Glare Filters: Eliminate annoying glare on your display screen, improve contrast and make reading easier on your eyes.

Non-Magnetic Copy Holders: Regular "magnetic" copy holders can wipe the copy right off of your disks. Don't take that chance! Get a non-magnetic type.

SAFT UPS: We all have our ups and downs, so be prepared for a power failure and guard against a total loss of information with an Uninterrupted Power Supply unit. It helps your computer shut down in an orderly fashion.

Touch 'N Go Pads & Antistatic Mats: Don't let static strike the information from your diskette records. Guard against shocks and the damage they can cause with these useful items. (Static electricity is especially prevalent in cold climate areas with low humidity).

A PRODUCT YOU SHOULD KNOW ABOUT

The Polaroid Instant Slide Kit—What would you do if you discovered, 15 minutes before your slide presentation on the fiscal budget, that someone put a decimal in the wrong place and threw off all your figures? Or what if you found a damaged slide 10 minutes before your important out of town meeting was scheduled to begin?

If your answer to the above questions is "PANIC," then you'll be happy to know about the Polaroid Instant Slide Kit. It comes with everything you need to develop and mount professional-looking slides in minutes without messy chemicals or a darkroom!

Meeting planners, communications professionals and others in offices throughout the country are discovering the advantages of using this instant kit. It's more than fast and convenient; it also reduces confidential information leaks and provides the immediate feedback that can really make your presentation a success.

For example, at an industry convention held in California recently, a production agency put together an 18 minute slide show, using 15 projectors, in only 1½ hours from the time the photographer began taking pictures. The audience was amazed to be viewing things they did just an hour or so before!

Quill is proud to be the only mail order office products dealer authorized to carry this product. And it happens to be one of our featured items this month. (See page 35D). At only $119.88, the Polaroid Instant Slide Kit is a product you can't afford to be without the next time you give a slide presentation, whether it's for business or pleasure.

HOW TO AVOID RETURNS: THERMAL VS. REGULAR ADD ROLLS

PROBLEM: The adding machine rolls you ordered don't work in your machine. You measured carefully, so they're the right size. But nothing happens when you try to print. What did you do wrong?

SOLUTION: Provided your machine is operating properly, chances are that you are trying to use regular add rolls with a thermal machine, which prints only through a heat transfer process on specially treated, thermal paper. Thermal machines became popular about six years ago, but have slowly given way, once again, to the standard machines that use impact printing.

There are still many thermal calculators out there, though. And as you may have discovered, regular add rolls won't work on them. The solution seems so obvious, you're probaby wondering why we're bothering to bring up the subject. Well, sometimes even the obvious manages to escape us.

According to our returns analysts, many of our customers inadvertently order regular tape for thermal machines or simply aren't aware that they have a thermal machine. With tax season just around the corner, we want to remind you to do a machine check now!

(continued on other side)

Figure 24. Typical free newsletter used to support direct marketing (Courtesy Quill Corporation)

148

quarterly or even "occasionally," which means whenever they decide that the newsletter is getting stale and a fresh edition is needed.

The overall purpose of using such a free newsletter is to induce the recipient to read it, of course, rather than to discard it as just advertising. So obviously, while such a newsletter is certainly going to include your sales appeals and promote your marketing efforts, if the newsletter is to serve you well, it must not be 100 percent advertising matter; it would not then be a newsletter, of course! You must include a generous proportion of useful information that is appropriate to whatever it is that you sell, as well as advertising matter. *The Quill*[R] *Pen–Pal* of Figure 24, for example, discusses office automation, suggesting products useful in the automated office, talks about shipping rates and the jargon of the shipping industry (e.g., "tailgate delivery"), answers customer's queries, and offers a few assorted ideas to improve office operations. It thus manages to promote Quill's products quite discreetly and tastefully, while still furnishing useful information to readers.

One refinement many newsletter publishers use is to have the printer "punch" holes in the newsletter for binding in a 3-hole binder. (Actually, printers *drill* the holes, rather than punch them, using a special paper drill that is not unlike the drill press found in a machine or woodworking shop.) This encourages readers to save each issue for future reference, instead of discarding it, which is to be desired for your purposes.

Many publishers of free newsletters include a price printed near the head of the first page. The purpose of this is to provide an intrinsic value for the newsletter, of course, despite the fact that all copies are distributed without charge. However, some newsletters that were free originally proved so popular that their publishers later began to charge subscription fees and made a substantial business of newsletter publishing itself. (In some cases, such as that of newsletter publisher Bernard Gallagher and *The Gallagher Report*, the publisher found the newsletter so successful as an enterprise that he abandoned his original venture—selling securities—and devoted his full time to newsletter publishing!)

WHEN AND WHERE TO USE—AND NOT TO USE—NEWSLETTERS

Publishing your own newsletter, whether free or not, has several benefits and advantages, arising from the basic characteristic of control—

control of what is in your newsletter and of who has the opportunity to read it. Of course, there are certain disadvantages also: There are severe limits to how many readers you can reach, for one, and the newsletter is not suitable as a PR medium in all cases, for another.

The newsletter is inherently a specialized publication covering a specialized field or interest that is not well served by other, commercial, media, such as newspapers, general-interest magazines, and radio and TV. For example, if you are selling wrist watches and fountain pens to the general consumer, it is likely that you will find it difficult to develop a newsletter that is useful—related to those kinds of products and read with enthusiasm by your prospects. On the other hand, if you are selling vitamins and/or other health products, there is a good chance that prospects with a special passion for health foods and health-related activities (who are your best prospects normally) will be interested in reading a newsletter on the subject. (Newsletters have a great deal of appeal to those for whom their special interest is virtually a passion, for they usually are hungry for all the information they can get on the subject.)

Too, a newsletter is most useful when you are shooting for customers, rather than sales—when it is published in the interest of selling items that are repeat items, for example, office supplies, travel services, and diet pills, rather than one-time-only items.

There is an exception to this. When the one-time-only item is a truly big-tag sale—a house, a luxury automobile, an expensive fur coat, etc.—the typical buyer does not buy casually nor hastily, but buys only after much shopping about and much consideration. Such customers need all the information and help they can get in reaching a decision, and are thus good candidates for a newsletter that helps them in this respect. Real estate developers and brokers therefore often use free newsletters effectively, as do computer manufacturers and others selling major items.

OTHER SOURCES OF PRINT PUBLICITY

One way to overcome that inherent disadvantage of limited readership is to gain exposure in other, more widely circulated periodicals. That is the purpose of the press release, of course. But the press release is not the only way to make an appearance in newspapers and magazines. There are at least these other ways to make those other PR appearances:

Contributing articles to periodicals

Writing letters for the Letters to the Editor feature

Writing a book

Contributions (letters) to regular columnists and feature writers

Getting yourself or your venture written about

Writing Articles

I do not suggest here that you try to compete with professional freelance writers who earn their livings writing articles for periodicals that pay them for their contributions. You are not likely to succeed in getting your articles published in *Reader's Digest* or *TV Guide*. But there are a great many publications in which you can have your article published without great difficulty and, normally, without payment to you. There are, for example, a great many association newsletters and even elaborate magazines published by many associations who welcome contributions, as long as the contributors do not demand payment for their articles. But there are also a number of commercial publications—special trade publications, quite often—that welcome such free articles.

Quite a number of entrepreneurs who publish newsletters, magazines, tabloids, and other periodicals of a similar nature depend on free contributions for most of their editorial content, and will welcome you to the ranks of their contributors. There are also a number of periodicals that will give editorial space to regular advertisers, permitting them to write promotional articles as editorial features. And even if you do not have any good ideas for articles, some publications of the above types welcome guest editorials—opinion pieces—which are, of course, much easier to write.

Letters to the Editor

Anyone can write a letter to the editor. It's quite similar to writing an editorial: It's an opinion piece. Such letters are often far more widely read (and often by other than casual readers) than you might imagine. When published in a widely read periodical your letter may draw a great deal of attention, especially if the subject or your handling of it is controversial. I can recall instances of being challenged by others who read my letters, requiring me to respond and sometimes even inspiring the editor to call or write with a special request that I respond. And in one case an acquaintance of mine was invited by a publisher to write a book, as a result of his letter in *Nation's Business*!

Writing a Book

Writing a book almost always produces important results when the book is a commercial success, but even the book that does not make a great splash can produce useful results. It is not easy, of course, to write a book, and it is even more difficult to persuade a commercial publisher to invest the substantial sums of money required for commercial publication as a risk venture (although that should be a first objective, ordinarily, and more than a few professionals and executives have succeeded in doing that). However, there are other ways to exploit the book-writing idea.

The word *book* is a flexible one. On the one hand it may refer to a formally bound massive tome such as Tolstoy's *War and Peace*. But it is also used to refer to paperback and even stapled volumes of a relatively few pages and otherwise modest size and modest production. Wealthy executives, heading major corporations such as the late Willard Marriott, Senior, often arrange to have their biographies written for them or, at least, to have collaborators assist them in writing their autobiographies for formal publication, which they may or may not subsidize. However, many entrepreneurs self-publish small volumes on a much more modest scale, and not necessarily biographies, either. These can be on virtually any subject that furthers your PR objectives, published in the same philosophy as the free newsletter—as promotional material for distribution to any and all who appear to be reasonably good prospects.

For example, a number of computer manufacturers have published small volumes to guide prospects in selecting a system. The typical such volume explains the basics of computers and computer systems, all with reference to the manufacturer's own models, of course, and with the invitation to call or write for more specific help in making purchasing decisions. But the computer manufacturers are not alone in publishing such material. Many others do so also.

Letters and Contributions to Columnists

Many newspaper and magazine columnists get at least some of their material from readers, and some (such as "Dear Abby") get all or nearly all their material that way. Those whose columns are based on answering readers' letters obviously solicit your letter, and more than one entrepreneur has gotten a bit of helpful PR through mention and even approbation in such popular columns as Dear Abby. But even those columnists who do not normally solicit letters from readers often mention readers and their letters when it is in their interest to do so. Writing to a columnist may pay.

In one case I succeeded in getting a columnist who was syndicated in 75 newspapers to mention me and my enterprise. What I was doing at the time was publishing (and selling by mail) certain information products—reports, newsletters, and books—of interest to job seekers. In persuading the columnist to become interested in what I had to say, I offered to send a free report to any of her readers who would send me a self-addressed, stamped envelope (usually referred to as "SASE"). It was fortunate that I made this proviso because I received over 3,000 requests for this information! (Even at 18 cents for first-class postage, this represented a substantial cost, added to the cost of the information booklet and advertising materials.)

Offering some premium, such as a useful report, is an effective means for both persuading columnists to run your notice and for inducing readers to respond. Columnists like to do things for their readers, of course, and readers like to get anything that is free.

There are columnists writing about a great variety of subjects. (Not all write about politics and world affairs.) The one I referred to above writes about people and their careers, but there are columnists writing about automobiles, stamp collecting, restaurants, travel, flying, woodworking, and literally hundreds of other subjects. There are columnists writing in newspapers, tabloids, magazines, trade journals, house organs (in-house publications), newsletters, and sundry other kinds of periodicals—even catalogs.

Most columnists welcome useful contributions, and will run them most gratefully. The work of getting mentions in these is largely the task of seeking out all these publications and their columnists. A trip to the public library and a few minutes spent with the librarian will reward you richly in this regard. Librarians can direct you to directories that list many such publications and will do so most willingly upon request. (You will probably be surprised at how eager librarians are to help in this.)

Getting Yourself Written About

There are at least two ways to get yourself written about, other than through the press release. One is to persuade a professional freelance writer to mention you or your venture in an article or two, or even to focus an article on you or what you do. The other approach is to induce an editor, especially a newspaper editor, to assign a writer or reporter to "cover" you or your venture.

Sometimes this is a chance occurrence, as it was in the case of Gary Dahl. His $25 booth in a trade show drew the attention of a *Time* reporter who wrote an amused piece for *Time* about Dahl's novel Pet Rocks offering, resulting in a reported $1 million for Dahl in 90 days. More to the point, however, such coverage can be engineered, as in my own case, when I wrote to a reporter on the (now-departed) *Washington Star*, suggesting that my own venture of helping others win government contracts might be of interest to his readers. The reporter persuaded his editor to authorize the story, and the result was a story in the business-news pages. (And this led to other, follow-up stories in other periodicals and to some other PR, as a result.)

What you must do is simply find the angle that ought to interest an editor, and then pursue the appropriate editors or writers, explaining why they should cover the suggested story. It's a marketing challenge, of course, and should be handled as such by showing the editor why and how it is in his or her own interest to cover the story.

THE PRESS KIT

Something called a press kit or media kit is a must for serious PR activity. This is a prepackaged kit of publicity materials you would normally make available to the media as a core element of every PR activity such as a press conference or any event— conference, convention, seminar, demonstration, or other—which is to be covered by the press. And such kits are also often mailed out to anyone inquiring into your activities or seeking information about your activities.

In any case, the kit normally includes two types of material: Standard materials that are normally included in all of your press kits, and materials that have been especially developed for the occasion. Among the kinds of items normally found in press kits are any or all of the following, as appropriate:

Photographs (of yourself or whatever you wish to publicize)

Releases

Brochures

Biographical data

Prepared statements/"white papers"

Reprints of articles/news items by or about you/whatever you are publicizing

Catalog sheets/specification sheets

Broadside

Circulars/flyers

Release (permission to quote/reproduce, not press release!)

Most editors prefer 8 x 10-inch black and white glossy photographic prints, although 5 x 7 and 4 x 5 are usually acceptable too. It is best to have the photographs made by a professional photographer.

It is advisable to provide a form giving permission to quote and/or reproduce your materials, despite the fact that such permission is clearly implied by the very fact of a press kit and/or news release. Such a form is often referred to as a "release," not to be confused with the press or publicity release, for the latter is a release of information, while the permission form is a release of rights.

Such a permission form need not be complicated. Figure 25 illustrates a form that is usually satisfactory for this purpose.

NEW-PRODUCT COLUMNS

Photographs are also invaluable for another kind of publicity. Many periodicals have new-product columns in which are described new products, with photographs where that is appropriate, and usually with prices and where- or how-to-order information. Sending photos and product information—the news release is suitable for this, but you can send a simple typed statement, using the release format—will get you a great deal of valuable free advertising in these columns.

In this connection many periodicals have specialists who will actually try out new products and write reviews of them, sometimes rather lengthy reviews. Where this is a practice and is appropriate to your own product, you may send a sample of your product to the appropriate columnist. (Major items, items that are too costly to give away freely—for example, computers and automobiles—are generally loaned to columnists, to be returned at some future time.) Computer products, especially software programs, are usually offered to computer periodicals for review, for example, as are new books and many other items. Be sure,

---

PERMISSION TO USE

Permission is hereby granted to reproduce and/or quote from material
supplied herewith, as indicated, with the understanding that attribution is
to be made.

_____   _____
(Typed/printed name/title)   (Signature)

_____   _____
(Company/division)   (Date)

Figure 25. Simple release form

when you send photographs of products, that they are properly identified, but do not depend on the enclosed release or statement for this
because it may become separated from the photograph. The only sure
and safe way of doing this is to attach a description of the item to the
photograph cemented or taped to the back that is. It also does no harm
to send more than one photograph of the item if you have more than one
useful view. In fact in the case of some items it is necessary to show more
than one view.

RADIO AND TV APPEARANCES

Getting on radio and TV to talk about and/or to demonstrate your product is excellent PR, but it is not easy to do. As in other cases of seeking
PR opportunity, it requires some work.

The most popular and most obvious target for such PR is the talk
show, of which there are many on both radio and TV. That is not the only
kind of radio/TV show possibility for PR. I have appeared on news programs and the programs of electronic columnists, as well as on talk
shows, although I admit I could not find a great deal of difference among
these. Nor is there any great difference in when they air; they air at any
and all hours of the day and night, and I have been surprised at how
many people have reported seeing or hearing me during the small hours
of the morning. (Of course, many of these shows are taped and broadcast
later.)

Contrary to what most people believe, the host or star of the show is
not the person to whom you should make your appeal. Probably he or

she could arrange to get you on, if he or she wanted you badly enough, but it is ordinarily the producer of the show, not the host, who makes the arrangements. And most producers are quite jealous of their authority and rights, and do not look too kindly on requests forwarded to them from the host. (In fact, if the host is not particularly well known and therefore not especially powerful, his or her recommendation may do you more harm than good!) The producer may have a great deal more sway than the host does. It is not that unusual. Producers will usually like you a great deal more if you recognize (and show respect for) their authority and rights by approaching them directly, instead of by some indirect means. Nevertheless, this is not to say that this will greatly improve your chances of appearing on that show. In spite of doing everything right you will still need to be quite persistent, and you will have to think up many reasons for being on the show, if you are to succeed in doing so. Producers are always weighing all prospective guests, trying to select the best ones—those guests who are likely to be the most interesting ones for the viewers, for that is their ultimate criterion of success as producers. Too, they tend to "book" more guests than they can use because these shows are often rather loosely formatted, with the host deciding spontaneously whether a guest is interesting enough to keep chatting for a while longer or is to be to cut off and gotten rid of. (And if the show has a live audience in the studio, audience reaction often determines whether a guest is kept on longer.)

Because of such considerations you may wind up quite often in the "ready room," waiting throughout the show without being called. That may result in your coming back another time, or it may result in your never being called. On the other hand, one reason producers overbook these shows is that some guests cancel at the last moment or simply do not show up at all, so the producer needs an emergency reserve. Therefore, if you have indicated that you can usually be available on very short notice and are able to reach the studio in a few minutes, you may get a panic call at the last minute.

To succeed in getting on these shows you must write and call the producers frequently, reminding them of your availability. And, as in almost everything else, persistence and perseverance will pay off: You will—must—eventually succeed if you stick with it long enough. (Sometimes you simply wear the producer down through your perseverance!) It is, in fact, almost a mathematical certainty that if you persevere long enough you will ultimately prevail. However, serendipity also plays a role: If you call often enough, you will "just happen" to call at the precise moment that the producer is frantically trying to find a last-minute replacement, but has not thought about you. Only your unceasing calls finally produce the result. It was in this manner that I finally broke through and got my face and voice on a TV show for the first time.

No celebrity I, I have nevertheless so far appeared on this (Washington's *Panorama*), and several other TV shows, and dozens of radio shows, some in person, some via telephone interviews. This latter method is, in this electronic and tape era, an increasingly popular mode of interviewing and presenting guests on radio and TV. Recently I recorded a two-minute public service videotape with a local TV personality. This tape will be shown six times a week for the next eight months! Recording it was easy enough. I prepared a script, rehearsed it with my TV host for only a few minutes, and then recorded it for air play.

One approach you might consider is that of listening to and participating in "call in" shows, as a kind of break-in experience. There are many such shows on TV and radio, especially on local stations, so it is not difficult to "get on."

The opportunities for media coverage are much greater than you realize. The many media—the thousands of publications, radio shows, and TV shows—engulf and devour information at a truly incredible rate and are correspondingly ravenous for more. Skeptical although editors and producers are (made so by the abundant supply of charlatans and fakers in our society), they are still hungry for fresh information if it appears at all interesting to their public: readers, listeners, and viewers. Offer information of value and you will be welcomed—eventually. (It may take some time and effort to win recognition and appreciation, but it must happen eventually for the dedicated and persevering.)

A FEW METHODS

In searching out opportunities in the electronic media, you must do your research first:

1. Seek out the programs, radio and TV, of interest
2. Call the studios and determine who the producers are
3. Send the producers releases and/or complete press kits
4. Follow up with telephone calls
5. Persist and persevere. Don't get discouraged, for persistence and perseverance are the keys to success in this.

11

SPECIAL OFFERS, METHODS, AND DEVICES

The "special offer" is to direct marketing what cream is to coffee—used by most as a matter of course. But there are also special methods and devices to consider.

EVERY DAY IS SALE DAY FOR SOME MARKETERS

A mainstay of marketing strategy in direct mail is the "Special Offer!" It is an inherent and virtually automatic concept, for many marketers, such as those who market a single item in each campaign. And it is especially the case for those who can not normally expect any volume of repeat orders and who must therefore manage to turn a profit on each individual order and on the campaign generally, as distinct from those in catalog sales and other campaigns where repeat business and, therefore, establishing new customers is the main objective.

But even in the latter kinds of campaigns, the marketers offer "specials" of various kinds, just as retail stores do. Quill$^{(R)}$ Corporation, for example, sends out a thick semiannual catalog, but also sends out a smaller monthly catalog listing many specials, and makes additional mailings of brochures and other sales literature listing specials. And at least a half-dozen mail-order vendors of computer equipment and supplies send me catalogs regularly, usually listing their own specials.

A FEW TYPICAL SPECIAL OFFERS

These special offers can and do take many forms. A few of those in rather common use are listed as Column A in Worksheet 21. Note that many are based on special prices—discounts and sale prices—and others on giveaways of various kinds. However, customers are not as naive as they once were. The special offer must be justified and explained to the customer before the customer will accept it as a truly special offer, although some of these special offers explain themselves. For example, the offer that says this is the last chance to get whatever it is at the old price, before the impending price rise, explains itself. We have become accustomed to inflation, and we expect prices to rise, so we are likely to accept that. On the other hand, a flat claim that this is a 40-percent reduction in price is likely to not be believed unless a rationale is provided. In any case, the average customer is far more likely to accept a special offer as genuinely special and act on it if you provide a persuasive explanation, so the rationalization tends to make the offer far more effective and should be considered a necessity.

Some of the many rationalizations used commonly to explain or justify the specials so as to persuade customers to believe that they are true specials indeed are listed as Column B in Worksheet 21. Try match-

INSTRUCTIONS: Write the numbers of Column B items in the boxes following
Column A items, matching each Column A item with a Column B item.

COLUMN A		COLUMN B
Heavily discounted items--perhaps		1. Special buy
loss leaders	[ ]	2. Discontinued item
Three for the price of two	[ ]	3. End-of-year closeout
Unique item--not available		4. Clearing inventory
anywhere else	[ ]	5. Special marketing test
Bonus--something free with		6. Introducing new product
quantity orders	[ ]	7. Introducing new supplier
Last call before price rise	[ ]	8. New-customer drive
Free trial	[ ]	9. 25th Anniversary sale
Double your money back guarantee	[ ]	10. Under new management sale
Free samples	[ ]	11. No explanation needed
Contests and prizes	[ ]	12. Discontinued model
Accumulating "credit" balances		13. To show our appreciation
or stamps for premiums	[ ]	14. Going out of business
Discount coupons for credit on		15. Bankrupt manufacturer
future purchases	[ ]	16. Summer clearance

Worksheet 21. Some typical special offers

ing the two columns up—the special offer with the rationalization—to
train yourself to think in these terms. Note that in many cases a special
offer can have more than one sensible rationalization, and many
rationalizations can fit more than one special offer. In this exercise,
choose your first-priority matches. Note too that there are more
rationalizations than there are special offers because there are no
"school solutions" here. There are only those choices you prefer to make,
and the only "right answers" here, as in real life, are whatever works
in practice.

A FEW EXAMPLES AND IDEAS FOR SPECIAL OFFERS

There can be few people left in America who are not now aware of the annual multimillion dollar prize contests by the two largest magazine distributors seeking new subscribers. (This year the first prize in these contests has reached $10 million.) In fact, one of these organizations mounts a major TV advertising campaign to persuade viewers to enter, with their "Come on, send it in" exhortation and display of winners of earlier years. Nor are there many who have not seen the TV commercials of the major weekly newsmagazines, especially *Time* and *Newsweek* who offer such gifts as cameras and calculators to seduce new subscribers. And there cannot be very many American households who have never received solicitations from the prominent Minnesota direct mail marketer, Fingerhut, who makes a standard practice of offering free gifts with every order.

Less highly visible, but nonetheless very much in evidence, are the thousands of other entrepreneurs who offer similar special inducements of their own to attract customers. The difference is much more one of degree than of kind, as a few examples will demonstrate.

The Globe Ticket Company of Horsham, Pennsylvania is a specialist in tickets and ticket systems for all kinds of events. The company sells tickets and related systems, including equipment that their mailer refers to as "ticket accessories," designed to both facilitate the efficient selling of tickets and to ensure that all the dollars collected for tickets find their way into their proper pockets. This piece is a patent self-mailer, 8-1/2 × 17 inches, folded down to a 6 × 8-1/2 inch packet. That includes a 6-inch order form and envelope, perforated for detaching. The envelope is a "BRE," (business reply envelope), preaddressed and with a permit indicia so that the buyer does not need to supply a postage stamp.

The front of the mailer is simple enough, and includes a box that bears the line: SPECIAL OFFER, a photo of what they call a Cash Ticket Case and a reproduction of a ticket, with the invitation to ask about one of their "revenue control systems" and the promise of saving money on this or other equipment they sell. The equipment and the various kinds of tickets are illustrated and explained on the inner panels of the mailer, with the promise of saving 25 to 50 percent on the equipment when bought with ticket orders, and a reminder to take advantage of the special offer. (It is easy to infer from the whole presentation that the company's main interest and primary business is printing and selling tickets, and the sale of equipment is a secondary interest undertaken in support of that primary interest.)

The piece is an excellent example: It is tasteful (no loud claims or hype), makes the offer quite clear (ensuring accountability for ticket sales, which they refer to as "revenue control"), it is easy to mail (a single piece and a self-mailer at that), it is easy to read (all in a single piece, with no thick parcel of brochures and circulars), and yet offers the customer the convenience of an order form and postage-free response envelope. A very neat package for someone who is selling an uncomplicated product or service.

Lasons Label Company of Chicago has a modest conventional mailing consisting of a letter, an order form, and a BRE, mailed in a regular number 10 business envelope. The letter is formally typeset and printed, and has a gold and red seal affixed to it announcing another company's tenth anniversary. It's an example of what Lasons is offering—custom-made anniversary seals, with a number of models shown on the order form and, as a special offer, Lasons promises to send 25 "happy-face" seals that say "We're happy for customers like you."

As in the case of the Globe company, the proposition is a simple and straightforward one, and the letter makes the offer clear: The seals are attention getters and lend distinction to the buyer's letters, invoices, brochures, and other such items sent out. And even the free premium, those happy-face seals, are leaders because the company also sells those happy face-seals to anyone who likes them well enough to want more of the same! That means that the happy-face seals do double duty as both a premium and an order-getting sample of another profit-producing product.

Card-deck mailings have become more and more popular as order-getters and lead-getters. The cards are simple—totally uncomplicated—and are easy for the customers to use since they can do double duty as order forms. So it is not surprising that there are numerous other free and discount offers, especially by card-deck advertisers. Presumably, the limited space of a card deck mandates a simple and easy-to-understand offer, although even that is no longer entirely true since mini-catalogs of 3-1/2 /x 5-1/2 inch outer dimensions have begun to appear in card deck mailings. However, here are a few typical offers found in card decks:

The card deck mailer High Tech Times[R] of Santa Barbara, California offers a free subscription. Unlike most cards, this one requires a postage stamp. (Almost all others bear permit indicia so that the respondent need not worry about postage.)

Computer Shopper, a monthly tabloid published in Titusville, Florida, offers a free sample issue, and makes that the main offer with the headline FREE ISSUE dominating the card.

Dynamic Graphics, Inc. of Peoria, Illinois, vendor of a subscription clip art service, offers a 24-page trial issue, asking the respondent to subscribe but with permission to cancel after the first issue is received. This organization also requires the respondent to supply a postage stamp.

The Januz Direct Marketing Letter of Santa Barbara, California offers two monthly issues free, but also requires that the respondent subscribe, with the privilege of canceling after the second issue and thereby owing nothing.

InfoWorld, a popular weekly tabloid devoted to computers, offers four issues free on those same terms—*free* means subscribing with the right to cancel after four issues, owing nothing. There are many such offers, and the theory on which such offers are based is that a great many who sign up will not cancel, even if they are not transported by the first issue or two.

The American Software Club of Santa Barbara claims 40,000 members and offers a one-year trial membership without obligation. Not very much information is offered on the card, and it is quite possible that the free software is, in fact, public domain software which is by its very nature free.

InfoSystems, a monthly magazine of Wheaton, Illinois offers free subscription.

A SPECIAL DEVICE

An item that has nothing to do directly with special offers, but is related to card decks merits mention here. John Wiley & Sons, Inc. a regular user of card decks to sell their technical, professional, and business books, has instituted a useful new idea, exploiting the principle of making it as easy as possible for the customer to order. Included in their card deck is a card that contains six copies (on self-stick labels) of the respondent's own name and address, so the respondent does not even have to go to the trouble of writing his or her name on the order form but may use the labels in responding! Of course, modern computer technology makes it possible to provide each addressee with such a convenience, and it seems like a rather useful idea, given the powerful influence of convenience as a motivator. But even that is not the only factor that makes this a valuable idea. There is also the secondary consideration of the positive effects achieved by *personalizing* the package in this way. It is the computer, of course, that makes such things as this possible.

A FEW SPECIAL METHODS

There are many ways to get your offers presented to prospects. The classic and conventional ways are the direct ones, of course: Radio and TV commercials (especially those late, late shows and cable programs) that solicit direct orders for records and tapes, jewelry, kitchen appliances, and other merchandise represent one significant media and method, and with the spreading popularity of cable TV and the convenience of taping video commercials for repetitive (and automatic) presentation, this kind of direct marketing is on the increase. There is also telemarketing, soliciting orders by telephone, and the computer has made it possible to automate making the calls, while the message may be on tape so that no human intervention is needed at all! But probably the most widely used method (at least in terms of total volume) is still the mailing of traditional direct-mail packages to names on mailing lists acquired by one means or another (to be discussed in greater depth later). Still, these are not the only methods; there are others, some of them variants on basic methods, used widely enough to merit discussion here.

Insert Programs

If you have ever received a credit card bill in an envelope that also contained a number of colored circulars or brochures for various kinds of merchandise offered by others than the credit card biller, you have had some first-hand experience with an insert program. Many organizations that do a great deal of mailing every week or every month rent their mailing lists, sometimes directly but more often through a list manager or broker, but some generate additional income by inserting others' sales literature for a fee.

In addition to credit-card organizations, those who offer insert programs include many kinds of organizations that send out literature and/or statements and invoices every month such as book clubs and other merchants of many kinds. Of course, they are usually selective and discriminate to some extent on what they will accept in their insert programs: They usually will not accept inserts that are directly competitive with their own offerings, and they will usually not accept literature they believe to be offensive to their customers, in bad taste generally, or otherwise contrary to their interests vis-à-vis their own enterprises.

Cooperative Mailings

There are, however, many companies serving the direct-mail business as professional mailers, who serve the direct-mail industry directly by making what some call "cooperative mailings." That is, the mailer has no merchandise of his or her own to sell, but provides a service to those who do have something to sell and who pay to insert their own literature. They are the principal customers of the mailer, and some of these mailers do this as a sideline to their main business of custom mailing for large-scale mailers, while others do this only. In fact, some mailers in this kind of enterprise refer to themselves as "direct-response publishers."

Some of these will accept any kind of insert from anyone, while others discriminate, promising to ensure that no mailing will include directly competitive offers (first come, first served), and no offensive materials will be included.

Card Deck Mailers

Many direct-mail ventures depend on post cards, either to solicit orders directly or to draw inquiries and (ergo) sales leads. These may be mailed as bound volumes, usually consisting of pages about three or four post cards deep, perforated for easy tear-out separation, or as a deck of separate cards packaged in a clear plastic wrapper. (The latter method has become the more popular one.)

Some large firms (such as John Wiley & Sons, Inc.) offer a wide enough array of items (business and professional books, in this case) to make up complete card decks of their own, which they may mail themselves or may entrust to professional mailers to handle. (And some firms do both.) Others wish to mail only a card or two and thus must depend on professional mailers if they wish to be included in large card

decks assembled for clients. A number of the "special offers" cited earlier in this chapter were made in cards of this latter class.

To give you some idea of the scope and magnitude of this kind of mailing service *DM News*, reported recently that one such mailer, Venture
Communications, had mailed four million card decks in 1985, and was
about to launch a 100,000-piece cooperative mailing (15 noncompetitive
participants) to VCR owners. The story reported also that Venture Communications targeted six million card-deck mailings for 1986, at the
rate of three mailings per month, and furnished a few statistics on card
deck mailings:

Forty to 60 participants (cards) per mailing

Response rates ranged widely—0.5 to 8 percent

Average mailing cost per deck was 12.5 cents (bulk rate)

Deck size could increase to 80 cards for the same mailing cost

Service firms offering such support services are numerous and can usually be located through their own advertising in the leading trade
periodicals (e.g., *DM News* and *ZIP Target Marketing*) and in telephone
book Yellow Pages. (A listing appears also in an appendix to this book.)
One firm offers direct marketers a useful device they call the "Insert
Program Guide." The firm is Qualified Lists Corp. (QLC) of Armonk,
New York, and the Insert Program Guide is a cardboard slide rule listing 44 insert programs and furnishing necessary statistics for each—
monthly and annual volumes of mailouts and charges for the service.
The Guide was offered free of charge to requestors in print advertising.

P.I. and P.O. Advertising

There are two special variants on this general scheme of piggybacking
others' mailings or participating in some type of cooperative mailing.
One of these is known as P.O. or per order advertising, and the other as
P.I or per inquiry advertising.

In this type of solicitation, a service organization sends out your solicitation, along with many others, using their own return address or
toll-free telephone number so that orders or inquiries are addressed to
them, rather than to you. Usually the mailer charges you a flat per-in-
quiry or per-order fee. For example, the Sunday newspaper supplement
Parade periodically runs a full page of announcements of items that are
free, charging the advertiser $2 per response. These are inquiry adver-

tisements, the free item is something inexpensive used to attract the inquiries, of course, and it is not unusual for such notices to attract as many as 2000 inquiries. On the other hand, the notices may solicit orders. In one case, a California company printed and mailed postcards, using copy I had prepared, bringing me many subscriptions to a newsletter I published at the time and billing me $5.00 per order received.

Most who use such services as these use them as a supplement or adjunct to their own direct mail and/or other advertising, rather than to replace their own direct efforts. For many, these are quite valuable services.

Drop Shipping

In a sense, drop shipping is another variant, although it resembles distribution through dealers and thus not direct marketing at all. However, it is direct marketing because in this mode of selling you do not sell anything to the middle operators who act as dealers or brokers nor do you ship anything (except advertising materials) to them. They merely solicit orders to be sent directly to them (often by simply including your sales literature in their own package, as in cooperative mailings) and deduct their commissions, sending you the balance and a shipping label (one that has their name and address on it), and you ship directly to the customer.

This is quite a common practice in many merchandising ventures, and has produced many notable successes. One individual in Washington, DC launched a small publishing business with a book he had written himself, selling it initially through a drop-shipping arrangement with a number of publishers of periodicals. He provided the full-page advertising copy and paid the participating periodical publishers a 50-percent commission, managing to sell many thousands of books that way. (Forty to 60 percent is a rather typical commission for such arrangements, so in most cases the viability of this mode of marketing requires a markup that permits commissions of this size.)

In another case, a firm used this method to sell a course of instruction, but with a special twist: They managed to persuade a number of periodical publishers to run their advertising in this manner, but when a particular periodical proved to be an especially effective advertising medium for their product, they then bought space in the periodical for future solicitations, thus pocketing all the proceeds of the orders. This gave them a cost-free way of testing the pulling power of each periodical before venturing their own advertising dollars!

Most periodical publishers will not admit that they accept such arrangements because they far prefer to sell their advertising space. In fact, they will stubbornly insist that they never deviate from selling their advertising space at whatever their normal advertising rates happen to be. However, when they have space left over—"remnants"—as they often do, they must either "waste" it by inserting additional editorial matter or dispose of it by another means. One of those other means is discounting, and direct marketers learn, sooner or later, that they can often bargain for remnants of advertising space. Failing that, however, publishers are often willing to accept cooperative advertising, such as that described.

It's not difficult to find publishers who do this, if you take the trouble to research magazines over a period of time. Eventually you come across advertisements that require the orders sent to the publisher, a sure sign that the arrangement is along the lines described here. This does not mean that the publication's advertising department will gladly make special deals with you, or even admit that they ever do so. However, knowing that they do so because you have the evidence of it, you can often persuade them to accommodate you, at least when they happen to have some unsold space to dispose of as best they can.

Some advertising agencies and perhaps even some others in related businesses, such as public relations, direct-mail support organizations, and consultants in these fields may be able to help you, but not all will be able to. In fact, Hubert Simon, a New York entrepreneur who had served his apprenticeship in advertising, relates how he made his start as an independent entrepreneur by compiling lists of radio stations that accepted P.I. advertising (radio and TV stations do it also!) and selling them to advertising agencies.

When selling merchandise through others, using drop shipping, it is common practice to provide reproducible copy to the brokers, from which to run print advertisements or print circulars, brochures, or other direct-mail copy. In some cases vendors print the direct mail copy themselves and supply it at cost to brokers.

RADIO AND TV MARKETING

What is true for print media and direct mail is true for radio and TV marketing, especially in the case of any kind of cooperative ventures. When you persuade a radio or TV station to enter into a P.I or P.O. deal, you have to furnish the advertising copy, preferably as a tape, or pay to have it made up so that the station can play it conveniently whenever it has time available. (Usually you can make a reasonable deal with the station to do this because they have the equipment and personnel who can handle it.) Even if you pay for air time at regular rates, you will do best when you provide your copy on audio or video tape. Not only will this normally cost you less than offering a script and leaving production up to the station, but you will have control over the presentation, and it will be what you want. (Having your print advertising "pubset"— made up at the judgment of the publisher—usually means dismay at the end-result, and this is as true in radio and TV, as it is in print media.) Videotape production does not have to be costly, however. Witness the late night TV offers for many items. They are usually quite simply done, often including little but basic product demonstration, with ordering information and most of the selling done via voice over.

TELEMARKETING

By now you may have been the recipient of one or more automated tele-marketing solicitations. Some systems are automated and dial numbers automatically (under computer control), while some more advanced ones (if "advanced" is the proper term for this!) are totally automated and use automatic tape players and recorders to deliver a sales message and record responses. (One called me recently and referred me to several other numbers to call for more information.)

Of course, telemarketing is not used only to solicit sales—direct orders—and gain leads for follow-up selling activity. Telemarketing is also used to make follow-up calls, using leads developed by any other means. However, the major activity referred to today by the term *telemarketing* is the use of the telephone and automatic equipment to launch total marketing campaigns, as you would in any other medium.

Of course, AT&T is in favor of telemarketing and strongly recommends its use. In fact, in some advertising of its own, designed to encourage the use of telephones as a marketing medium, AT&T mentioned a small catalog mailer, citing it as an example of success through telemarketing, and bringing the firm cited over 500 inquiries and orders immediately as a direct result of the great coverage AT&T provided. That firm's telemarketing had a strong and entirely unusual reward!

So far, telemarketing has not become as widely used as any of the other media for direct-marketing, although it is used by many thousands of direct marketers (estimated by one of my sources at 80,000), it is on the increase generally, and it is gaining more and more prominence in the direct-marketing field, as witness the increasing coverage of the subject in both editorial coverage and advertising matter in direct marketing trade journals. But there are special problems in telemarketing that do not exist with the other media, or at least not to nearly the same extent, so there are at least those differences.

One problem is that a great many people resent being solicited by telephone, especially when the call happens to come at an inconvenient time and represents an interruption. Compare this with the rather insignificant number of people who dislike receiving what they term "junk mail" enough to formally demand that their names be removed from mailing lists. Where one can simply ignore and discard such mail or set it aside to read at leisure, telephones must be answered when they ring, and that demands one's attention immediately. Many therefore resent calls from strangers as an invasion of their privacy under those circumstances, and some even have the same reaction to telephone calls from strangers no matter what the circumstances are. And the use of automation—computers and tape machines—is even more offensive to some.

This has led to an increasingly widespread introduction of legislation regulating the use of telemarketing. It was reported, for example, that well over 100 pieces of proposed legislation were introduced into legislatures during 1985 alone. One thing that such legislation proposes to control is the period during the day during which such calls can be made. But legislation aims also to regulate and control the use of automatic dialing equipment and related tape recorders and players. And, as in the case of mail, individuals would be permitted to require that their names be placed on "no call" lists or marked with asterisks in telephone directories to indicate their wish to be omitted from any lists of prospects for telephone solicitations.

Other matters come up. In Maine, for example, Sears was sued successfully by someone because Sears was allegedly guilty of misrepresentation in their telephone solicitation. A judge also stipulated that telephone orders were not binding contracts under Maine law because the law requires the customer's signature to make the contract binding. This compelled Sears to modify their campaign and methods.

Telemarketing has, on the other hand, the advantage of lending itself readily to automation, with computer programs dialing numbers, reading taped messages, and recording responses. To some, this is de-

172 SPECIAL OFFERS, METHODS, AND DEVICES

humanizing and a personal assault, but there is the compensating factor of almost unlimited numbers—sheer volume of solicitations—as well as cost advantages.

There is also the major advantage of being able to utilize a large pool of part-time help not otherwise available, such as housewives who are unable to leave home to go to work. Many of these housewives are willing to do telephone solicitations in their own homes.

As in the case of all other direct-marketing methods and media, there are numerous support services available to help you learn how to use telemarketing methods effectively and even to handle all the details for you. (Sources are cited in the appendixes.)

Forms For Monitoring Telemarketing Efforts

Aside from these special concerns, telemarketing is, in the abstract, similar to other methods of direct marketing and requires much the same kind of planning and control. Where in direct mail, you keep records of each mailout and each mailing list used, in telemarketing you must keep records of calls made and telephone lists used. In the case of non- or semiautomated systems, sales representatives make the calls and must therefore keep the records, whether they work from their own homes or on your premises.

At the same time, recording and recordkeeping can be quite different and rather specialized for telemarketing because there are many special conditions, conditions that do not exist in most direct-mail campaigns. For example, while many telemarketing campaigns are aimed at selling typical consumer items, usually small-tag items such as small household appliances, others are aimed at selling major items such as home renovations, automobiles, insurance, and major appliances. Moreover, telemarketing is used quite commonly to make commercial and industrial sales—business to business sales that is. And while many of these calls are first-time calls, in pursuit of initial sales, many are regular and periodic calls on established customers, seeking new sales. These factors impose their own requirements.

Figure 26 is a suggested format for a telephone call report, for example. The order number column is used only when an order has been placed, of course. The remarks column may be used to note such items as *no answer, call back, don't call again*, or other suitable notation. The order would have been written up on another form, of course, according to your normal business practice.

Daily Telephone Call Report

Day and Date _____ List Used _____ Sales Rep._____

Name	Tel. No.	Address	Order No.	Remarks

Page ____

Figure 26. Form for daily call report

There is need for other forms, especially for one to be used for follow up when follow up is appropriate. Figure 27 suggests a format for this. It is generalized and provides for a recommended final disposition, if the result is other than an order placed. Possible entries for this are suggested, with room for remarks and notes.

If you use only commissioned sales representatives working from their own homes, you may have no need for further forms, since your major selling expense is the commission paid on each sale. But if you are running an in-house telemarketing campaign, you are encountering costs that must be balanced against results. In that case, you can use a form somewhat along the lines of the forms used to monitor direct-mail results. Figure 28 suggests a format for this.

SPECIAL DEVICES AND GIMMICKS

My own mail brings me direct-mail packages containing new ideas almost daily. Some of these arrive unbidden, others are free items offered in advertising that attracted my interest enough to induce me to fill out the coupon or write a request for the item. This area of special devices is one of the greatest opportunities in direct marketing for creative brilliance.

FOLLOWUP CALL

Date to make call_____   Sales Rep_____

CUSTOMER_____

REASON FOR FOLLOWUP_____

_____

RESULTS OF CALL

ORDER _____

OBJECTIONS_____

_____

_____

OTHER_____

_____

_____

DISPOSITION/RECOMMENDATION:

Second followup   [ ] Date for followup:_____

Personal call   [ ] Date for call: _____

Mail formal quotation [ ] (Details for quotation attached)

Mail proposal   [ ] (Details for proposal attached)

Other: _____

_____

_____

REMARKS:_____

_____

_____

_____

Figure 27. Report of followup

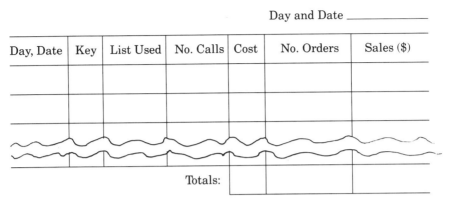

Figure 28. Daily form for recording results of calls

These devices are all aimed at getting attention and/or stimulating the desire to respond, of course. Ideally, they should all do both, but not all are suitable for doing both. Following are descriptions of just a few of the kinds of items I have found commonly used in these mailings and promotions:

A plastic card, embossed with the addressee's name, simulating a credit card

Samples of the product

Pop-up surprise items, such as an insert that pops up as a small box when released from the envelope

Useful tools, such as the cardboard slide rule described earlier

A notebook or appointment book embossed with addressee's name on the cover

A special discount certificate

A "check" that is really a discount coupon

A contest entry

A plastic wallet-size calendar

A free-trial offer

An invitation to a special luncheon or showing of some sort

A free demonstration in your own office

A coupon or certificate that must be mailed back to qualify for a free sample such as a computer disk or demonstration program

A humorous item such as a special "greeting card" that is relevant

A special "courtesy card" sent to established or repeat customers, promising special service, open account, testifying to creditworthiness, or other boon

A gift, not necessarily related to the item being sold such as major newsmagazines and others offer

Worksheet 22 lists these devices and asks you to think hard about what you can expect each to do and for what objective each is best suited, and then register your opinion, per the instructions supplied in the worksheet. The idea is to think about what each kind of device can be expected to do in soliciting orders or inquiries and in acting as a stimulant to ordering—a motivator—or is suitable only for arousing interest.

Some of the items listed are also "special offers," as you may have noticed. That is, they are devices that introduce or present special offers, usually in some novel or dramatic way, rather than in unadorned description in a letter or brochure. You can therefore combine the idea of making a special offer with that of using some special device to present the offer and dramatize it or draw special attention to it in some manner.

The check that is really a discount coupon is an obvious example. Anything that appears to be a regular bank check is bound to draw some special attention—and one hopes—generate some desire to "cash" it. And there are other ways of dramatizing special discount offers, so it is therefore fairly easy to combine the discount with a special device of one sort or another. On the other hand, however, a free demonstration in the prospect's own office is usually far more difficult (but not impossible) to dramatize with some kind of special device.

There are, of course, great advantages to be had by combining these ideas—by using a special device of some sort to support the special offer. One immediate advantage is drawing attention directly to the special offer. Another is to magnify the importance of the special offer. Still another is to make the offer more attractive by using a device that is motivating in itself—the simulated bank check or the special courtesy card, for example, each have their own special appeal and support the main offer you are making.

Obviously you can make these offers of discounts, free demonstrations, gifts, premiums, bonuses, and many other inducements in your letter, circular or brochure, but they rarely have the same impact then as when they are made in the form of a special device—a formal invita-

INSTRUCTIONS: Write A (for get Attention), D (for stimulate Desire), or B (for Both) in the first box provided beside each item in the left-hand column. Then, in the second box, write O (for Order) or I (for Inquiry).

SPECIAL DEVICE	YOUR RESPONSES	
Plastic "credit card"	[ ]	[ ]
Sample of product	[ ]	[ ]
Pop-up (surprise) item	[ ]	[ ]
Useful tools	[ ]	[ ]
Notebook or appointment book	[ ]	[ ]
Special discount certificate	[ ]	[ ]
"Check" discount coupon	[ ]	[ ]
Contest entry	[ ]	[ ]
Plastic wallet-size calendar	[ ]	[ ]
Free-trial certificate	[ ]	[ ]
Invitation to a special luncheon or showing	[ ]	[ ]
Free demonstration certificate	[ ]	[ ]
Coupon for free sample	[ ]	[ ]
Humorous item, as "greeting card"	[ ]	[ ]
Courtesy card	[ ]	[ ]
General gift item	[ ]	[ ]

Worksheet 22. Special direct-mail devices and what they can do for you

tion, an expensive-looking certificate or coupon, a raised-letter panel-card invitation, or other such device. These indicate that you attach a great deal of importance to the offer, and that rubs off on the recipient: It signals your feeling about this because it suggests that you thought the offer—and the recipient—important enough to justify what is obviously an expensive presentation. And it is important that the presentation be made on a reasonably good quality paper and printing if you expect the prospect to take you and your offer seriously. A presentation that has been obviously "made on the cheap" is self-defeating. But it is

----

SPECIAL OFFERS

Special discounts   [ ]   _____

Free demonstration   [ ]   _____

Free trial   [ ]   _____

Special of the month   [ ]   _____

Prizes   [ ]   _____

Credits for premiums   [ ]   _____

Double money back guarantee   [ ]   _____

Two for the price of one   [ ]   _____

Special sale   [ ]   _____

Special luncheon/cocktail party   [ ]   _____

_____   [ ]   _____

_____   [ ]   _____

_____   [ ]   _____

SPECIAL INSERT DEVICES

1. Wallet-size calendar   6. Pop-up item

2. Special courtesy card   7. Formal invitation

3. Engraved invitation   8. Pocket memorandum book

4. Humorous greeting card   9. Personal gift

5. Free sample   10. Rain check

Worksheet 23. Matching special offers with special devices

appearance that counts, and what is expensive in appearance is not always expensive in fact. There are, in fact, many ways to make a presentation appear to be far more expensive than it is. Earnest and unabashed conversation with your printer may bring you a few surprises in this respect!

Worksheet 23 is designed to help you think out the kinds of devices you might wish to use to support such special offers. It is designed to encourage you to match up special offers and special insert devices, but these are by no means holy: The form also provides space to use some imagination and write in your own suggested items in both categories— special offers and special insert devices.

The items provided are equal in number—10 each—but that does not mean that each special offer must match a special device. Quite the contrary, marketing is not an exact science by any means, and you should use your own judgment in making matches, totally uninhibited and uninfluenced by the limited number and variety of items and ideas listed here.

A FEW HAZARDS

Despite the many advantages of using special offers and special devices to support your offers, there are potential hazards to be aware of and to be avoided. A chief and most common hazard in using special offers and special attention-getters is that of obscuring what you are selling—that is, of selling the gimmick instead of the item you started out to sell. (It is quite easy to slip into this.) This, in turn, introduces a new potential hazard of its own: You may easily oversell the gimmick, in your enthusiasm, leading to customer disappointment. One research study, for example, demonstrated that sending sample copies of newsletters hurt sales, rather than helped them, because all too often the sample copy disappointed the prospect. Whether this is due to oversell by exaggerated claims or to customers reading their own wishes into your offer, the result is the same: Disappointment leads to buyer remorse, which leads directly to cancellations and returns. Ergo, the need to keep everything involved in your offer in proper perspective. Do use special offers and special devices, but do subordinate them to your main offer—to what you are really selling.

12

THE RIGHT
MAILING LIST

The right mailing list is important, but it is "right" only with
respect to the rest of the package.

HOW CRITICAL IS "THE RIGHT MAILING LIST"?

Again and again we hear from professionals in direct mail that the mailing list is the single most important item responsible for success or failure in a mailout—in an entire dm venture, for that matter. Not surprisingly, these sages generally turn out to be mailing list managers (brokers) or direct-mail people who base their campaigns primarily on heavy use of rented lists, so that their judgment is inevitably skewed by their own interests. And, to at least some degree, this philosophy is also propagated by those whose campaigns fail for one reason or another and who find it necessary to seek a cause that absolves them of any shortcomings in skill or industrious effort.

This is not to belittle the importance of the mailing list in any respect, especially for any direct-mail venture, but only to get it into proper perspective. For all marketing—all business ventures, for that matter—are based on certain basic principles and elements that are the same in all cases. In fact, the three general and most basic requirements for any venture are the following:

1. Knowing precisely what you wish to sell
2. Identifying the right prospects for what you wish to sell
3. A means for reaching those prospects and presenting your offer

The first item is not as absurd as it may appear. An amazingly large number of individuals decide to enter into a direct-marketing venture with only a most generalized notion of what they wish to sell, and an even more vague notion of what their marketing strategy is to be. You can hardly make intelligent decisions about the other items before you have settled the first one.

Note that as they are organized here (so organized because most ventures begin with an idea of something to sell, rather than with one of the other two factors), satisfying each numbered item depends on first defining the one before it. Defining the right prospects requires knowing what you are going to sell, and determining how to reach prospects requires that you first define the prospects, of course. That alone indicates that the right mailing list must be one that matches the other items—that enables you to deliver your presentation to people who are good prospects for what you are selling.

Still, even this is highly generalized. There are many other factors that influence the success of your campaign—the effectiveness of your copy and your package overall, the economic situation of the moment, the season, and perhaps totally unexpected and uncontrollable factors, such as sudden news stories that can be a boon or a disaster to your campaign.

The right mailing list is therefore highly important, but it is only one of several critically important factors. The successful direct mail campaign results from a properly integrated package of all these elements: they must match and complement each other—the right offer to the right prospect at the right time and at the right price. It would be impossible, normally, to choose the best mailing list without knowing and taking into account these other factors. And even that does not consider all the influencing factors.

CRITERIA FOR THE CHOICE

Choosing the right mailing list requires that you analyze your marketing situation, establish premises, and validate—test—those premises. For in the testing, you will learn that your experience, no matter how vast and deep, is often no substitute for testing. My own experience demonstrates this rather clearly:

My personal background in electronics engineering in the high-tech defense and space programs showed me clearly that the contractors who designed and built Buck Rogers weapons and depended primarily on government contracts for their survival were my best prospects. I decided that they needed me more than anyone. I therefore zeroed in on those prospects in marketing my services as a consultant, lecturer, proposal specialist, and newsletter publisher in that field, confident that I understood my contemporaries in the field and would be welcomed as a consultant and supplier of critically important services. How could they not eagerly clasp to their hearts this demonstrated winner of many government contracts?

The results were disappointing. I was not as warmly embraced by these arms merchants and space-hardware manufacturers as I had expected. I was forced to turn to testing, trying to learn where I had gone wrong, to salvage my vanity, as well as my enterprise. I was soon forced to admit that I had permitted my own interests and peculiar experience—hardware—to prejudice my judgment. The most receptive and enthusiastic respondents proved to be computer-software companies. Why? I know not, not even now, but I know that it is true because test mailings proved it. I had far better response from software developers than from any other single class of government contractors.

LISTS MUST BE TESTED

My personal experience leads me to believe that you cannot possibly know for a fact what are the right mailing lists for you until you have tested a few lists. You may and probably do believe that you know who your best prospects are, and you are probably entirely wrong (or you may believe that the list broker knows best what you need). But what we think is logical is not always accurate. For example, door-to-door salespeople learn, after a while, that the householder in the modest, factory-district home is more likely to be able to pay in cash for a purchase than is the "house-poor" middle-class white collar worker. (My early, depression-days experience as a a door-to-door salesman demonstrated this rather clearly to me.)

Still, despite this there are some verities. It is true that a large percentage of professional people today, especially successful physicians, are almost constantly in quest of investment opportunities (and that factory workers are not good targets for investments). It is true that the middle-class workers are the buyers of modern high-tech appliances, such as videocassette recorders and satellite dishes. It is also obviously true that neighborhoods of impoverished minorities are not likely to be highly productive when selling upscale products by mail.

But those are only rough measures. They are helpful as starting premises, but not as conclusions. They are premises to be tested by mailings, mailings to test (in this case) the lists, rather than the offer itself. What you know or think you know, and what list brokers advise—even *assure* you—are the premises to be tested.

Those are not the only things to consider and test, however. There are many factors, one of which is demographics—the social statistics of populations—and demographic trends. For example, demographers now tell us that America's senior citizens—those 65 or older—now have more discretionary income—spending money—than any other age group in the United States. Another trend, we are told, is that the once booming teenage market has begun to shrink (presumably the result of the now-ended baby boom), but it is still a substantial market. These and many other similar factors should be considered in choosing your lists, since they are critical market factors to consider.

Some list brokers make a point of promising a minimum percentage of "nixies"—undeliverable addresses—in their lists and guaranteeing to replace all such nixies with a larger number of new names and addresses. The quality of lists, in this respect, is a factor of how well they are maintained—"cleaned" by being purged of nixies and kept up to date—and how old the lists are. That, however, is a relatively minor factor, as long as the number of nixies is not excessive. What is much more important is that the list is what is represented to be such as a list of known buyers, as distinct from prospects not known to be mail order buyers, or a list of people in the income brackets claimed, rather than other income brackets.

Some of these are the most important factors. For example, a list of known buyers by mail is almost certain to produce better results than a list of mere inquirers, with no established record of buying by mail. (There are, in fact, many "big-mail junkies"—often shut-ins, youngsters, and others who are simply bored—who constantly send for catalogs, brochures, and other items that get their names proliferated onto many mailing lists, but who never buy anything.) These are not, of course, good prospects for you.

Even more important is further detailing of buyers. If you are selling books by mail, a list of individuals known to have bought books by mail in the past year is probably a premium list for you. But there are other factors by which mail-order buyers can be specified: These can be closer descriptions of items bought, for example, engineering books, or amount of money spent, for example, $50 or more, or other such measures and specifications.

Obviously, the more detailed the information you can get about the lists—or, conversely, the more detailed the specifications you can draw up and match your mailing lists to—the more valuable the lists are likely to be. That is, it is not only the nature of the specifications, that is, but the degree of detail that will be important in choosing your list.

WHAT, EXACTLY, ARE YOU RENTING?

Mailing lists are rarely, if ever, for sale; they are rented. The most basic rental arrangement is for the use of the list a single time, for some fee per 1000 names, usually with a guarantee to replace nixies. (Lists are "salted" to detect any unauthorized and unpaid-for second use of the list.) However, it is usually possible to order and pay for multiple uses, and some brokers even offer unlimited use for some given period, such as a year, for a suitable fee.

However, anyone on a list who buys from you—becomes your customer—naturally becomes a name and address you now "own," and can add to your own house list of customers. And of course you should do so immediately, for customer lists are certainly the most valuable lists. In fact, the lists are usually rated, in order of importance and value, as customer lists, inquirers, and cold prospects.

WHERE MAILING LISTS COME FROM

List managers are also list brokers. It's a matter of their relationships with you—whether they are renting your lists to others or renting others' lists to you that determines whether they are list managers or list brokers. That is, they are managing your lists or brokering others' lists.

Once you have built a mailing list of substantial size you have an asset that can produce income by rentals to others. But unless you are prepared for and able to undertake all the labor of renting your own lists (for it is a major undertaking, a business in and of itself), you do what most direct-mail firms do: You turn the task over to a list management firm, specialists in renting mailing lists.

That list manager arranges to market your list for a percentage of the rental fees. In organizing and marketing your list, the firm is a list manager. In renting your list to others and keeping a commission or percentage of the fees, the firm is a list broker. Ergo, you entrust your lists to the services of a list manager, but rent lists yourself from a list broker, although it is the same firm. Their advertisements in the trade journals of dm announce some of the lists they manage such as those of the Spiegel catalog firm, *Venture* magazine, or other organization that does substantial business by mail and thus builds lengthy lists of customers and prospects. (Of course, many list brokers build up some lists of their own, "house lists," over the years, and rent these out too.) So most of the lists rented out are brokered customer lists, including the subscription lists of many publications and inquirer lists. But there are also cold-prospect lists, lists of people about whom there is no information bearing on their "quality" as prospects.

In most cases, the brokers' catalogs and brochures describe their lists under a two- or three-level indexing system. For example, a first-level category of MANUFACTURERS might list under it Machinery—Non-

Electric, and under that, Ball Bearing Manufacturers, Computer Manufacturers, and so forth. Each of the latter terms identifies a given list, and the guide will list a number of names for each of these, frequently with an SIC (Standard Industrial Classification) code number.

Since all major list management today is handled with the aid of computers, the list broker is able to accommodate your desires in a variety of ways. You can usually get your lists customized in zip-code order, on labels, addressed by title or, in many cases, by individual names, and you can specify your list requirements by given zip codes—geographic selection, that is, among other choices you can make and specify.

At least one list broker, The Lifestyle Selector(R), takes advantage of this flexibility made possible by the computer and makes it the chief feature of their marketing strategy. They offer to supply you with lists completely customized to your specifications. In fact, they stipulate that they *create* lists for you. To support this idea they describe the parameters from which you may choose your specifications as these, with options listed under each category:

Hobbies/interests	Sex
Age	Income
Marital status	Home
Occupation	Children at home
Religion	Ethnicity
Credit cards used	Location

AN EMBARRASSMENT OF RICHES

Modern computers permit treating the lists as general databases, banks from which almost any kind of withdrawal may be made. That is, computerization provides such a high degree of flexibility that the possible selections and specification criteria become almost endlessly varied. Edith Roman Associates, Inc., for example, offers in only one of the firm's mailings (and in addition to their regular large bound catalog) a list of subscribers to a wide variety of U.S. business publications available by publication name or as a merged list, and recently offered two new lists, one of banking and financial executives and another of medical specialists.

Ed Burnett, a well-known list manager and dm consultant, furnishes a quite substantial (70-page) bound catalog of his offerings, with a preface that he titles "A Short Course in the How-To's of Direct Mail." He recommends in this "short course," among other things, the following common sense rules and other guidelines (all abbreviated here):

Rule 1: Determine your objective first

Rule 2: Turn to experts—consultants, for example—for guidance

Have the list (on labels) delivered to you, not your mailer, so you can check it over to verify that it is what you ordered

Mail the entire list in one drop to make an accurate "half-life" measurement

Make all test mailings together, in a single drop, to avoid differences in results due to differences in timing

Insist on postal receipts to verify quantity of mail out each day

This goes on to describe his "half-life" system of measurement, with graphic illustrations. Burnett also offers to send his complete 3-part article, written for *Folio on the Rules for Testing Lists*, to anyone making a request on a formal business letterhead to his publicity department. (Burnett's address is in directory of mailing list managers appearing in the appendix.)

On the other hand, there are a number of relatively small list brokers, who furnish simple circulars or brochures, rather than catalogs and directories to list and describe their offerings. The list descriptions are equally simple. Here are a few typical list descriptions from which you are invited to make your selection:

Extra-income seekers	Opportunity seekers
Real estate seminar attendees	Book buyers
Tape cassette buyers	Magazine subscribers
Overseas-job applicants	Do-it-yourselfers
Loan applicants	Credit card holders
Computer owners	Software buyers

Another broker, Claritas, offers a market targeting system they call PRIZM, which offers you choices on the basis of geography and demographics, or what they refer to as geo-demographic segmentation. The system is based on Census Bureau data, and identifies five broad categories of affluence, social status, and other factors. It then divides the population into 12 social groups and 40 clusters (sub-groups). Together, the system enables you to draw up a set of specifications for your lists based on those factors.

List managers/brokers are not the only source of rental mailing lists. Some organizations with their own large mailing lists opt to be their own list managers and rent their lists out directly. Dun & Bradstreet is one major example of such an organization, and they happen to be a "natural" for this: The nature of their work in the business/industrial/financial world centers on amassing detailed data on individuals, companies, industries, and organizations of other kinds. Inevitably they not only compile extensive and detailed databases, but their work is such that the databases are automatically maintained and kept up to date, making their lists virtual premium lists (and enabling them to command excellent fees for rentals).

COMPILED LISTS

There is still one other kind of list broker: one who compiles lists from directories of various sorts—telephone yellow pages, membership lists, and computer online databases, as well as from various other sources, including the U.S. Government, for example, which has provided many mailing lists under the statutory requirement of the Freedom of Information Act (albeit reluctantly in many cases). I have been able to get government-supplied lists of Navy contractors, minority-owned firms, subscribers to the government's *Commerce Business Daily*, and government consultants, and lists of government buyers, among others.

Companies who carry out surveys, such as R.L. Polk and the Donnelley Corporation (a subsidiary of Dun & Bradstreet), are in a good position to compile mailing lists, and they do so. They are particularly well positioned to compile the "resident" lists, which enable some marketers to blanket entire neighborhoods, cities, or entire geographic areas with "resident"-addressed consumer appeals. Ergo, some of the lists offered are compiled lists, and in many cases, little detail about those prospects, other than geographic data, is available as descriptive or specification data. This does not mean that these lists are not useful, but they are not very well targeted, except most generally in geographic terms, although those terms may strongly suggest other factors, such as economic status and ethnicity.

On the other hand, some compiled lists are already segregated into categories defined inherently by the source. The members of many associations have a common denominator—they are all CPAs or all electronics engineers, for example—and that may be all you need to know if you are selling some specialized item that is useful to only a class of customer defined by occupation or special interest. When I published a newsletter on marketing to the federal government, my first choice in selecting lists was lists of companies already contracting with the government. My second choice was lists of those whom I might persuade to try to contract with the government. And even in the case of the first choice, I soon learned that lists of those who provide custom computer-programming services to the government were usually more productive for me than were the others.

LIST RENTAL FEES

Rental fees for mailing lists vary widely, according to many factors, such as the nature of the list, the number of names ordered, and the number of uses paid for in the original order. Fees range from a low of $20 per 1000 names to as much as $90 per 1000 names, although there are exceptions to even these extremes. However, probably the mean is about $40–45 per 1000 names for lists of good quality. In list rentals, as in most things, you may or may not "get what you pay for," but you are most unlikely to get more than you pay for. Good lists—and that means lists that are up to date, comprehensive, and accurate—are not cheap. But the quality and the price of lists are also factors of the basic nature of the list. A list of mail-order buyers who have spent $50 or more in the past 90 days will normally be more valuable than one of buyers who have spent only $10 or have not bought by mail for six months or more. And a list of buyers will generally cost more than a list of inquirers. So while it is possible to get some lists for $25 and less per 1000 names, they are usually lists of lesser quality. Even given all the other factors you might wish to specify in deciding who your best prospects are, you should consider these factors when comparing the offerings available to you. But remember too that while lists are most commonly rented for one-time use only, other arrangements are also possible, such as renting for more than one use or for unlimited use for some period of time. The value of any given list is therefore not a simple matter to establish, making it somewhat difficult to make objective choices among competitive offerings.

There are no absolute measures of quality and value, of course; in the end, subjective judgment must be exercised. However, it is possible to establish a few guidelines or general standards, such as those offered in Worksheet 24. This worksheet is offered as an aid to comparing competitive mailing lists when you must choose among several offerings to

LIST NAME, TYPE, OR OTHER ID

SPECIFICATION ITEM	LIST A	LIST B	LIST C	LIST D
Size of list				
Cost per 1,000				
Buyers or inquirers?				
MO buyers?				
Type of items bought				
If buyers, size of sale				
Recency of sales/inquiries				

NOTES:_____

_____

Worksheet 24. Checklist for comparing competitive lists

INSTRUCTIONS: Check off and/or write in your options or best estimates (they
will be estimates, in some cases) as at least a preliminary checklist for
specifying and evaluating mailing lists.

LIST SPECIFICATIONS/EVALUATION CRITERIA

AGE GROUP

Teenagers   [ ]   Yuppies [ ]   Mature Middle aged   [ ]

Senior Citizens [ ]   Other (detailed) _____ [ ]

ETHNIC CHARACTERISTICS

White [ ]   Black [ ]   Hispanic [ ]   Other _____ [ ]

OCCUPATIONAL CRITERIA

Executives   [ ]   Professionals   [ ]   Craft workers   [ ]

Skilled workers [ ]   Unskilled workers [ ]   Semi-skilled workers [ ]

Other (detailed or specific) _____ [ ]

INCOME LEVEL

Upper [ ]   Middle [ ]   Lower [ ]   Specific $_____ [ ]

GEOGRAPHIC PREFERENCE

Metropolitan [ ]   Suburban [ ]   Small town [ ]   Rural [ ]

SOME MISCELLANEOUS CHARACTERISTICS

Estates and servants [ ]   Furs and jewelry [ ]   Pools and patios [ ]

Minority yuppies   [ ]   Coaltown   [ ]   Corntown   [ ]

Agribusiness   [ ]   Pickups and guns [ ]   Union stalwarts [ ]

Levittown dwellers   [ ]   Millworkers   [ ]   Hill folks   [ ]

Worksheet 25. Guidelines for specifying mailing lists

decide which is best suited to your needs and which is the best value.
The measures suggested will also alert you to the kinds of questions you
might wish to ask the list broker, if that information is not supplied in
the descriptions of the lists.

Whether you are renting lists from a list broker, choosing lists for
some particular campaign from among your house lists, or compiling
lists from directories and/or via inquiry advertising, you can't do an intelligent job without having set some criteria for—specifications of—

what you believe you want and need to do the job properly. But you must plan, and Worksheet 25 will help you do that, especially when used in conjunction with Worksheet 24. And again, as in earlier worksheets, you need not make all final decisions here and now, but you can make up a rough estimate on a preliminary worksheet—that is, in fact, what a worksheet is really for—and then refine your plans on additional worksheets until you are satisfied that your plan is workable and is what you need to do the job.

You do not have to make an entry for every item listed, but only for those which are appropriate.

13

COMPILING AND BUILDING YOUR OWN HOUSE LISTS

Despite the almost limitless number and variety of mailing lists available for rental, there are occasions when compiling house lists of your own is the most practical and productive approach.

HOUSE LISTS

Not everyone's list is for rent. Some firms do not permit their own lists—
house lists—to be rented at all, fearing that their lists will fall into the
hands of competitors who will draw business away from them far
beyond the value of the income they might earn from such rentals.
Many others who have built up extensive mailing lists of their own do
not use rented lists at all, since house lists are generally considered to
be far more valuable than any rented list is likely to be (although probably most firms continue to do at least some mailing to others' lists,
which they have rented). But the value of house lists is not absolute,
either; it varies according to many circumstances, as direct-mail consultant Shell Alpert explains in a published article, "How much is your
HOUSE LIST really worth?," (*Zip Target Marketing*), that first, while
any list built up by, and belonging to, an individual or organization is
a house list by definition and probably an asset of some sort, the mere
fact of being a house list does not confer any specific immediate or absolute value on it. He discriminates among customer lists, inquirer lists,
compiled lists, hot leads, subscribers, patrons, donors, homeowners,
coupon clippers, members, and many others. He discriminates also on
both the pragmatic value—how often a given list can be used profitably—and the rental potential—how easily a list can be rented. But he
makes the point, nevertheless, that house lists almost always outpull
rented lists. It is rarely less than a 2-to-1 ratio, he says, and often as
much as 3- or 4-to-1. And he goes on to offer detailed methods for cal-
culating values for house lists. (See appendix listing of consultants for
Alpert's address to order reprint of article.)

TABLE 2. Rented Lists Versus Your Own
Compiled Lists

Factor	Rented Lists	Own Lists
Large quantities available immediately	Y	N
Virtually unlimited supply	Y	N
Known history of list	Y	N
Customized to special needs	?	Y
Cost of acquiring relatively low	Y	N
Cost of subsequent uses low	N	Y
List becomes your fixed asset	N	Y

Inevitably, as you do business, you begin to acquire your own lists—house lists. Even if you begin with rented lists they will contribute to your house lists because every one who places an order with you becomes a member of your customer list, the most valuable list you can have. And anyone who writes you subsequently to inquire about anything becomes a name you "own," whether that individual learned of you through mailings to a rented list or by other means.

However, it is possible to begin with house lists, lists built through compilation by various means, and some find it necessary to begin this way. This raises the entire question of whether you should or should not begin by renting mailing lists.

SHOULD YOU USE RENTED MAILING LISTS?

Conventional wisdom about direct mail and mailing lists tends so strongly to accept and even advocate the use of rented lists as a premise that the question of whether you should rent lists might not even be taken by some to be a serious question. But not everyone agrees with the premise. Hollywood columnist Rona Barrett reveals, for example, that when she marketed a newsletter of her own earlier in her career, she rented lists but they did not pull as well for her as did lists she compiled herself. My own experience parallels this, in at least one of my mail-order ventures. However, in all fairness it is possible that Barrett did not choose the right lists for her needs, and it is true that, in my own case, I was not able to find the precise lists I needed for this particular venture, which were lists of individuals and organizations who contracted with the government or were interested in learning how to contract with the government. I was compelled to compile my own lists, and often found myself hard pressed to find useful sources that I could afford to utilize. (Cost of compilation is a large factor, and we will consider here only some of the more economical ways of compiling and acquiring names and addresses of prospects.)

That, however, was not the only case in which I was forced to choose. There were others, cases in which I actually used both rented lists and lists I had compiled myself. Again, I found that my own compiled lists pulled significantly better results than did the lists I had rented.

That should not be surprising, despite the fact that it conflicts with conventional wisdom. There are good arguments for using rented lists, as there are also good arguments for compiling your own lists. In fact, some basic pros and cons of rented lists versus your own compiled lists are offered for consideration in Table 2. Items are listed as Y (yes), N (no), or ? (uncertain or to limited degree).

SHOULD YOU COMPILE YOUR OWN LISTS?

It should now be evident that there is no hard and fast answer to the question of where you should turn for your lists or from what source come the most dependable lists. There are too many variables to make this selection of lists a science. For some or in some situations, rented lists are your only practicable approach to a direct-mail campaign. In other cases, you will be far better off to compile lists of your own. And, of course, you may very well profit by doing both, as many do, using a mix of rented lists and house lists you have compiled, and often testing them to determine whether one pays off better than another. (But the payoff should be calculated in actual dollars as ROI—return on investment—rather than in response percentages, which are of no real consequence.)

In my own case, publishing a newsletter for marketing to the government, I did not have much success in renting lists that were truly targeted for me because there is no simple way for those who are not thoroughly immersed in government marketing to select such prospects. (That has changed since, and at least some list managers—Dun & Bradstreet, for example—now offer such lists.) But then, if I wanted such lists, I was compelled to compile them myself; the alternative would have been to use general lists of businesses, and that would have been highly inefficient because only about 2 or 3 percent of American businesses pursue government contracts consistently enough to have made them good prospects for me. (I tested such lists, in fact, and found them to be truly unproductive.)

THE BASICS OF COMPILATION

There are really four ways to compile and thus acquire your own house lists:

1. Compile from a variety of directories and miscellaneous other print sources.
2. Acquire names and addresses that are suitable as mailing lists or can be easily converted into mailing lists.

3. Gather names and addresses of inquirers by using inquiry advertising and PR, while accumulating your own customer lists.
4. Swap mailing lists with other direct marketers whose lists are suitable for your use, while the two of you are not directly competitive with each other.

I used all of these methods. The following were among my major sources of names and addresses:

The subscription list of the federal government's *Commerce Business Daily* (It was then possible to get it under the Freedom of Information Act)

The Small Business Administration's list of minority contractors

A list of Navy contractors (made available by the Navy)

Names of contractors listed in the awards section of the *Commerce Business Daily*

Display help-wanted advertising by firms I could easily identify as government contractors (This was a continuous source, and is even easier to use today with the advent of several specialized publications for job seekers)

SOURCES

The sources I used were peculiar to my needs. But more significant than that is the fact that I wished to address business organizations of various kinds—for-profit companies and corporations, principally, but not exclusively: There are many labor unions, associations, and other such nonprofit organizations who are awarded government contracts and derive much of their income from such contracts. These were among my many prospects and, ultimately, customers.

We must therefore distinguish between the need to compile lists of business organizations, both for- and nonprofit, and lists of private individuals. (Of course, many of these individuals find themselves on both kinds of lists, getting many of the same appeals at the office that they do at home.) "Yellow pages" directories and such directories as Standard & Poor's and the Thomas Register help in discovering business organizations to add to your lists, but they are of little help when you want to reach the average householder—private citizen—with a typical consumer item. For those you need to turn to other resources, such as the many "Who's Who" directories, membership rolls of associations, individual subscribers, and other such listings.

I learned, as I proceeded, that some associations will not release names of their members, while others will sell copies of their membership lists—often as bound directories published every year—for quite reasonable prices. And because I lecture regularly to associations, as well as to others, I have often been handed copies of membership directories when they would not have been available to me at any price otherwise. But I found, too, that in some cases membership directories of associations are distributed freely at their annual conventions and conferences. Attending such an annual event may deliver many thousands of names and addresses of good prospects into your hands.

If you are compiling lists of business organizations various periodicals are quite useful. I used the display help-wanted sections of the *Wall Street Journal*, the Sunday edition of the *New York Times*, the *Washington Post*, and a few others that had substantial such sections, although I sometimes found the classified advertising sections also quite helpful in compiling my lists. On another occasion, when I was selling a resume-writing service via mail order I used the reverse strategy: I found the "situations wanted" advertisements quite helpful in producing names of prospects. And in selling a different kind of newsletter I found it helpful to scan the general advertising of small firms and add their names to my lists. In fact, I launched this newsletter entirely on the strength of names acquired in this way. In general, however, if you need to build mailing lists of individuals, these methods are quite limited in what they can do for you. You need to turn to other sources, such as inquiry advertising.

INQUIRY ADVERTISING

Inquiry advertising is simply advertising designed solely to elicit inquiries from individuals. These inquiries then become sales leads, in the case of those enterprises where each such inquiry is to be followed up by the personal and individual efforts of a sales representative (usually a "big tag" sale such as home modernization or an automobile), or part of a mailing list, in the general case of direct-sales programs. And this is often the best way to build highly responsive mailing lists, if the inquiry advertisements have been well designed.

Well-designed inquiry campaigns are those that produce inquiries from those truly interested in—truly good prospects for—whatever you sell, so the response to your sales literature following up the inquiries should be quite good. The objectives and criteria for inquiry advertisements are, therefore, that you not only get a good percentage of response to the advertisements but that the respondents are good prospects for you—*qualified* prospects, in fact.

Inquiry advertising does not have to be costly. In fact, many effective inquiry campaigns are carried out with classified advertisements alone. The "secret" of effective inquiry advertising is to offer something that is attractive but is free or available for a most nominal cost, and to advertise in the right media—those read (or watched and listened to, in the case of broadcast media) by the kinds of people you want to reach. That is, to maximize the response to inquiry advertisements you must offer some effective inducement—a special report, a sample of the products, or a free newsletter, for example, or perhaps a useful tool such as a cardboard slide rule or engineering nomograph. Even when what you offer is free, you must "sell" it to your readers. The more attractive the special offer, the bigger the response, of course.

On the other hand, inquiry advertising must be designed to draw inquiries from only qualified prospects. There is nothing but grief ahead for you in drawing inquiries from and mailing literature to idle curiosity seekers, children, and those "big-mail junkies." You can draw a large response to your inquiry advertising and a disappointingly small response to the mailout of sales literature to those inquirers if you do nothing to control the kinds of responses you get.

The way to avoid or at least to minimize this problem is simple enough, in principle: *Qualify* inquirers. There are several ways to do this:

1. The inducement should be such that it is likely to appeal to or be useful for only those who are good prospects. That should rule out such generally useful items as calendars and notebooks. Offer highly specialized reports, newsletters, engineering slide rules and nomographs, for example. Few big-mail junkies will be interested in those.

2. If your appeal is to professionals or business people of some sort, require that respondents make their request on their business letterhead or enclose a business card.

3. Advertise only in media that reaches the right people, the ones you want to reach.

4. Make a small charge, stipulating that it will be refunded or credited to any future order. (In fact, *Reader's Digest* learned in a test mailing of inquiry advertising many years ago that a small charge actually increased response because the small charge increased the perceived value of the offer.)

WHAT VALUABLE GIFTS CAN YOU OFFER?

Although a free gift of some kind is an excellent gambit for eliciting responses from readers—words such as FREE, BONUS, and SALE seem to never lose their appeal—it is not always necessary to offer a literal gift item to induce readers to respond. *Information* is itself a valuable commodity in the right circumstances, and can often be made an even greater inducement than a fancy free notebook or other such item. That is, the information may be itself a gift, whether it is delivered to the inquirer as a formally bound book, a brochure, a recorded telephone message, an audio cassette, a video cassette, or information in some other form. All of these have been and are being used today. For example, one firm has placed printed circulars under the windshields of automobiles in parking lots, which invite the reader to call a telephone number. That results in a recorded message inviting the caller to a free seminar.

Everyone has personal problems, fears, and aspirations. And those in responsible positions in organizations, whether they are owners or executives, all have also problems, fears, and aspirations related to the organization. The "special report"— free information—is always welcome, but especially so when the reader perceives it as something that correctly identifies his or her problem, fear, or aspiration and appears to offer directly related help. The hazard is in overgeneralization—trying to do too much and promising a panacea. It doesn't work well. What works best is the information focused sharply on a specific problem or aspiration. Moreover, in many circumstances, if you plan carefully enough, you can make the offer of information appear to be *unique*, which further enhances its value.

Consider the examples of Tables 3 and 4, offered to illustrate how free information can be offered to attract prospects for given items. Table 3 addresses individual consumers, as private citizens, while Table 4 addresses business owners and executives, offering the same items. Note the change in orientation or slant of the free report offered, according to the kind of customer-prospect.

TABLE 3. Free Information With Personal
Appeal

Items Offered for Sale	Free "Special Report" (Information) Offered
Tax manual	15 little-known tips for saving up to $3000 *extra* in income taxes
Personal gifts	The idea book of gifts for every occasion and every pocket
Vocational training	Complete list of jobs and typical salaries you can qualify for after training
Personal computer	27 ways to use computer know-how to advance your career and earn more money
Investment newsletter	New ideas every month to make the safest investments

It is essential to always remember that you are addressing *people*, not numbers, not demographic abstractions, and not even companies or other organizations. People make the decisions, and it is people who must be motivated to respond with inquiries. If the proper motivators are not there, the responses will not take place.

Worksheet 26 is designed to make you think a bit about this. It includes a number of examples of good and bad inquiry advertising—good or bad in terms of whether the advertising includes a sensible motivator. All examples are taken from actual inquiry advertisements, specifically inviting the reader to send for more information. They are paraphrased or rephrased and abridged, but enough information is retained to identify the item where the copy does so identify it or the headline is represented, along with the invitation to send for more information. The motivational strategy may or may not be clearly apparent, but may have to be inferred. In passing judgment on the quality or effectiveness of the copy (in copy, effectiveness is quality!) consider both the clarity of the copy (what is the offer all about?) and the motivational effectiveness of the invitation to inquire further.

Although print advertising is commonly used for inquiry advertising, other advertising methods can be and are also used for the pur-

TABLE 4. Free Information With
Business-Oriented Appeal

Items Offered for Sale	Free "Special Report" (Information) Offered
Tax manual	15 little-known tax-saving tips even few accountants know about
Personal gifts	The idea book that solves the problem of what to give special clients; for every occasion
Vocational training	How to use training to increase productivity and reduce costs: three case histories
Personal computer	27 ways to use an inexpensive desktop computer to do in-house what you have been vending out
Investment newsletter	Investment ideas every month that can be applied to your company cash flow

pose—radio and TV commercials, card packs, and even PR, especially press releases. The principles are the same: Offering something that is likely to induce readers to respond to your invitation to send more information or some other useful gift. In fact, designing a press release to draw inquiries can make the release even more acceptable to the editors because it offers something to their readers. It is possible to write such inquiry advertisements and inquiry PR as to induce readers to write and ask for more information, but it is even more productive of inquiries when you promise to send some item of value to every inquirer, as touched on earlier.

Worksheet 27 is designed to help you organize a structured plan to create your own mailing lists by compilation from directory resources and through inquiry advertising. Fill in specific names, as suggested by leads, making best guesses, which you can refine by making up additional worksheets, until you are satisfied that your plan is workable and final.

INSTRUCTIONS: Rate each item from 1 to 10, 1 the lowest mark and 10 the highest for effectiveness of the copy in eliciting inquiries.

COPY	RATING
BE A COMPUTER EXPERT. Be in business for yourself with our agent program. No fees; supplies & training furnished.	[ ]
NEWSLETTER FOR WRITERS. Sample $3. Free details, SASE.	[ ]
GET A GOVERNMENT JOB. Call for current list.	[ ]
WRITER TRAINING COURSE. Send for free writer's aptitude test.	[ ]
WRITER TRAINING. Become published. Send for "Writer's Guide to Publishing."	[ ]
TERMINAL EMULATOR. For communications flexibility. Send for more information.	[ ]
WORD PROCESSING SYSTEMS. FREE word processing training guide and training program disk.	[ ]
NECKTIES AND SCARFS WITH YOUR CORPORATE LOGO. Call or write for free brochure.	[ ]
TELEMARKETING SERVICES. FREE copy of "22 Ways to Stimulate Your Marketing Promotions."	[ ]
SCHEDULE BOARDS. Write or call for brochure explaining kits.	[ ]
LIST MANAGEMENT. Free book on how to get maximum income from rental of your mailing lists.	[ ]
BECOME A GUIDANCE COUNSELOR. Call for free brochure.	[ ]
BUSINESS OPPORTUNITY "SUCCESS BUSINESS." Free audio cassette.	[ ]
MAIL ORDER BUSINESS PLAN. Free book and sample catalog.	[ ]
PUBLISH YOUR OWN BOOK. Free booklet and manuscript report.	[ ]
BE A MONEY BROKER. Write for free details.	[ ]

Worksheet 26. Typical inquiry advertisements

INSTRUCTIONS: Write in specific names, even if only preliminary estimates or hypotheses for each category listed in both sections of worksheet. Use this first sheet as a preliminary plan, then make up additional worksheets, as necessary, to refine estimates and arrive at final working plan.

<u>COMPILATION SOURCES</u>

MEMBERSHIP LISTS

*Associations: _____

_____

DIRECTORIES

Yellow pages _____   Online databases _____

**Other_____   _____

_____   _____

<u>INQUIRY ADVERTISEMENTS</u>

MEDIA

Print _____   _____

Broadcast _____   _____

Other _____   _____

INDUCEMENT

Newsletter _____   Report _____

Other _____   _____

NOTES: _____

----

*Names of relevant associations from whom you can get membership lists
**<u>Thomas Register</u>, <u>Standard & Poor</u>, other such directories

Worksheet 27. Plan for compiling house lists

14

MANAGING THE DIRECT-MARKETING CAMPAIGN

Only disasters happen spontaneously. Good things happen
only by design—by *management*—by being **made** to
happen. For that, in the end, is management: making
things happen.

WHAT IS MANAGEMENT?

Over the years, a great many attempts have been made to sum up definitions of management, often in clever little aphorisms insisting that management is the art of getting other people to do what the manager wants them to do. Of course, that's patent nonsense. We all must sometimes undertake to carry out tasks and programs entirely unaided and alone—without other people. We have no one other than ourselves to persuade to do what we want to get done, but we are pledged to get it done anyhow. And the job must be managed, no matter how many or how few people work on it. So management may or may not have something to do with other people. (Even when others are involved, management is not getting others to do what we want them to do, but *supporting* "the troops," the ones for whose work the customer really pays. But that is another matter.) In fact, if management is anything, it is the art of carrying out the mission successfully with the available resources, whatever they may be. But we must carry the definition a step further and define more clearly the two factors of management identified but not themselves defined: *mission* and *resources.*

THE MISSION

Every organization, program, or task has a mission. Perhaps it is more helpful, however, to call that a *goal* or an *objective.* And that is simply a statement or identification of the result sought—what we want or need to accomplish. For planning and control purposes it is most useful to think in terms of both a goal and an objective or set of objectives. For example, in planning a marketing campaign your goal is to gain either sales, customers, or leads. It is important that you decide about that in advance, that you have a clear understanding of what result you really want, if you are to have any reasonable probability of achieving it. Otherwise, the result comes about by chance, not by design or purpose. That isn't management at all, and it is almost certain to lead to disaster ultimately.

With the goal firmly established, you can set objectives. You can set a schedule, a budget, a set of milestone targets (dates or elapsed time) for the various events and steps required, all of which are objectives marching toward the goal, whatever that is.

All of this makes up the mission. And stated in this manner, it seems so obvious that this is essential ordinary wisdom or common sense that

it seems unnecessary to say it. And yet every day people launch programs without any truly clear goals or objectives, hoping to somehow
stumble into a success.

THE RESOURCES

Resources are assets. They are whatever can be used to accomplish
something. They are time, money, material, equipment, fixtures, other
facilities, people, imagination, talent, energy, and perhaps even other
resources. One of the less well-known cliches of management has it that
you can accomplish anything you wish, given unlimited resources. But
in practice you never have enough of anything you need, and the real
test of management is the ability to get the job done—carry out the mission successfully—despite the inadequacy of the resources. True managers get the job done without enough time, without enough help, without
enough money, and without enough of anything, and great managers
do so under the most difficult circumstances.

One resource we all have in at least nominally equal quantity is time.
It is the one resource that we cannot regain or replace: once lost, it is
lost forever. Maximum effort should therefore be made to budget it with
great care and use it to greatest effect.

The resource of money is not necessarily literally cash in hand. It
may be and more often than not is credit. Some of us have more cash
and/or more credit than others. However, like time, money should be
managed and husbanded with the greatest of care. Carelessness here is
one of the most common causes for the ultimate disaster.

Some of the resources, such as material on hand, are simply other
forms of money and must be treated as if they were, in fact, cold cash
or credit. Others, such as equipment, fixtures, and other physical facilities, are related to time and money: used properly, they can conserve
time and money, and so might be considered to be extensions of those
resources.

The most valuable resources and the ones most difficult to quantify
and budget are your own internal resources of talent, imagination,
creativity, and personal energy. These are imponderables, impossible to
measure, calculate, or even estimate, and therefore impossible to factor
into any equation. Again and again such resources as these produce almost unbelievable results. So we will not attempt to take these resources into account here, in designing tools for management, but we
will bear their potential always in mind. To fail to do so would be to

deprive ourselves of what often proves to be the most valuable resource of all: human imagination and creativity.

Setting your goal overall is entirely up to you; it is an arbitrary decision. However, there are some guidelines that will help you make the decision, and they are presented in Worksheet 28. This is a rather simple form, but an important one.

Ignore the first item, *Goal*, for the moment. It is logically the first item on the form, but is not the first item to make a decision about. We'll return to it later. Describe first, in a brief statement, what you wish to sell.

The next consideration is the size of the sale. Yours may be a situation in which the price is fixed—there is only one possible price—or a variation in price may be expected. The form of the worksheet allows for that. Enter the price, the estimated amount of the average sale, or the probable range of most sales, as appropriate, whether these sales are the direct goal or can be realized only later, after follow up.

INSTRUCTIONS: Check off and/or write in appropriate responses to the items called for. Try to be thoroughly objective in your judgments and estimates, and avoid the trap of wishful thinking.

Goal: Make sales [ ]   Get leads [ ]   Make new customers) [ ]

        Build mailing list [ ] Other: _____ [ ]

Sale item(s): _____

_____

Type item(s):   Big-tag [ ]   Consumer item [ ]   Loss leader [ ]

Other: _____ [ ]

Expected size of typical sale: $_____ - $_____

Probability of immediate sale: _____ - _____ %

NOTES:_____

_____

_____

Worksheet 28. Deciding on the basic goal

Next estimate the probability of closing sales directly as the result of the mailing advertisement, or commercial, without follow up of any kind. This calls for hardheaded honesty, not wishful thinking. If the order runs to several hundred dollars the likelihood of an immediate sale without follow up is small, and if the item runs to four or five figures, you may be sure that you are extremely unlikely to make a sale without one or more follow ups—that your goal ought to be focused on getting sales leads, not on making direct sales. Big-tag sales often require a half-dozen or more calls, solicitations, and presentations before you can close them properly and get the order. Be honest in estimating the percentage of probability here. It is likely to save you time and money. Finally, room is provided to make any appropriate notes you wish to, if there are data you believe should be made part of the record and no appropriate boxes have been created for that information.

All of that done, it is time to return to the first item and decide what your true goal is. You have at least four choices. You can be trying to make sales directly, trying to get inquiries to build a mailing list, trying to get sales leads for follow up via personal calls or telephone, or trying to expand your customer base by using loss leaders or other inducements. (One prominent and successful mail-order company has for many years built their mailing lists through selling loss-leader name-and-address labels at an almost nominal price in print advertisements.) All of these are perfectly legitimate and honorable goals, and you may even get unexpected results on some occasions such as getting a large number of direct sales where you expected only to generate a few leads to follow up. But you can't count on unexpected bonanzas; you must exercise reasonable prudence in deciding what a sensible goal is—what you have a right to expect from your campaign. Helping you do that is the entire purpose of this worksheet.

OBJECTIVES

With a goal established, you need to set objectives—milestones marking the way to achieving the goal—because a great many steps must be taken and a great many things accomplished before you achieve the goal.

Sound management practice requires that you do these several things:

1. Establish and define clearly the specific objectives.
2. Set target dates for their achievement.

3. Have a mechanism for monitoring progress and—especially important—an early-warning system that detects problems almost immediately.
4. Establish contingency programs to cope successfully and promptly with the problems.

Philosophically, this means that you expect things to go wrong, as "Murphy" cautioned us they would. We therefore acknowledge a need to monitor progress so as to detect problems at an early stage, while they can still be corrected. (Most disasters are the result of not perceiving the problems until it is too late to prevent them from screwing everything up.) To complement that early-warning system, you must have a set of contingency plans—ready-to-go remedial measures, measures that can be implemented immediately because they were prepared in advance. In terms of specific management instruments or tools, this calls for at least the following kinds of items:

1. A planned schedule of some sort, in tabular or chart format, showing the optimal dates and/or the "drop dead" (absolutely latest) dates.
2. A CPM (Critical Path Method) diagram showing the alternative routes to the goal when the optimal route is blocked or impeded.
3. A calculated appreciation of all the possible or probable problems.
4. Alternatives for every possible problem of item 3.

Obviously the specific items on the schedule or chart will vary from one case to another, depending on what you are trying to do. Following (Figures 29, 30, and 31) are some specimen tabular schedules, as examples or models you can adopt and adapt to your needs. They are, of course, somewhat generalized, to fit as wide a variety of needs and situations as possible. For your own case or for any given application, you will probably not use all the items suggested, and you may find it necessary to use the blanks provided for your own write-in items.

Because they are broken into classes of activity, the list of dates will not be in strict chronological order. That is something of a drawback. There is a distinct advantage in having schedule dates in chronological order. For one thing it facilitates monitoring progress. But there is also an advantage in grouping milestone objectives by functional categories, and advantage you can appreciate best perhaps when you tackle the job

		OPTIMAL DATE	DROP DEAD DATE
	ITEM		

I: CREATIVE

1. Letter _____ pages

2. Brochure _____ size/pp

3. Order form _____ size

4. Envelopes, teaser copy, _____ size

5. BRE, _____ size

6. Photography, field

7. Photography, studio

8. _____

9. _____

II: ART/PREPARATION

1. Roughs

2. Comprehensives

3. Camera ready

III: PRINTING

1. Copy to printer

2. Ready-to-mail/to mailing house

3. Mailing begins

4. _____

5. _____

IV. MISCELLANEOUS

1. Mailing lists

2. _____

3. _____

Figure 29. Schedule form for direct-mail program

213

	ITEM	OPTIMAL DATE	DROP DEAD DATE

I: CREATIVE

    1. Copy, draft, _____ words/column inches

    2. Review, changes

    3. Final copy

    4. Photography, field

    5. Photography, studio

    6. Drawing(s), roughs

    7. Follow-up copy ready

    8. _____

    9. _____

II: ART/PREPARATION

    1. Final drawings

    2. Final photo selections

    3. Rough layouts

    4. Comprehensives

    5. Camera ready copy

    6. _____

    7. _____

III. MISCELLANEOUS

    1. Insertion order placed, verified

    2. Copy to publication (deadline)

    3. _____

    4. _____

Figure 30. Schedule form for print-advertising program

	ITEM	OPTIMAL DATE	DROP DEAD DATE

I: CREATIVE

    1. Narrative script, draft, _____ minutes

    2. Video storyboard, draft, _____ no. frames

    3. Final copy

    4. Photography, field

    5. Photography, studio

    6. Drawing(s), roughs

    7. Follow-up copy ready

    8. _____

    9. _____

II: ART/PREPARATION

    1. Final drawings

    2. Final photo selections

    3. Taping

    4. Editing

    5. Final tape(s) ready

    6. _____

    7. _____

III. MISCELLANEOUS

    1. Air time order placed, verified

    2. Tapes to studio(s)

    3. _____

    4. _____

Figure 31. Schedule form for broadcast-advertising program

of setting up contingency plans to cope with problems that are likely to arise.

Use these forms as preliminary schedules—rough worksheets, designed primarily to help you analyze the needs and estimate the times required—and then convert the results into chronological schedules that you will use to actually monitor progress.

This approach gives you the preliminary (by function) schedules as aids to monitoring and troubleshooting problems, while it also provides a more convenient means of monitoring progress overall. However, the chronological schedules overall, as distinct from those chronological-by-function schedules, are probably most useful when they are graphic, as in the form of milestone charts.

Figure 32 is an example of such a milestone chart. In this case it is based on the first schedule, Figure 29, but the model can be adapted readily to any schedule. This model is based on a 90-day—13 week—schedule, but it can be modified to be based on any time period, of course. It is a generalized milestone chart for overall monitoring of a campaign, most suitable for the relatively small organization or small campaign. For truly major campaigns, a separate chart should be generated for each functional area (see Figure 33, for an example), with an overall chart for the entire campaign. However, for truly complex programs, something based on the Critical-Path Method (CPM) is even more helpful.

CRITICAL-PATH METHOD CHARTING

CPM tools are used commonly in the construction business, where there are many factors operating at one time, requiring close control, if schedules are to be met and budgets controlled. The idea overall is to set forth on paper all the critical factors, such as deliveries of materials and completion of tasks on time and determine which factors are—must be, by the nature of things—sequential and which can be concurrent. For example, printing cannot be carried out until camera-ready copy is available, and camera-ready copy cannot be created until writing and art work are complete. Ergo, these are necessarily sequential functions. On the other hand, the process of creating a brochure or designing the carrier envelope can be carried out while the letter is being developed, so these are functions that can be parallel.

The milestone chart shows this clearly enough, and even suggests the possible time relationships by judging which task takes 10 weeks,

PROGRAM: _____

(Start date: _____)

WEEKS----------------------------------->

```
0    1    2    3    4    5    6    7    8    9    10   11   12   13
```

```
|----------------------------1-----------2---------3---------4-----------5----6
    Letter

|----------------------------1------2----▲--3-----4---------------5-----6
    Brochure

            |------1----------2---|
                Photography

                |---------1-----2----------3-------4-------5--▸--6
                    Envelope teaser copy

                    |----1----------2------3-----4--------5-----6
                        Order form

                    |--------------------------------5------6
                        Mailing lists

                            |--------5--------6
```

```
|--------------------------------|
    Other (e.g., broadside, catalog)
```

Legend:

1. Roughs/drafts
2. Final copy
3. Camera ready
4. To printer
5. Ready to mail
6. Mailing date

Figure 32. Generalized model of milestone chart

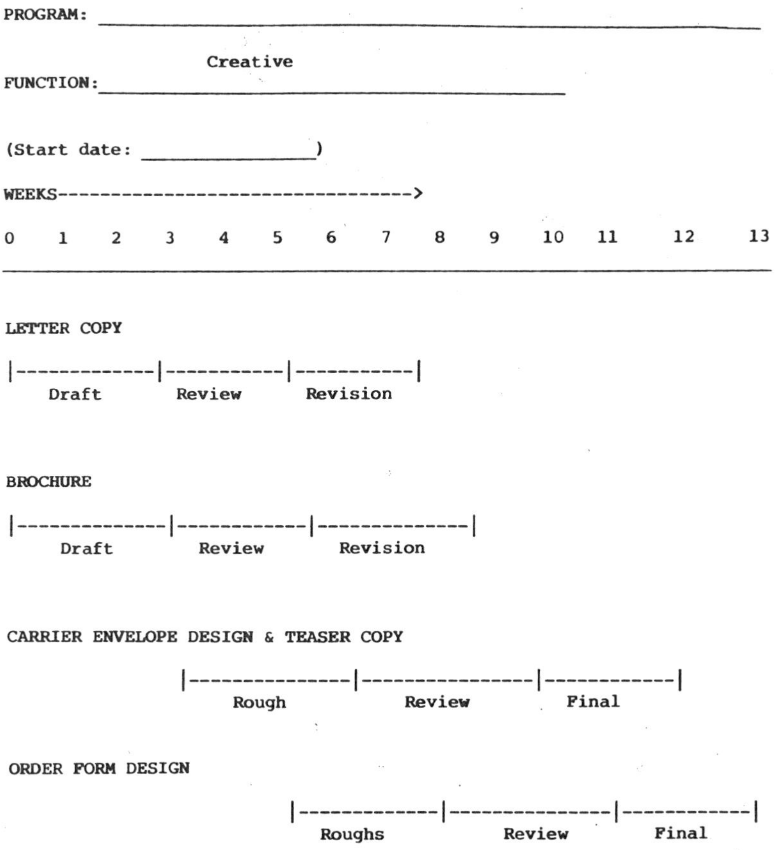

```
PROGRAM: _____

                  Creative
FUNCTION:_____


(Start date: _____)

WEEKS--------------------------------->

 0    1    2    3    4    5    6    7    8    9    10   11    12    13
_____


LETTER COPY

|-------------|-----------|-----------|
     Draft       Review      Revision


BROCHURE

|-------------|-------------|--------------|
     Draft        Review        Revision


CARRIER ENVELOPE DESIGN & TEASER COPY

              |---------------|-----------------|------------|
                    Rough             Review          Final

ORDER FORM DESIGN

              |-------------|----------------|------------|
                   Roughs            Review        Final
```

Figure 33. Model of milestone chart for creative function only

which 4 weeks, when each job can be scheduled, and so forth, and plotting each on the chart that way. However, CPM charting shows this in a somewhat different manner that many managers prefer. In fact, the purpose of CPM charting is not only to plan the most efficient ways and schedule to get a job done, but also to help monitor and manage the work every day, especially when there are interruptions to the schedule and it is necessary to troubleshoot problems and resort to alternative measures.

To illustrate this, a CPM plan for the use of writing labor on the project is offered as Figure 34. A single writer can begin with a first, rough draft of the letter, and turn to a first, rough draft of the brochure as soon as the letter is handed over to management to review. Then when management reviews the brochure draft, the writer goes to prepare the final copy of the letter. This careful planning of phases of tasks continues enabling a single writer to handle it all, if no trouble arises. However, if something comes along to hang up the letter—disagreements and lengthy discussions of what should be in it, for example—the writer can be assigned to leapfrog over the original planned work progression and go on to one of the other tasks. Or, as an alternative, another individual can be assigned to help with writing. Or, as still another alternative, some or all of the writing might be assigned to a consultant or contract copywriter. In fact, this kind of chart might be used to manage consultants and/or vendors or contractors, as well as staff personnel, and, in the construction business, most management problems do involve the subcontracts and subcontractors.

The chart provides an overview of what was planned and what the alternatives are for unforeseen contingencies. In this example, it plots the critical path for writing, but it could be designed to plot a critical path for other functions or aspects of work, and it could also be made larger and more complex and cover all phases and aspects of the program, if desired.

FLOWCHARTS

These several types of schedules and charts are all helpful in planning and managing projects of all kinds. However, this supposes that you know in advance all or most of the steps, phases, and functions you will encounter and must anticipate in drawing up these charts and schedules. For many, especially those who are not completely experienced in planning and carrying out a campaign, some preliminary study and planning are necessary. And for this purpose, the flowchart is especially helpful as an analytical aid and planning tool.

The flowchart is, in its simplest form, a presentation of the logical and sequential series of steps in a process. Figure 35 is an example of such a simple flowchart, in this case, describing the flow of activity involved in preparing a formal proposal in response to a request, and beginning (upper left hand corner) with the analysis and decision to submit a bid or proposal. (In many ways this is an unusually appropriate

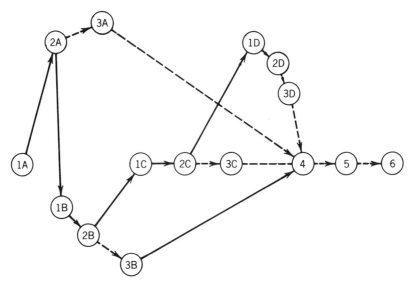

Figure 34. CPM plot of writing function

example, because it describes the development of an important tool used in direct marketing of custom-tailored products and services, and involves many of the steps used in developing a direct-mail program—sales strategy development, writing, and production of a printed end-product.) This type of chart can be used at the very outset of the planning, developing the chart as a logical flow of things to do—things that *must* be done, in fact—to achieve whatever goal or end-product is indicated in the final box of the chart.

Figure 36 shows a similar chart describing the required steps and functions in a typical direct-mail campaign. Again, the chart is straightforward and uncomplicated. But that is because it deals with all functions on a macroscopic—overview—basis, ignoring realities. That is, it suggests that each task is a simple one that is accomplished quickly and efficiently, as shown. It assumes, also, that each step takes place in the sequence shown and is done and over by the time the next task shown is undertaken.

Of course, the real world does not function that way. Even when you carry out a complete program by yourself, you juggle several things at a time, you return to tasks you thought you had finished or to problems you thought you had solved to do some more work on them, and even

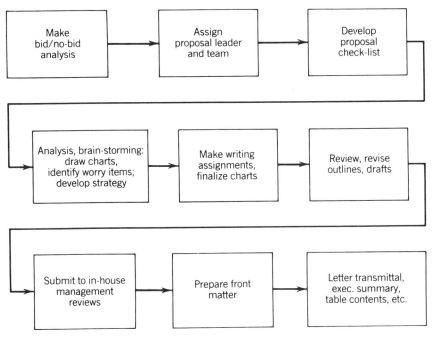

Figure 35. A typical flowchart

when you think the whole job is done and is at the print shop, you get a frantic call from the printer advising you that something is out of kilter and requires your efforts immediately to straighten it out.

Such contingencies can be and generally are shown in flowcharts by indicating both where and what iterations are likely. Moreover, flowcharts are not necessarily entirely sequential in presentation but, as in the case of the network and milestone charts, flowcharts can easily be made to show which tasks are or can be made to be concurrent, as well as which are necessarily sequential.

A brief example of this is shown in Figure 37, which is a small portion of Figure 36 expanded to show in greater detail how the work is likely to flow in actual practice. Program materials—letters, brochures, order forms, and other elements—are not designed and written in a single action, of course, but are drafted in rough form, reviewed, redesigned, and rewritten, and this iteration may be repeated many times before everyone is satisfied with the end-products.

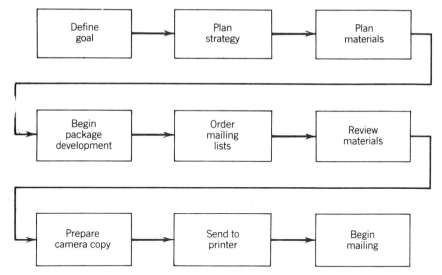

Figure 36. A flowchart for a typical direct mail development

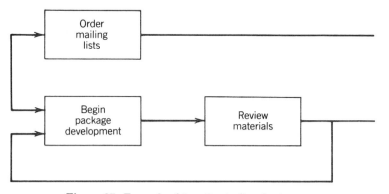

Figure 37. Example of iteration in flowchart

This iteration and reiteration is represented by the line showing the feedback from review of materials to package development. At the same time, a parallel path shows that ordering mailing lists is (logically) a concurrent activity, and that it is presumably not dependent in any way on other activities, except that it must follow early planning, during which you must decide who your proper prospects are—what mailing lists you want to order, that is. But as soon as you know what mailing lists you want, you may proceed to investigate the availability of those mailing lists and order those you think most suitable for your strategic needs.

But even that is not an absolute: Perhaps you can not or should not decide arbitrarily who your prospects are to be and what mailing lists you will want to order. That assumes that you know in advance what mailing lists are available and/or will be available to you, and so can judge which are best for your needs. But you cannot assume that. You must determine what is possible—what mailing lists you *can* find and rent—before you decide firmly exactly who you will target as prospects. So while Figure 38 illustrates the concept of Figure 37 applied to the flowchart overall, Figure 39 carries the idea further. It demonstrates that a survey of available mailing lists ought itself to be a preliminary of, and contribution to, strategy formulation.

You must always remember that no matter how well you know what mailing lists are currently being offered, new lists become available constantly, and one of the most recently available lists may be far better suited to your needs than those offered last week or last month. The decision as to which mailing lists you will use, may have a decisive effect on your sales strategy, so it would be foolish to firm up a sales strategy before being sure of the mailing lists you will use. That latter decision may drastically change the strategy you would otherwise have employed.

CONTINGENCY PLANNING

Direct-marketing campaigns are complex operations. They entail a large number of functions that must be carefully integrated, per the established schedules and budgets. Only when all come together as planned can the campaign have a maximum chance for complete success. Every failure to come together as planned jeopardizes the campaign and lessens its chances for complete success. Minimizing such failures—aberrations in the overall plan—must be a target of management, and can be accomplished by contingency planning. Contingency

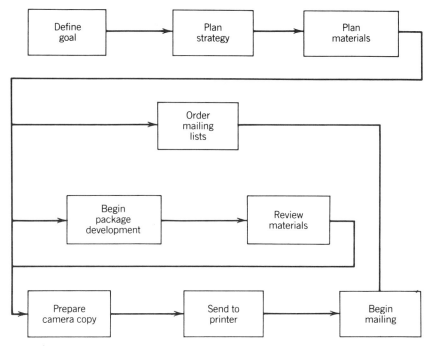

Figure 38. The overall effect of determining concurrency of ordering mailing lists

planning is, in fact, a most important part of campaign planning and management control. And it is based on distinguishing carefully between that which is under your own direct and total control and that which is not under your direct and total control—that which depends on others. Identifying each and every function, including the development of your marketing-products (e.g., salesletters and brochures), in terms of whether the function is or is not under your own direct control, requires a bit of explanation and definition:

You might believe that because you are the customer and you are paying for having some service performed or some product developed by a contractor, vendor, or consultant that the function is under your direct control. Not true. It is only *nominally* under your control. All too often the limits of your control over things will become painfully apparent to you, as a supplier fails to deliver something on schedule, a contractor fails to deliver at all, a consultant becomes ill or otherwise incapaci-

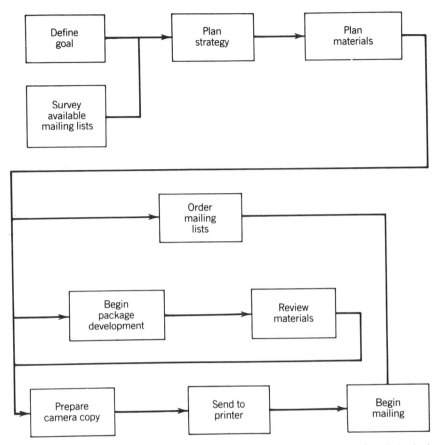

Figure 39. The overall effect of determining mailing-list availabilities as inputs to strategy formulations

tated, or any of a thousand other disasters prophesied by "Murphy" materializes.

In fact, to some degree you are not even in total control of work and products being prepared by your own in-house staff. My own experience bears this out. Aside from the fact that even your own staff can become incapacitated unexpectedly, staff members sometimes leave your employ abruptly and before they complete their work, and it is not always easy for someone else to take over and "get up to speed" quickly on the job. (I have even known staff people to waste many weeks and even months of an employer's time and money and then resign abruptly because they came to realize that they could not do the job acceptably well and feared being exposed and fired.) So bear in mind that to at least some degree everything said here can apply to your staff and in-house work.

The larger and more complex the program is, the greater the problems and the greater the risks are: The number and complexity of their functions are usually in some proportion to the size and complexity of the programs overall. That increases the number of possibilities for trouble, of course. But a great deal of money—risk investment—is at stake, too, and every delay costs money, increasing the risk overall by decreasing the order margin. Usually you literally cannot afford problems that threaten your schedules because they almost automatically threaten your budgets and investment too.

Increasingly in this area we find contractors and suppliers indifferent to our needs and to their own moral and legal obligations. It is a highly frustrating situation, but it is possible to combat the problem successfully: After deciding in advance which are the functions over which you do not have total control, prepare alternative measures— that is, anticipate that such things will happen and be prepared to skirt the problem with a solution that you can put into place immediately.

I like to think of this kind of planning as similar to a Chinese restaurant menu, with columns A and B. Column A is the original plan, and column B is the alternative plan.

In its simplest form, it consists of having alternative sources identified in advance. For example, whenever I had a printing or typesetting job with a critical schedule requirement vended out, I had identified at least one other source (I usually tried to identify three acceptable sources before I chose one) that would be available to me on short notice.

I did the same with other suppliers and vendors of services—consultants, writers, illustrators, and/or others. I made it a firm principle to always have an alternative source firmly identified (and in some cases I had even identified myself the alternative source) for everything not done in-house by in-house staff.

But even that is not always enough. There is the matter of lead time. If a printing job is going to require four weeks to do, no matter who does it, by the time you find that you will not get delivery on schedule it is too late to salvage the situation completely, even with an alternative source, and even with premium payments for accelerated service. But there is an answer for this too: You must identify such special hazards as this— functions with long lead times—and make special provisions to "cover" these special kinds of functions. There are three ways to do this:

One, you might manage to compel your printing contractor to post a performance bond, which might be sacrificed by failure to deliver on schedule. That kind of penalty is usually rather effective, although it is not easy to induce suppliers and service vendors to post such bonds because performance bonds and penalties are not traditional in printing and in providing most other services relevant to direct marketing programs. Another and probably more practical way in most cases is to allow for long lead time when you place your original order, so that you have at least some time cushion when and if you have to turn to an alternative source.

A third way, which is something of a variant on the second way suggested, is to set up a schedule for and order partial or phased deliveries whenever possible so that you can detect any slippage in service at an early stage. This can be done by setting up special schedules or by incorporating these deliveries in the schedules overall (as by making changes in Figures 32 and 33 to show interim deliveries, for example).

In fact, to some degree these are already built into schedules for certain kinds of work (especially all creative functions) which normally go through one or more drafts and reviews before settling on final copy or designs. In these cases, especially when the work is being done under contract, rather than by in-house staff, be alert for and alarmed by any slippage or indication of panic deliveries of drafts and roughs.

Note that the alternative may be to identify someone in-house (even yourself) as an alternative, particularly in emergencies. This is an especially good alternative or emergency measure because you have complete or nearly complete control over it. But it works both ways: On the other hand, don't neglect the possibility that an in-house resource may fail you for any of the reasons already cited, and that the alternative to that may be an outside source—a consultant, contractor, or vendor of some sort.

Worksheet 29 is offered as a form to use in taking the first step in your contingency planning. Of course, not all items will be relevant or applicable in any given case, and perhaps some items will never be relevant to your needs. On the other hand, you may have special items you must write in, using blanks provided for the purpose. For creative services and functions you may enter either the projected dates or required times for the first draft, or you may enter both those dates/times and the final dates/total time required. However, it is that first-draft or elapsed time that is most important, for if there is slippage there, in that first draft, a warning is (should be) sounded immediately.

Worksheet 29 is in two parts. Part I, the first sheet, is an aid for only the first step. Part II, the second sheet, is offered as an aid to taking the second step in preparing for contingencies. Write in the appropriate items (salesletter, brochure, broadside, etc.) for each function/service you must perform, especially those you are buying, and establish your second and third alternative sources, whether in- or out-of-house.

Summation of Campaign Management and Control Measures

A final management control worksheet is provided as Worksheet 30. It is a simple worksheet, a reminder list. You should be able to answer Yes to each question on it. If you cannot do this, you have probably overlooked or neglected something important to a successful marketing campaign.

Name/description of program: _____

Target date for printing: _____   Target date for mailing: _____

ITEMS REQUIRED

Salesletter [ ]   Brochure [ ]   Order form [ ]   BRE [ ]   Broadside   [ ]

Mailing lists [ ]   _____ [ ]   _____ [ ]

OUTSIDE SERVICES

Creative: Consulting [ ]   Writing [ ]   Illustrating [ ]   Design [ ]

Production: Layouts   [ ]   Mechanicals [ ] Typesetting [ ]   Printing [ ]

Mailing lists [ ]   Mailing [ ] Consulting [ ] _____ [ ]

DUE DATES OR TIME REQUIRED (IN WEEKS)

Salesletter: Writing _____   Design _____

Brochure: Writing _____ Design_____ Illustrating _____

Broadside: Writing _____ Design _____ Illustrating _____

Order form: Writing _____ Design _____ Illustrating _____

Mailing lists _____

LONG-LEAD ITEMS & SERVICES

Salesletter: _____ weeks   Brochure _____ weeks

Broadside: _____ weeks   Order form: _____ weeks

Mailing lists: _____ weeks   Writing: _____ weeks

Design: _____ weeks   Illustrating: _____ weeks

_____ : _____ weeks   _____ : _____ weeks

NOTES: _____

(a)

Worksheet 29. Contingency planning: *(a)* First step

SERVICE/ITEM	FIRST SOURCE	SECOND SOURCE	THIRD SOURCE

WRITING:

_____   _____   _____   _____

_____   _____   _____   _____

_____   _____   _____   _____

_____   _____   _____   _____

DESIGN:

_____   _____   _____   _____

_____   _____   _____   _____

_____   _____   _____   _____

_____   _____   _____   _____

ILLUSTRATING:

_____   _____   _____   _____

_____   _____   _____   _____

_____   _____   _____   _____

_____   _____   _____   _____

LAYOUT, MECHANICALS:

_____   _____   _____   _____

_____   _____   _____   _____

_____   _____   _____   _____

_____   _____   _____   _____

BRE: _____   _____   _____

MAILING LISTS: _____   _____   _____

PRINTING: _____   _____   _____

CONSULTING: _____   _____   _____

NOTES:_____

(b)

Worksheet 29. Contingency planning: (b) Second step

230

THE MANAGEMENT CHECKLIST

1. Have you set a budget overall for your program?   Y [ ]   N [ ]

2. Have you identified all major elements of your program

   and listed them in your budget and master schedule?   Y [ ]   N [ ]

3. Have you defined/identified your overall goal?   Y [ ]   N [ ]

4. Have you defined and committed yourself to a complete set

   of objectives as milestones marking the way to the goal?   Y [ ]   N [ ]

5. Have you planned all your activities for achieving each

   objective, setting up schedules and budgets, anticipating

   possible problems, and preparing contingency plans?   Y [ ]   N [ ]

6. Do you have your "Chinese menu"--primary and secondary

   sources identified--and on a standby if needed?   Y [ ]   N [ ]

7. Does your plan provide for you to monitor all functions

   through all phases carefully so as to spot a schedule- or

   budget-threatening problem almost immediately?   Y [ ]   N [ ]

8. Can you institute the corrective action immediately when

   such a problem arises?   Y [ ]   N [ ]

Worksheet 30. Checklist for management and control

15

COMPUTERIZING
OPERATIONS

The modern desktop computer is one of the most valuable
and useful tools available to even the smallest
direct-mail program.

COMPUTERS AND MAILING LISTS, AN EARLY MARRIAGE

A large portion of the direct mail industry turned to computers some time ago—to mainframe computers, before the advent of the personal or desktop computer of the past decade. Probably mailing list managers and brokers (and others who managed lists such as professional mailers fulfillment services and in-house list managers of major publishers and large mail-order firms) were among the first to do so. Computers enabled them to diversify their lists and customize their services almost immediately: Through computerization they could code, sort, and organize lists to deliver a wide variety of list products from a single database of names and addresses. It was now possible to sort in zip code order, alphabetically, by street name, by occupation, by economic class, by history as a buyer, or by almost any other parameter or search term, according to how the list was originally coded. In fact, it was rapidly becoming possible to deliver to each user a product that was almost completely customized to the user's unique needs.

The desktop or personal computer has been even more revolutionary in many ways. Now even the smallest business can afford a computer, and desktop computers can do most of the things their mainframe brethren can do, even if not quite as rapidly or as efficiently. However, this has not detracted in any way from the work done by the larger machines but has made life easier for the small organization and enabled that small organization to do many things previously available only to those with access to a mainframe computer.

By far the most popular use of desktop computers has been word processing. Word processors, however, are not machines; they are software—programs—that are loaded into computers. There are a few "dedicated" word-processing computers, machines designed to do word processing only, but almost all word processing is being done today on desktop general-purpose computers that can do many other jobs by simply loading other programs into them. You can, for example, use your desktop computer to compile, sort, organize, reorganize, and print out your own mailing lists on labels or even directly on envelopes. You can prepare a standard or form letter, and have your machine individually address and type out a copy for each person on your list. You can manipulate figures as readily as you do words, and with some printers, you can create your own headlines (admittedly they will be of somewhat lesser quality than formal typesetting would get you). You can also develop graphics—charts and plots of many kinds—in black and white or in color.

Despite all this, by far the greatest use you will (probably) make of your desktop computer is word processing in developing copy. And while you will probably want to use formal typesetting for brochures, order forms, broadsides, and perhaps other literature, you can use a letter-quality printer to "set type" for your salesletter. Typewriter quality such as you normally get from a letter-quality printer is usually perfectly acceptable for salesletters.

Composition or typesetting, however, is not the issue and not the chief reason for or benefit of using word processing. The chief benefit lies in the judicious use of word processing and what it can do for the writing process—for the *quality* of the written product. That is a very much misunderstood facet of word processing, unfortunately, so that a great many users of word processing are getting only a small fraction of the total benefits possible.

The all-too-common error of word-processor use is in using the system as a kind of automatic or super-typewriter, thereby failing to understand its real significance. Where once, before word processing, executives and others writing in offices scrawled their ideas on lined yellow paper and turned the holographic manuscript over to typists to type on their IBMs, they now scrawl their ideas on lined yellow paper and turn the holographic manuscript over to "word-processor operators" (typists!) to type on their word computer keyboards for printing out ultimately.

Little has changed thereby. It is now easier, faster, and more efficient to make changes in the copy. Less retyping and less proofreading are required now because only the changes have to be proofed. It's also easy to create more than one original copy, but that is not too much of a boon because office copiers can now turn out perfect copies, sometimes copies that are even *better* than the originals.

Those little benefits are not worth the cost of the machine, not to mention the difference between salaries paid typists called typists and typists called word processor operators. The real benefit of word processing is realized only when the writer works at the keyboard, for the true benefit is not what word processing—"wp"—does for typing but what it does for writing—what it contributes to the actual writing itself, as well as for the greater efficiency of all work related to writing in the office. Unfortunately, this is not well understood, and merits a brief discussion here:

There are, first of all, a couple of cliches that are relevant. One has it that all good writing is rewriting. Only tyros at writing believe that they can produce writing of adequate quality in a first draft. Professional writers operate from a premise that a first draft is written solely for the purpose of getting raw or basic ideas down to study and reorganize in a second draft. Perhaps a second draft will be acceptable, but even second drafts are rarely of the quality they could be and should be. And many writers are not satisfied until they have written several drafts. But even then they believe that they must edit their work one more time and polish their manuscript a bit more.

A second cliche recognizes that it is much more difficult to write effective short copy than it is to write effective lengthy copy. The reasoning is simple enough: It is more difficult to deliver a message in perhaps 50 words than it would be to deliver that message in 200 words. And that is particularly true in this case, especially when you are trying to persuade a reader to spend money on something, sight unseen. It takes a great deal of writing and rewriting to produce effective copy that is short.

Of course, "short" is a relative term. A short letter might be a single page or even a half-page—perhaps 200 words. But a short print advertisement may be 25 words, or a short radio/TV commercial 10 seconds. However, whatever "short" means in actual number of words or time in any given case, it also means working at writing and revising the copy almost endlessly, until it has maximum impact and can do the job.

WRITING AT THE KEYBOARD

All this writing and rewriting is a somewhat wearisome job at best, especially when you have to literally *write* and *rewrite*, whether in longhand or by typewriter. And this is where the word processor shines, for it is so much easier to revise and rewrite with a word processor that it is almost fun. But even that isn't a complete description of what wp — word processing—can do for you, for while word processing offers a whole bagful of tricks—shortcuts and aids—there are many shortcuts and aids that can be added with auxiliary software programs that enhance word processing generally. Here are just a few typical things you can do with these programs:

Insert and delete words and longer expressions
Automatically search for words, terms, or other material in files
Automatically replace or correct mistakes via find-and-replace functions.

Make various expressions, whole phrases, and even whole para-graphs standardized and available at the press of a single key when wanted

Readily customize prototype or standardized basic material for al-most instantaneous creation of new materials

Check spelling and also help greatly in proofreading thereby

Copy files or portions of files readily and almost instantaneously

Provide convenient and easy combination or recombination of di-verse materials from several sources

Index your materials (for catalogs, for example)

Footnote materials

Catalog whole collections of files

Create forms of all kinds, both from scratch and via customizing older forms stored in your computer archives

HOW TO WRITE PUNCHY, SHORT COPY

Short copy is never written; it is *rewritten* as short copy. That is, the method is to write your message out in as much detail and as great a length as you wish—in your first draft. The purpose of the first draft is to get it all down, everything you wish to say, all the features you want to describe, all the benefits you wish to promise, all the arguments you wish to make. Even if you plan a one-page letter you should probably write a two- or three-page draft. At least.

Go over that first draft, and keep adding whatever it is that you think adds weight and substance to it as persuasive copy. Only when you can think of nothing more to add is it time to go on to the next step.

The next step is to sort the ideas. You will probably find some redun-dancies, the same idea expressed more than once, although perhaps in different words each time. In some cases, it is perfectly sound to say the same thing—especially to reinforce some arguments or benefit prom-ises—more than once. In others, it is unnecessary and may even prove tiresome to the reader. You will have to make the value judgment on this and decide how much redundancy to edit out of your copy.

You will have to weigh the various benefits promised and the argu-ments made. Copy can easily be weakened, rather than strengthened by too many promises and/or promises that are too extravagant. Re-member that you must provide some kind of evidence that you can and will deliver on those promises. Eliminate those promises you cannot back up convincingly. Far better to make moderate promises that you can back up than to make extravagant promises that you can't back up. In fact, it's a good practice to focus primarily on one major benefit and make all other promised benefits supportive of and subordinate to the major benefit.

Cut the hyperbole—those superlatives—and minimize your use of other adjectives and adverbs. Stick to noun and verbs. (Adjectives and adverbs come across as claims and opinions, where nouns and verbs are much more likely to be accepted as facts—are inherently more credible.) State the benefits quietly—the promise is usually easier to believe if you are not shouting—and then back them up by making the *facts* dramatic.

A CHECKLIST

The following is a brief checklist of things to do in editing and rewriting your copy:

Get rid of all passive words
Use active voice
Make your statements sound positive
Use simple language
Use "you" and talk *to* the reader

Figure 40 illustrates some of this in a small sample. It is the beginning of mail-order copy describing a new book. The figure shows first an "A" version, the original, and then a "B" version, the shortened and rewritten copy. Note what has been changed, how the reader is addressed directly in the revised version, and how much more dynamic the copy has become generally when the copy is purged of unnecessary words.

Forms

One of the most useful aspects of desktop computers and word processors is the convenience they afford in making up forms. Many special graphics programs are available to draw a variety of plots and charts, many of which are helpful both in presenting information to readers and in managing your programs. However, ordinary word processing

A: Original Version

Today's explosion of information—the advent of the so-called information industry—has resulted in the creation of a host of money-making opportunities for all kinds and sizes of businesses based somehow on information. Any of those who wish to capitalize on today's demand for specialized information and knowledge will surely welcome this new and practical help describing and discussing all phases and aspects of launching a new information-based enterprise or extracting more profit out of an existing such venture.

* * * * * * * * * * * * * * * * * * * *

B: Revised Version

New opportunities for wealth are waiting for you in today's information industry, and this practical new book shows you how to cash in directly on the boom. Whether you wish to launch a new information-based venture or increase the profitability of an existing one, this author guides you through every step necessary.

Figure 40. Before and after copy

programs can be used to make up many of these kinds of graphics, as well as many other forms and figures that are beyond the scope of those special graphics programs. In fact, most of the forms and figures used in this book were made up originally via WordStar word processing software. And in many cases they were adapted from earlier wp-composed models residing in my floppy-disk archives of earlier books and my own direct mail ventures.

It is possible to make up many forms and figures that are excellent for draft manuscripts and even adequate in some cases for final manuscript and camera-ready copy. Once a basic model of any form exists, it is usually quite easy to adapt it to a new use. (In addition to the many forms that have already appeared in these pages, a miscellany of others are offered in the next chapter.)

The Asset of Complete Archives

You will find it very much to your benefit to create archives—stored copies on floppy disks—of everything you create for each campaign. (Those using high-capacity hard disks often use tape for backup files, but this is to make true archives, backup records that will probably not be used again, unless some disaster wipes out disk files, so floppy disks are far more convenient and practical for the use recommended here.) Even if you use a pen to mark up final copy for typesetting and printing, you will be wise to update your disk/tape files to reflect the final version of your copy. As these archives grow they represent an ever more valuable asset.

One of the greatest advantages word processing confers on you is the ability you now have to create a different kind of archive. And perhaps that is not even the right term for this. *Archives* connotes dusty files of rarely used records, and what is referred to here is more in the nature of a resource library, a repository of materials that can be used over and over.

What makes these archives so useful lies in the nature of computers and word processors in two basic characteristics: the ability to make exact copies instantly, and the ability to make changes readily. The capability so represented can make your work grow constantly easier, as the archives or reference library of resource materials grows. For while it is fairly laborious to create many of these materials in their original versions, it is usually easy to adapt them later to other needs, making the original time and effort expended a true investment, one that pays handsome dividends in subsequent uses.

In general, the procedure is to make a copy of the original and modify the copy, leaving the original intact. Aside from the fact that this creates a new original to add to your archives ultimately, it is a great help when something goes wrong with your revision effort. Sometimes it is easier to start over, in such cases, than to fix the problem, because it takes only a moment to scrap the effort and make a new copy of the original. So, because it is so easy to make copies, you need never tamper with or disturb the original beyond copying it.

There are different ways to establish these archives or library files. First of all, you will probably want a simple library copy of all the materials and records of each campaign, and it is good "insurance" to have such a permanent record of the original. However, for utility in future programs, these are not the most convenient records to turn to. Probably the number of classes of archives ought to be somewhere between four and 10, depending on what kinds of campaigns you conduct and the kinds of materials you use. Following is a suggested list of archives that should be built:

1. Charts, plots, and diagrams
2. Forms

3. Miscellaneous figures/illustrations composed by computer
4. Sales letters
5. Print advertisements
6. Brochures
7. Broadsides
8. Order forms
9. Catalog sheets
10. Miscellaneous copy

Of course, you may wish to subclassify some of these, depending on your own situation and needs. You might wish, for example, to keep a file of all print advertisements for each medium in which you advertise. You may also find it useful to make notations of the results each archived item (or the campaign in which it was used) produced, as a possible index for future use or adaptation of the item.

16

MISCELLANEOUS FORMS AND REFERENCES

Tying up a few loose ends and supplying some useful
reference materials.

SOME PRACTICAL CONSIDERATIONS IN ADVERTISING

Unless you buy a great deal of space or air time, as major corporations do, thereby making it possible for an advertising agency to do all your creative work and buy space/time without cost to you, you must do all the creative work and handle all the administrative detail yourself. That is the typical case for direct marketers. Of course, you can get some assistance from publishers and broadcast studios, but that is not an unmixed blessing because they work in their own interests, not in yours.

Unless you happen to be well experienced in typography, you will almost surely find the vast array of typestyles and typefaces bewildering, for example, and that may induce you to gratefully accept the help of the newspaper or magazine staff in choosing type and even in laying out the copy as "pubset"—set by the publisher, rather than by the advertiser (you). Unfortunately, the publisher's editorial staff are expert enough in layout and typography, but they are not marketers. The result of having your copy set by the publisher is far too often a deep and costly disappointment. You are usually far better off providing camera-ready copy to the publisher.

There are two ways to do this. You can hire a specialist to do this work for you: There are many individuals and small graphic arts shops that will work closely with you so that you get what you personally prescribe and/or approve. Or you can learn to do the work yourself, and do it in-house. But actually, there is a third way that most use: a hybrid in which you get expert help with some aspects and do some of the work yourself. Help is offered here for this.

What is true for print advertising is equally true for radio and TV commercials. You can get studio help in preparing your audio or video tapes, but you lose control if you turn the entire job over, and you will be well advised to arrange to either do it yourself or have it done in some arrangement that permits you to control the outcome. There are specialists available to help you with this, too, support vendors who can do any part or all of the work you need done to prepare audio and video tapes for broadcasting your commercials. (Many announcers and commentators on local radio and TV stations moonlight to help advertisers.) They usually can supply you the names of actors, narrators, and professional presenters to record your tapes.

PLANNING ADVERTISING AND COMMERCIALS

There are a number of factors to consider when ordering print advertising. In ordering newspaper advertising, for example, specifications of the day on which it is to appear, the section of the paper in which it is to appear, and the position in which it is to appear are often as important as—and perhaps even more important than—the size and content of the advertisement. Space in the Sunday edition is usually more expensive than space in weekday editions, for example, because Sunday circulation tends to be greater, and circulation is the principal determinant of advertising rates. Too, Sunday editions of many newspapers carry special sections that do not appear in weekday editions. The section is important in all cases, however. If you wish to appeal primarily to women readers, you are likely to miss a great deal of your audience by advertising in the sports pages. On the other hand, not many men read the foods section or news of local social events. And for placement or position, you may want your copy in a left- or right-hand page, centered, or on one side or the other of the page, but many advertisers specify that the advertisement must appear "above the fold"—in the upper half of the page—because it is more prominent there.

Figure 41 is a suggested form for specifying all important details of your print advertising. Of course you can use more than one copy of the form if you are going to run your copy in more than four periodicals. "Placement" details will vary according to type of periodical. In newspapers size and costs are generally in terms of column-inches, at least for smaller advertisements. Large advertisements may be measured and priced as they are in many magazines, by the page or fraction of a page. There are also many special publications, some of them annuals such as directories of various kinds or the yearbooks of some organizations. Usually magazines and special publications such as those referred to here have some premium placements, such as back cover, insides of the back and front covers, and centerfold.

Figures 42 and 43 are similar forms for broadcast media—radio and TV—but are similar in suggesting the decisions you should make when planning commercials. As in the case of Figure 41, space is provided to decide when to run these spots, and you can use additional forms if you are going to use more stations than there is space to record on the forms.

In all cases it is important to identify the campaign and the copy. In the case of print advertising you can attach a printed copy of the advertisement to the form and identify the copy so that it can always be identified, should it be necessary in the future. Similarly, you should use some kind of identifying title on the videotapes or audiotapes for future reference.

Of course, part of the data for these forms comes from the media. It is those publishers and broadcasters who will have to tell you what the

SPECIFICATIONS FOR ADVERTISEMENT, PRINT MEDIA

Date: _____ Campaign/project: _____

Copy identification (note if copy attached):_____

_____

Publication #1: _____

Size and placement:_____

Date to be submitted:_____

Dates of insertion:_____

Who sets:_____

Publication #2: _____

Size and placement:_____

Date to be submitted:_____

Dates of insertion:_____

Who sets:_____

Publication #3:_____

Size and placement:_____

Date to be submitted:_____

Dates of insertion:_____

Who sets:_____

Publication #4:_____

Size and placement:_____

Date to be submitted:_____

Dates of insertion:_____

Who sets:_____

NOTES:_____

_____

Figure 41. Planning/specification sheet for print advertising

SPECIFICATIONS FOR COMMERCIALS, RADIO

Date: _____ Campaign/project: _____

Station #1:_____ Length of spot:_____

Dates & times to run:_____

Who furnishes tape:_____

Date to submit tape:_____

Station #2:_____ Length of spot:_____

Dates & times to run:_____

Who furnishes tape:_____

Date to submit tape:_____

Station #3:_____ Length of spot:_____

Dates & times to run:_____

Who furnishes tape:_____

Date to submit tape:_____

Station #4:_____ Length of spot:_____

Dates & times to run:_____

Who furnishes tape:_____

Date to submit tape:_____

Station #4:_____ Length of spot:_____

Dates & times to run:_____

Who furnishes tape:_____

Date to submit tape:_____

NOTES:_____

Figure 42. Planning/specification sheet for radio advertising

SPECIFICATIONS FOR COMMERCIALS, TV

Date: _____ Campaign/project: _____

Station #1:_____ Length of spot:_____

Dates & times to run:_____

Who furnishes tape:_____

Date to submit tape:_____

Station #2:_____ Length of spot:_____

Dates & times to run:_____

Who furnishes tape:_____

Date to submit tape:_____

Station #3:_____ Length of spot:_____

Dates & times to run:_____

Who furnishes tape:_____

Date to submit tape:_____

Station #4:_____ Length of spot:_____

Dates & times to run:_____

Who furnishes tape:_____

Date to submit tape:_____

Station #4:_____ Length of spot:_____

Dates & times to run:_____

Who furnishes tape:_____

Date to submit tape:_____

NOTES:_____

Figure 43. Planning/specification sheet for television advertising

248

deadlines are—when copy or tapes must be furnished—for the advertisements or commercials to run as you wish them to run.

YOUR OWN ADVERTISING AGENCY

If you are one of the many direct marketers who advertise consistently but whose purchases of space and time are not large enough to merit the services of the established, large advertising agencies you may choose to set up your own advertising agency, with yourself as your own sole client. You can thereby reduce your advertising costs by the amount of the agency commissions, typically 15 percent. (This helps to defray your costs for creating camera-ready copy and broadcast tapes.) Most publishers are well aware that many advertisers do this, and some publishers even encourage the practice quite openly, since you are certainly morally justified in doing this.

In practice, setting up your own advertising agency is simple enough. You need only think up an agency name—no great problem, of course— and create an insertion form and suitable stationery, such as a letterhead and envelope. Examples of such insertion forms appear as Figures 44 and 45, and they may be modified to suit your own situation, of course.

Actually, you may be able to reduce your advertising costs even further, since you can often get 1 to 3 percent additional discount for prompt payment—payment within 10 days of being billed—making the total reduction in advertising costs even more substantial.

LAYOUTS

If you are to take a hand in making up your copy for printing, even if it is only communicating with contractors who help you, rather than being more directly involved in doing the actual work of preparing copy, you must gain at least a basic understanding of the processes. Although they are not especially complex, there is a great deal of jargon used in the related editorial and printing trades, and it can be quite confusing if you don't have an at least general idea of what is referred to.

Just as text copy goes through draft stages before reaching its final stage, where it is composed or typeset prior to being printed, illustrations go through similar stages as "roughs" before they become final

SILVER CITY ADVERTISING AGENCY

415 North Mother Lode Avenue

Silver City, CA 97003

INSERTION ORDER

TO: The Silver City Post   Order No. 329

   83 First Street   Date: Feb 6, 1987

   Silver City, CA 97002   Advertiser: Triple A Catalog Sales

==

INSERTION DATE(S): Mar 28-30/87   NO. INSERTIONS: 3 Times

SPACE: 6 column-inches   RATE: $65

PLACEMENT: Financial pages   POSITION: Above the fold, RH page

SPECIAL INSTRUCTIONS: None

TOTAL SPACE COST: $1,170

15% AGENCY COMMISSION: $175.55

NET DUE: $994.45

NOTES: Camera-ready copy enclosed.

Figure 44. Typical form for insertion order

and ready for printing. And layouts, the combination of all the elements of type—headlines, captions, and body copy—and other matter—photographs and drawings—also go through similar stages of development: the rough layout, the comprehensive layout, and the mechanical layout. The rough layout is a preliminary plan, the comprehensive is a more detailed plan, and the mechanical is the actual camera-ready copy pasted down in final format, ready to be photographed for making into printing plates.

Figure 46 is another representation of a rough layout (an earlier one was shown as Figure 16) and Figure 47 shows this developed as a comprehensive layout. The difference is not great: The rough layout is tentative, while the comprehensive layout is somewhat more detailed and represents commitment, including copy fitting, usually with headlines

SILVER CITY ADVERTISING AGENCY

415 North Mother Lode Avenue

Silver City, CA 97003

INSERTION ORDER

TO: WABC-TV   Order No. 46

45 Oxide Avenue   Date: Feb 6, 1987

Silver City, CA 97005   Advertiser: Triple A Catalog Sales

==

INSERTION DATE(S): Mar 28-30/87   NO. TIMES: 3 daily (9 total)

RATE: $132   LENGTH: 60 seconds   TIMES OF DAY: Late night

SPECIAL INSTRUCTIONS: Breaks in late, late show (movie)

TOTAL COST: $1188

15% AGENCY COMMISSION: $178.20

NET DUE: $1009.80

NOTES: Videotape supplied

Figure 45. Typical form for buying air time

and captions inserted. These figures represent copy for a rather simple print advertisement, whereas often the layout will be for a large brochure, broadside, catalog or other mailing piece and therefore will include one or more full pages, with many headlines, captions, pieces of copy, photographs, drawings, and sometimes even other elements. But the principle is the same in all cases: a general plan, followed by a more detailed plan and commitment to it, and finally a paste up of the actual copy to match the comprehensive, ready for printing.

Handling photographs is a special problem because photographs often include matter that is not of interest and may even detract from what you really want the photograph to present. You may, for example, want to select an individual from a photograph of a group, or a single product from a display of many products. This is done by what is referred to as *cropping* the photograph. Figure 47 illustrates how this is done by professionals in such work:

Photo

Figure 46. Rough layout

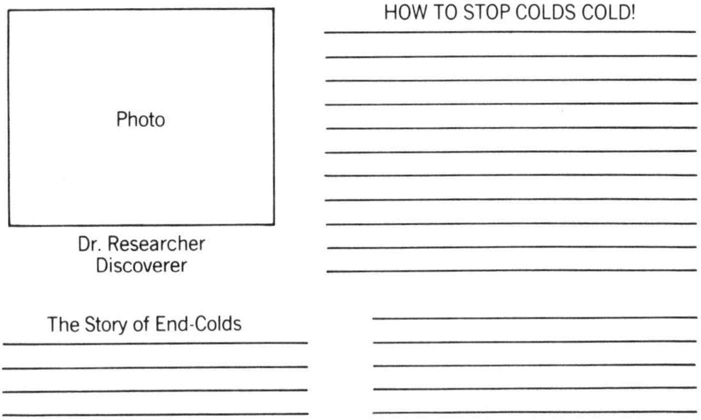
HOW TO STOP COLDS COLD!
Photo
Dr. Researcher
Discoverer
The Story of End-Colds

Figure 47. Comprehensive layout

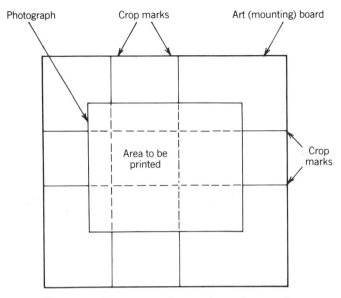

Figure 48. Arrangement for cropping a photograph

The photograph is first mounted—pasted down—on a stiff backing, such as artists use. Then lines are drawn on the backing, as shown in the figure. The solid lines in the figure represent the actual lines drawn on the mounting board, and the dashed lines represent the imaginary lines—extensions of the solid lines—on the photograph itself. The area of the photograph enclosed by the imaginary lines where they cross each other is the portion of the photograph that is to be reproduced. The printer understands this and will set the camera so as to photograph only that sector of the photograph. (The photograph will be copied through a screen that breaks the photograph down into a pattern of dots, so that it is printed as what the trade calls a *halftone*.)

APPENDIX

CREATIVE SERVICES

Marketing in general is a virtual industry unto itself, and direct marketing is especially peopled with large numbers of consultants, specialists, and services of many kinds. Some of these services are offered by individual consultants, others by organizations of many sizes, some of them large corporations.

Several lists of such support services appear in this appendix. The first list, for example, is that of consultants and others who offer what are generally designated as *creative* services. The listing is something of a potpourri of individuals and organizations offering creative services to support direct marketing. It is virtually impossible to subclassify the list adequately because there is too great a diversity of characteristics and services offered to do so effectively. Suffice it to say that all of the following individuals and organizations offering creative services of various kinds for direct marketing, although they differ from each other in many ways such as the size of their organizations and the kinds of services they offer. Most offer consulting services and a great many are also advertising agencies, graphic arts shops, copywriters, and mailers. Many are generalists in support of or services for direct marketing. Also included among these listings are those who are also list managers/ brokers and offer mailing and fulfillment services, as well, although others offering these services will appear in separate lists.

Some are individual consultants who specialize in counseling clients and helping plan campaigns, but most offer creative services such as copy writing, testing, campaign planning, and design.

The lists are by state and in alphabetical order.

ALABAMA

Global Marketing Services
3639F Logtrail
Birmingham, AL 35216
(205) 987-7647

Ronnie McDonald & Associates
Box 1751
Florence, AL 35631
(205) 766-9233

MultiService
111 S. Sparkman Street
Hartselle, AL 35640
(205) 773-2082

ALASKA

Concept Marketing
Box 813
Fairbanks, AK 99707
(907) 479-7708

ARIZONA

Abacus
4747 N. Seventh Street
Phoenix, AZ 85014
(602) 279-4276

Cramer-Kassell Southwest
3300 N. Central Avenue

Phoenix, AZ 85012
(602) 277-0600

Gilbert Advertising
3216 N. Third Street
Phoenix, AZ 85060
(602) 234-2948

Hanson, Eaton, & Associates
Mountain Road, #15
Sedona, AZ 86336
(602) 282-1735

Interstelle Communications
48 N. Tucson Blvd.
Tucson, AZ 85733
(602) 795-5351

The National Switchboard
2150 E. Thomas Road
Phoenix, AZ 85064
(800) 262-5389

W.B. Nelson, C.B.C.
Box 41630
Tucson, AZ 85717
(602) 296-3334

Thorne Shepard & Rodgers, Inc.
3001 N. Second Street
Phoenix, AZ 85012
(602) 279-3306

Trey Ryder
Box 2112
Scottsdale, AZ 85252
(602) 835-1885

Southwest Direct Marketing
1638 E. Candlestick Drive
Tempe, AZ 85283
(602) 839-9911

Starcourt Graphic Design
Box 9681

Phoenix, AZ 85068
(602) 992-6118

T.A.P. Graphics
5016 W. Avalon Drive
Phoenix, AZ 85031
(602) 247-2563

Usry Advertising
5503 N. Calle Del Santo
Phoenix, AZ 85018
(602) 840-2704

WFC/Westcom
655 N. Alvernon
Tucson, AZ 85711
(602) 795-4580

ARKANSAS

Heritage Publishing &
Telemarketing
4100 Heritage Drive
N. Little Rock, AR 72119
(501) 945-5000

Kirkpatrick & Associates
600 Centre Place
Little Rock, AR 72201
(501) 378-0382

The Media Market
285 College Street
Batesville, AR 72503
(501) 793-6902

CALIFORNIA

A.B. Concepts
16776 Bernardo Center Drive
San Diego, CA 92128
(714) 485-0601

Ad Systems International
Box 2109

Sausalito, CA 94966
(415) 332-4252

Advertising Plus/Myra Lookabill
2174 W. Falmouth
Anaheim, CA 92801
(714) 535-2495

Advertoon
Box 1272
Santee, CA 92071
(619) 286-8233

Alba Advertising
1377 Ninth Avenue
San Francisco, CA 94122
(415) 665-1198

All-Media Services
13415 Ventura Boulevard
Sherman Oaks, CA 91423
(818) 995-3329

A & M Direct Mail Services
441 Borrego Court, Box 216
San Dimas, CA 91733
(818) 966-1013

American Bookdealers Exchange
5746 Kiowa Drive
La Mesa, CA 92041
(619) 462-3297

AMS Response
1422 Liberty Street
El Cerrito, CA 94530
(415) 232-8850

Analog Enterprises
1484 N. Kraemer Boulevard
Placentia, CA 92670
(714) 529-5480

Analytical Solutions
40401 Strathern Street
Canoga Park, CA 91306
(818) 341-6063

Anderson-Miller
Communications
846 California Street
San Francisco, CA 94108
(415) 986-1739

Arnold Associates
11 Willow Glen
San Carlos, CA 94070
(415) 595-8766

Arrow Production Art Design
Library
2521-F N. Grand Avenue
Santa Ana, CA 92701
(714) 631-1813

Arts Unlimited
16105 Gundry
Paramount, CA 90723
(213) 634-6484

ASAP Advertising
32129 W. Lindero Canyon Road
Westlake Village, CA 91361
(818) 707-2727

Azimuth Communications
11030 Santa Monica Boulevard
Los Angeles, CA 90025
(213) 478-5048

Baker Advertising & Mailing
3923 W. Sixth Street
Los Angeles, CA 90020
(213) 385-2939

Ball Group
4167 Eastlake Avenue
Oakland, CA 94602
(415) 482-1959

Banning
11818 Wilshire Boulevard
Los Angeles, CA 90025
(213) 477-8517

BASIC/Bedell Advertising
2040 Alameda Padre Serra
Santa Barbara, CA 93103
(805) 963-1501

Gary Beals Advertising
4141 Fairmount Avenue
San Diego, CA 92105
(619) 284-1145

Joseph Behm Associates
700 Larkspur Landing Circle,
#199
Larkspur, CA 94939
(415) 461-6388

Aleon Bennett & Associates
1345 Ventura Boulevard
Sherman Oaks, CA 91423
(818) 990-8070

Bick International
Box 854
Van Nuys, CA 91408
(818) 997-6496

Ralph Bing Advertising
16109 Selva Drive
San Diego, CA 92128
(619) 487-7444

Terry Brand & Associates
10712 Hastings Drive
Villa Park, CA 92667
(714) 639-6918

Buchanan/Vinson/Rosenfield
Direct
1335 Hotel Circle S.
San Diego, CA 92108
(619) 293-3940

Burridge & Doty Advertising
928 E. Carpinteria Street
Santa Barbara, CA 93103
(805) 963-8688

Bernice Bush
15052 Springdale Street
Huntington Street, CA 92649
(714) 891-3344

Business Communications
Associates
2275 Republic Avenue
Costa Mesa, CA 92627
(714) 548-5470

Business Extension Bureau
1335 S. Flower Street
Los Angeles, CA 90015
(213) 749-0151

Business Management Research
1668 Lombard Street
San Francisco, CA 94123
(415) 776-2664

Business Passcards
11 Village Center
Carmel Valley, CA 93924
(408) 659-4550

Business Promotion Group
1000 Kenfield Avenue
Los Angeles, CA 90049
(213) 472-9207

Campbell & Associates
850 Second Street
Santa Rosa, CA 95404
(707) 528-7520

Carlson & Associates
Box 2601
Culver City, CA 90231
(805) 496-7284

Catalyst Marketing
1252 Randol Avenue
San Jose, CA 95126
(408) 998-3121

Charandon Advertising
1352 Grand Avenue
San Rafael, CA 94912
(415) 456-1001

Leo Chick & Associates
1962 E. Loma Alta
Altadena, CA 91001
(818) 797-9898

Chris Christensen & Associates
Box 2863
Santa Rosa, CA 95405
(707) 539-0126

James Churchill & Associates
2229 Butte Place
Davis, CA 95616
(916) 758-9725

Clark, Meyer, Charters & Howell
16052 Beach Boulevard
Huntington Beach, CA 92647
(714) 841-1886

Coast Envelope
240 Littlefield Avenue
San Francisco, CA 94080
(415) 761-4455

William Cohen, Ph.D.
Professor of Marketing
California State University, L.A.
Los Angeles, CA 90032

Cole, Webber, & Associates
17501 17th Street
Tustin, CA 92680
(714) 730-6677

Comco/Goodfellow Management
25829 Mission Boulevard
Hayward, CA 94544
(415) 887-8993

Communication Consultants
24765 Camino Villa
El Toro, CA 92630
(714) 951-1705

Communicators Group
67 Boronda-L
Carmel Valley, CA 93924
(408) 659-4828

Conant: Direct Sales
Consultations
4111 Lincoln Boulevard
Marina del Ray, CA 90292
(213) 392-8881

Connections
846 Higuera Street
San Luis Obispo, CA 93406
(805) 544-8448

Considine & Associates
521 S. Madison Avenue
Pasadena, CA 91101
(818) 449-4210

Crane Advertising
431 Cheyenne Place
Placentia, CA 92670
(714) 961-8746

Creative Associates
1350 Grand Avenue
San Marcos, CA 92069
(619) 744-8832

Creative Direct Marketing Group
25550 Hawthorne Boulevard
Torrance, CA 90505
(213) 373-9408

Creative Marketing Design
2391 Ardem Way
Sacramento, CA 95825
(916) 924-0769

Creative Response Marketing
3423 E. Chapman Avenue
Orange, CA 92669
(714) 639-6918

Creative Sales Promotion
10042 Fullbright Avenue
Chatsworth, CA 91311
(818) 885-0270

Creator's Rep
1314 Bush
San Diego, CA 92103
(619) 296-3434

Cronan Advertising
Route 2, Box 3866
Tehachapi, CA 93561
(805) 822-6797

Cundall/Whitehead Advertising
3000 Bridgeway
Sausalito, CA 94965
(415) 332-3625

D'Anna & Associates
1299 Old Bay Shore Highway
Burlingame, CA 94010
(415) 340-8955

Data Marketing
1885 De La Cruz Boulevard
Santa Clara, CA 95050
(408) 970-0555

Data Source/Sales Lead
Marketing
631 S. Brookhurst
Anaheim, CA 90254
(714) 778-3580

Datatronic Systems
Box 144128
Panorama City, CA 91412
(818) 988-5290

Robert Day Communications
8826 Dorrington Avenue
Los Angeles, CA 90048
(213) 858-0520

Demographic Research
233 Wilshire Boulevard
Santa Monica, CA 90254
(213) 451-8583

Desert Mailing Services
Box 1763
Palm Springs, CA 92263
(619) 321-1790

Diablo Direct Mail & Printing
1381 Franquette Avenue
Concord, CA 94520
(415) 687-7375

Direct Mail Advertising of
America
2133 S. Bundy Drive
Los Angeles, CA 90064
(213) 820-0474

Direct Mail & Marketing
Associates
1516 W. Redwood Street
San Diego, CA 92101
(619) 692-4042

Direct Mail Marketing Services
144 Townsend Street
San Francisco, CA 94107
(415) 543-4305

Direct Mail Programs
1013 E. 145th Street
Los Angeles, CA 90021
(213) 627-0491

Dorius & Assoc., Mktg.
Communications
74-420 Buttonwood

Palm Desert, CA 92261
(619) 568-5942

Uri Dowbenko & Associates
Box 1201
Agoura Hills, CA 91301
(818) 706-8838

Dwan Typography
7203 Bodega Avenue
Sebastopol, CA 95472
(707) 829-5442

The Emco Group
5236 Yarmouth
Encino, CA 91316
(213) 996-3484

ERS Media Services
24009 Ventura Boulevard
Calabasas, CA 91302
(818) 704-5300

J.W. Estay Advertising Services
11847 Teale Street
Culver City, CA 90230
(213) 390-4061

Evans/Weinberg
5757 Wilshire Boulevard
Los Angeles, CA 90036
(213) 653-2300

Febbo & Graffweg Advertising
Assoc.
655 Woodland Avenue
Chico, CA 95928
(916) 895-8648

Federal Products
622 W. Princeton
Fresno, CA 93705
(209) 227-3782

Fonetik
1826 32nd Avenue

San Francisco, CA 94122
(415) 661-9325

Forms
745 15th Street
San Diego, CA 92101
(619) 233-9742

Ben Franklin Advertising
1424 Lincoln Boulevard
Santa Monica, CA 90401
(213) 451-8973

J. David Fraser, Persuasive
Commun.
14551 Linden Avenue
Irvine, CA 92714
(714) 551-1849

Neal L. Friedman
22030 Sherman Way
Canoga Park, CA 91303
(818) 340-4700

Geisz International
11500 W. Olympic Boulevard
Los Angeles, CA 90064
(213) 478-0251

Mark Geller & Associates
941 Oakwood Avenue
Fullerton, CA 92635
(714) 529-4628

Howard Goldstein Design
7031 Aldea Avenue
Van Nuys, CA 91406
(213) 987-2837

Golomb Group California
227½ Coral Avenue
Newport Beach, CA 92663
(714) 673-2043

Graphic Marketing
558 Pilgrim Drive

Foster City, CA 94404
(415) 574-2525

Great Pacific Trading
Box E
Santa Barbara, CA 93101
(805) 963-3673

Guzman/Gerrie Advertising
222 W. Main Street
Tustin, CA 92680
(714) 838-0234

Hammer Industries
5482 Oceanus Drive
Huntington Beach, CA 92647
(714) 898-7324

Hedberg & Associates
3606 Terrace View Drive
Encino, CA 91436
(818) 789-2079

Stu Heinecke Comedy
Advertising
Box 34803
Los Angeles, CA 90034
(213) 837-3212

Holmes-Hally
7460 Bandini Boulevard
Los Angeles, CA 90022
(213) 728-3311

Craig Huey
Infomat, Inc.
25550 Hawthorne Boulevard,
Suite 304
Torrance, CA 90505

Bob Hum Advertising
28120 Peacock Ridge Drive
Rancho Palos Verdes, CA 90274
(213) 541-3166

Hurley Associates
1330 Monument Street
Pacific Palisades, CA 90272
(213) 454-0234

IC Direct List Brokerage/Direct
Mkt.
3248 Summit Avenue
Mill Valley, CA 94941
(415) 381-6116

Idea
3150 Ducommun Avenue
San Diego, CA 92122
(619) 452-7465

Ingram & Associates
12858 Caminito En Flor
Del Mar, CA 92014
(619) 481-0600

International Direct Marketing
18 E. Canon Perdido
Santa Barbara, CA 93101
(805) 963-8888

International Gaming Promotions
20201 Sherman Way
Canoga Park, CA 91360
(818) 998-2121

Intrec Marketing
48 Paul Drive
San Rafael, CA 94903
(415) 492-9226

J & D Expo Productions
7334 Topanga Canyon Boulevard
Canoga Park, CA 91303
(818) 999-4070

J & K Productions
5601 27th Avenue
Sacramento, CA 95820
(916) 456-6005

J.W./Estay Advertising Services
1847 Teale Street
Culver City, CA 90230
(213) 390-4061

Johnson Design Associates
1250 Oakmead Parkway
Sunnyvale, CA 94088
(408) 773-9347

Lawrence Kay & Associates
30820 Oakrim
Westlake Village, CA 91362
(213) 453-1800

Jerry S. Kaye Associates
20410 Chapter Drive
Woodland Hills, CA 91364
(818) 347-2894

The Kelley Group
1965 San Ramon Street
Mountain View, CA 94043
(415) 964-7373

Kimbal Trading & Marketing
980 Bush Street
San Francisco, CA 94109
(415) 441-0800

Kresser & Robbins, Inc.
2049 Century Pk. E.
Los Angeles, CA 90067
(213) 553-8254

Krupp Taylor
12800 Culver Boulevard
Los Angeles, CA 90066
(213) 306-3646

Lavy Reis & Hamilton
Box 4012
Tustin, CA 92681
(714) 551-8142

Richard Lee & Company
Box 277

Palo Alto, CA 94302
(415) 328-5044

Lewis & Mayne
645 Harrison Street
San Francisco, CA 94107
(415) 543-7385

Linkin Communications
10710 National Place
Los Angeles, CA 90034
(213) 837-8400

M-Car Advertising
30506 Palos Verdes Drive W.
Palos Verdes, CA 90274
(213) 377-1387

Joel A. MacCollam
530 Monte Vista Avenue
Glendale, CA 91202
(818) 242-4782

Magni
2401 E. 17th Street
Santa Ana, CA 92701
(714) 630-6042

Market Demographics
2101 Geer Road
Turlock, CA 95380
(209) 668-9341

Marketing Intelligence
10675 S. De Anza Boulevard
Cupertino, CA 95014
(408) 446-3040

Marketing Support Services
2040 Laguna
San Francisco, CA 94115
(415) 346-3004

MarkeTrends
4455 Torrance Boulevard
Torrance, CA 90503
(213) 371-8684

Marx Advertising
112 W. Ninth Street
Los Angeles, CA 90015
(213) 626-3153

The Marz Group
15445 Ventura Boulevard
Sherman Oaks, CA 91403
(818) 986-2000

Matrix Marketing Strategists
459 Hamilton Avenue
Palo Alto, CA 94301
(415) 322-2999

Bill McGrew & Associates
635 Lowell Avenue
Palo Alto, CA 94301
(415) 327-7136

McLean Public Relations
652 Bair Island Road
Redwood City, CA 94063
(415) 369-3070

Media
2450 San Juan Road
Hollister, CA 95024
(408) 636-2010

Meeker Direct Marketing
Box 3315
Saratoga, CA 95070
(408) 973-0848

Mega Media Associates
9555 Warner Avenue
Fountain Valley, CA 92708
(714) 963-8007

Mellmark Advertising
8150 Firestone Boulevard
Downey, CA 90241
(213) 861-0911

The Merchandising Group
6930 Owensmouth Avenue

Canoga Park, CA 91303
(818) 999-6515

Merit Media
Box 61853
Sunnyvale, CA 94088
(415) 968-1506

Mint Print/CHA Direct
54 Mint Street
San Francisco, CA 94103
(415) 337-1525

Mirkin & Associates
13416 Magnolia Boulevard
Sherman Oaks, CA 91423
(818) 784-4177

Donald Moger Direct Marketing
Box 69219
Los Angeles, CA 90069
(213) 852-1154

Money Mailer
15472 Chemical Lane
Huntington Beach, CA 92649
(714) 898-9111

John D. Morgan
4460 Via Alegre
Santa Barbara, CA 93130
(805) 964-8588

Mowen & Associates Advertising
888 N. First Street
San Jose, CA 95112
(408) 297-7500

MPA Associates
5306 Beethoven Street
Los Angeles, CA 90066
(213) 822-9966

Paul Muchnik
5818 Venice Boulevard
Los Angeles, CA 90019
(213) 934-7986

N & N Industries
19000 Sherman Way, #15
Reseda, CA 91335
(818) 345-2931

Don Nagle Enterprises
Box 3013
San Rafael, CA 94912
(415) 454-2019

National Decision Systems
539 Encinitas Boulevard
Encinitas, CA 92024
(619) 942-7000

Nefe-Armedia Direct Response
25 Van Ness Avenue
San Francisco, CA 94102
(415) 621-6961

Nelson Panulio Jutkins Direct
Mktg.
2121 Cloverfield Road
Santa Monica, CA 90404
(213) 829-3444

Newport Marketing
1731 Kaiser Avenue
Irvine, CA 92714
(714) 261-6101

Mark Nolan
139 G Street
Davis, CA 95616
(916) 758-9688

Palisades Advertising &
Marketing
845 Via de la Paz
Pacific Palisades, CA 90272
(213) 459-1713

P & L Direct Marketing
9255 Sunset Boulevard
Los Angeles, CA 90069
(213) 858-8875

Richard Parker & Associates
680 Beach Street
San Francisco, CA 94109
(415) 441-6866

PMA Enterprises
1136 Sea Bluff
Costa Mesa, CA 92627
(714) 722-8077

Ray Pope Advertising
15010 Ventura Boulevard
Sherman Oaks, CA 91403
(213) 344-3440

Richard Potter & Associates
23140 Los Encinos Way
Woodland Hills, CA 91367
(818) 769-9844

Melvin Powers Mail Order
Advertising
12015 Sherman Road
N. Hollywood, CA 91605
(215) 875-1711

Professional Media Services
18530 Beach Boulevard
Huntington Beach, CA 92648
(714) 964-0542

Pro Graphics Advertising
14111 E. Freeway Drive
Santa Fe Springs, CA 90670
(213) 921-3100

Pro Mail Services
1341 W. Brooks Street
Ontario, CA 91761
(714) 984-5722

Publishers Mini-Systems
1327 Alita Lane
Escondido, CA 92027
(619) 747-8327

Quorum
5230 Carroll Canyon Road
San Diego, CA 92121
(619) 457-3300

Rable Advertising
1821 Delaware
Huntington Beach, CA 92648
(714) 536-7617

Reeds, Faris, Lewis, & Maisel
2801 Cahuenga Blvd., W.
Los Angeles, CA 90068
(213) 874-2801

Russ Reid
2 N. Lake Avenue
Pasadena, CA 91101
(818) 449-6100

Jay R. Reiss Advertising Agency
2444 Wilshire Boulevard
Santa Monica, CA 90403
(213) 453-8859

Response Advertising
1815 Via El Prado
Redondo Beach, CA 90277
(213) 540-5446

Rogers & Associates
2049 Century Pk. E.
Los Angeles, CA 90067
(213) 552-6922

RRH Communications
Box 610
Alta Loma, CA 91701
(714) 946-4700

Andra Rudolph Design
1545¹/₂ Pacific Garden Mall
Santa Cruz, CA 95060
(408) 425-0765

Rullman & Munger Advertising
7060 Hollywood Boulevard

Los Angeles, CA 90028
(213) 463-6871

Ryan's Express
Box 17280
S. Lake Tahoe, CA 95702
(916) 577-3377

Sackheim Enterprises
170 N. Robertson Boulevard
Beverly Hills, CA 90211
(213) 652-0220

Lillian Sale Communication
Services
Box 48439
Los Angeles, CA 90048
(213) 655-5460

Sales Overlays
20530 Earlgate
Walnut, CA 91789
(714) 595-5551

Richard W. Salzman
1352 Hornblend Street
San Diego, CA 92109
(619) 272-8147

Diane R. Schaffler Sale Promotion
10042 Fullbright Avenue
Chatsworth, CA 91311
(818) 885-0270

Schmidt-Cannon
1208 John Reed Court
Industry, CA 91745
(818) 961-9871

SCW
20433 Nordhoff Street
Chatsworth, CA 91311
(818) 882-7200

Selmore
1017 N. La Cienega Boulevard

Los Angeles, CA 90069
(213) 657-1214

Carl W. Sickler Advertising
1201 Park Avenue
Emeryville, CA 94608
(415) 655-9295

Richard Siedlecki Direct
Marketing
Box 817
El Toro, CA 92630
(714) 768-5830

Smith-Hemmings-Gosden
3360 Flair Drive
El Monte, CA 91731
(818) 571-6600

Smith Miller Moore
15130 Ventura Boulevard
Sherman Oaks, CA 91403
(818) 995-6060

Source View
835 Castro Street
Martinez, CA 94553
(415) 228-6220

Southwest Marketing
Corporation
Box 1027
Imperial, CA 92251
(619) 352-3251

Spirit of the Future Unlimited
3027 22nd Street
San Francisco, CA 94110
(415) 821-7800

Edgar S. Spizel Advertising & PR
1782 Pacific Avenue
San Francisco, CA 94109
(415) 474-5735

Christopher Stagg
26150 Hidden Hill Road

Carmel Valley, CA 93924
(408) 659-4997

Stamp Master
18525 Sherman Way
Reseda, CA 91335
(818) 881-5010

Stanberry Promotions
Box 384
Roseville, CA 95661
(916) 786-5646

David J. Steckel
795 Folsom
San Francisco, CA 94107
(415) 442-5433

B.J. Stewart Advertising
3300 Irvine Drive
Newport Beach, CA 92660
(714) 756-1560

Stone Associates
444 Castro Street
Mountain View, CA 94041
(415) 966-1202

C.J. Street & Associates
24301 Southland Drive
Hayward, CA 94540
(418) 782-8520

Strom-Hill Marketing
Box 420877
Sacramento, CA 95842
(916) 338-0157

Russ Tilford Associates
2223 El Cajon Boulevard
San Diego, CA 92104
(619) 692-1230

Tomorrow Today
3279 20th Street
San Francisco, CA 94110
(415) 641-4103

Unidyne Direct Mail
365 W. Bradley Avenue
El Cajon, CA 92020
(619) 588-6747

Universal Advertising
2248-2 Main Street
Chula Vista, CA 92011
(619) 429-8254

Vis/Aid Marketing
Box 4502
Inglewood CA 90309
(213) 688-8383

Wakeman and deForrest
4770 Campus Drive
Newport Beach, CA 92660
(714) 476-2992

Mal Warwick & Associates
Box 1282
Berkeley, CA 94701
(415) 843-8011

Washington & Associates
1960 Cedar Crest Drive
Merced, CA 95340
(209) 383-4443

Western Graphics
7614 Lemon Avenue
Lemon Grove, CA 92045
(619) 466-4157

Westland Communications
6060 Sunrise Vista Drive
Citrus Heights, CA 95610
(916) 722-8900

Willheim Marketing Services
13711 Raywood Drive
Los Angeles, CA 90049
(213) 472-6621

The Williams Group
221 Caledonia Street

Sausalito, CA 94965
(415) 331-8154

Earl I. Wilson & Associates
6355 Topanga Canyon Boulevard
Woodland Hills, CA 91367
(818) 340-6201

Neal Woods Associates
3316 Jefferson Street
Napa, CA 94558
(707) 253-1313

WS & C Advertising
656 Fifth Avenue
San Diego, CA 92101
(619) 235-6361

S.K. Zack & Associates
17371 Sandalwood
Irvine, CA 92715
(714) 786-3040

COLORADO

Art Service
342 E. Third Street
Loveland, CO 80537
(303) 663-1724

Concept Promotions
1311 S. College Avenue
Fort Collins, CO 80524
(303) 484-6200

Decals
Box 208
Wheat Ridge, CO 80033
(800) 433-2257

Directory Service
950-52 S. Sherman Street
Longmont, CO 80501
(303) 530-9650

Finley Terman Creative
2049 Broadway

Boulder, CO 80302
(303) 449-2921

GWL Associates
169 S. Buchanan
Louisville, CO 80027
(303) 665-9630

Rhino Products
4134 Garfield
Denver, CO 80216
(303) 355-6161

Tamara Scott
19062 Two Bar Road
Boulder Creek, CO 95006
(408) 338-9683

Maxwell Sroge Publishing
731 N. Cascade Avenue
Colorado Springs, CO 80903
(303) 633-5556

Tracy-Locke Direct
5600 S. Quebec Street
Englewood, CO 80111
(303) 733-3100

Trimark of the Rockies
7985 W. 16th Street
Lakewood, CO 80215
(303) 233-2669

Wren Marketing
609 W. Littleton Boulevard
Littleton, CO 80120
(303) 794-8699

CONNECTICUT

Anderson & Lembke
4 Landmark Square
Stamford, CT 06901
(203) 357-1189

V. Anthony Agency
418 Main Street
Middletown, CT 06457

Astra Associates
86 Sanford Avenue
Bridgeport, CT 06601
(203) 334-7002

B & B Associates
45 Royalwood Court
Cheshire, CT 06410
(203) 239-4644

Barry Blau & Partners
1960 Bronson Road
Fairfield, CT 06430
(203) 254-3700

Bremer Advertising
Windy Hill, RR2, Box 624
Old Lynn, CT 06321
(203) 434-9838

Charlie Browne Communications
Hawthorne Hill Road
Newtown, CT 06470
(203) 426-0287

Business Communications
41 Heritage Drive
Woodbury, CT 06798
(203) 263-4200

Coogan Associates
17 Elm Street
New Canaan, CT 06840
(203) 972-0040

Corcillo Direct
6 Eversley Avenue
Norwalk, CT 06851
(203) 854-5777

CRT Associates
348 Peddlers Road

Guilford, CT 06437
(203) 453-0354

Daniels Productions
1155 New Britain Avenue
W. Hartford, CT 06110
(203) 233-9611

Malcolm Decker Associates
180 Hills Point Road
Westport, CT 06881
(203) 226-5301

DEZ Associates
190 Weston Road
Weston, CT 06883
(203) 226-6626

Dickison Rakaseder
205 Main Street
Westport, CT 06880
(203) 226-1296

The Direct Marketing Agency
1 Dock Street
Stamford, CT 06902
(203) 357-7895

Donnelley Marketing Information
Svcs.
1351 Washington Boulevard
Stamford, CT 06902
(203) 965-5400

Fairfield Consulting Group
Box 1643
New Canaan, CT 06840
(203) 966-6366

Frigitronics of Connecticut
770 River Road
Shelton, CT 06484
(203) 929-6321

Greenwich Direct Marketing
38 Locust Road

Greenwich, CT 06830
(203) 531-5208

Don Hansen Advertising, Inc.
21 Bridge Square
Westport, CT 06880
(203) 227-9567

Holaxis
968 Farmington Avenue
W. Hartford, CT 06107
(203) 524-4571

Integrated Marketing
International
181 Post Road W.
Westport, CT 06880
(203) 226-3662

The Kaplan Agency
11 Forest Street
New Canaan, CT 06840
(203) 972-3600

Keiler Advertising
304 Main Street
Farmington, CT 06032
(203) 677-8821

Joe Kizis Organization
428 Clark Lane
Orange, CT 06477
(203) 795-3089

James B. Kobak & Co.
774 Hollow Tree Ridge Road
Darien, CT 06820
(203) 655-8764

Lavin Associates
12 Promontory Drive
Cheshire, CT 06410
(203) 272-9121

Jim Mann & Associates
9 Mount Vernon Drive

Gales Ferry, CT 06335
(203) 464-2511

Marcom, Inc.
18 Thompson Road
Broad Brook, CT 06016
(203) 623-9856

Marketing Concepts Group
134 Patrick Avenue
Norwalk, CT 06851
(203) 846-3809

Marketing East
520 West Avenue
Norwalk, CT 06850
(203) 866-2234

Mirbach & Company
21 Charles Street
Westport, CT 06880
(203) 226-7988

North Castle Partners, Inc.
20 Bridge Street
Greenwich, CT 06830
(203) 622-1122

Passavant Seminars &
Consulting
193 Main Street
Middletown, CT 06457
(203) 346-3003

Pharmagram
24 Twin Hills Road
Stamford, CT 06903
(203) 322-8488

Phoenix
Box 788
Sharon, CT 06069
(203) 364-0511

Progressive Grocer Information
Sales
1351 Washington Boulevard

Stamford, CT 06902
(203) 325-3500

Reaves Stroble Direct Response
Mktg.
Stevenson Road
Deep River, CT 06417
(203) 526-2671

Roll Out Marketing
11 Mill Broad Road W.
Stamford, CT 06902
(203) 357-7238

Route One Graphics
Box 925
Darien, CT 06820
(203) 655-2440

Sales Systems Specialists
2437 Albany Avenue
W. Hartford, CT 06117
(203) 233-0658

School Market Research Institute
Saybrook Road, Box 10
Haddam, CT 06438
(203) 345-8183

Shanneer & Pappas
528 Clinton Avenue
Bridgeport, CT 06605
(203) 576-1516

Ray Smith Associates
316 Arnold Lane
Orange, CT 06477
(203) 795-5721

Smith, Dorian & Burman
1100 New Britain Avenue
W. Hartford, CT 06110
(203) 522-3101

Thermal Resources
360 Granfield Avenue

Bridgeport, CT 06610
(203) 334-5979

William R. Tynnan & Associates
224 Farmcliff Drive
Glastonbury, CT 06033
(203) 633-9949

Tyson Associates
52 Aspen Ledges Road
Ridgefield, CT 06877
(203) 431-8905

Walsh
21 Charles Street
Westport, CT 06880
(203) 227-0896

Weintz
50 Water Street, Dockside
S. Norwalk, CT 06834
(203) 866-2687

William F. Welch
Box 426
Greenwich, CT 06836
(203) 428-5945

Westport Direct
21 Charles Street
Westport, CT 06880
(203) 227-2656

W.I. Mail Marketing
212 Elm Street
New Canaan, CT 06840
(203) 972-0721

Word Communication Systems
33 Main Street
Ellington, CT 06029
(203) 875-7373

Yankelovich, Skelly, & White, Inc.
969 High Ridge Road
Stamford, CT 06905
(203) 322-7600

L.R. Yelding Associates
Greathill Road Industrial Park
Nawgatuck, CT 06770

DELAWARE

Beach Publishing and Printing
Route 26 & Central Avenue
Ocean View, DE 19970
(302) 539-3728

Cimino Creative
2506 Normandy Court
Newark, DE 19713
(302) 368-2540

Jay Gundel & Associates
300 Foulk Road
Wilmington, DE 19803
(302) 658-1674

Lyons Direct
715 Orange Street
Wilmington, DE 19899
(302) 654-6146

Joseph J. Sheeran
507 Silverside Road
Wilmington, DE 19809
(302) 798-0675

DISTRICT OF COLUMBIA

Albertella Associates
777 14th Street, NW
Washington, D.C. 20005
(202) 347-2396

Colortone Press
2400 17th Street, NW
Washington, D.C. 20009
(202) 387-6800

Columbia Direct Marketing
2100 M Street, NW

Washington, D.C. 20037
(202) 466-3055

Creative Options
1730 K Street, NW
Washington, D.C. 20006
(202) 785-9377

Creative Strategy
1511 K Street, NW
Washington, D.C. 20005
(202) 628-9508

Daly Associates
918 16th Street, NW
Washington, D.C. 20006
(202) 659-2925

Daly Direct Marketing
918 16th Street, NW
Washington, D.C. 20006
(202) 659-2927

Direct Marketing Services
4117 Davis Place, NW
Washington, D.C. 20007

DKA Advertising
3106 Cleveland Avenue, NW
Washington, D.C. 20008
(202) 296-1478

Haber & Associates
1771 T Street, NW
Washington, D.C. 20009
(202) 328-0888

International Development
Marketing
750 13th Street SE
Washington, D.C. 20003
(202) 546-1900

Charles R. Mann Associates
818 18th Street, NW
Washington, D.C. 20006
(202) 466-6161

Market Development Group
1200 Potomac Street, NW
Washington, D.C. 20007
(202) 298-8030

The Master List
729 Eighth Street, SE
Washington, D.C. 20003
(202) 543-8801

Maxon Administrators
117 C Street, SE
Washington, D.C. 20003
(202) 546-6484

Stanley R. Mayes Associates
1101 New Hampshire Avenue, NW
Washington, D.C. 20037
(202) 466-2578

Power House Communications
1000 Potomac Street, NW
Washington, D.C. 20007
(202) 333-7400

Preferred Advertising & Lists
499 S. Capitol Street, SW
Washington, D.C. 20003
(202) 484-5004

Public Communications Group
227 Massachusetts Avenue, NE
Washington, D.C. 20002
(202) 543-3550

J.F. Schramm & Associates
2550 M Street, NW
Washington, D.C. 20037
(202) 429-9580

Wright Idea
Box 5649
Washington, D.C. 20016
(202) 686-1276

FLORIDA

Advertere
Box 999
Fort Lauderdale, FL 33302
(305) 764-7001

The Advertising Works
1104 E. Robinson Street
Orlando, FL 32801
(305) 841-7840

Alba International
51 SW LeJeune Road
Miami, FL 33134
(305) 445-5331

American Advertising
Distributors
516-C Douglas Avenue
Altamonte Springs, FL 32714

American Advertising
Distributors
8326 U.S. Route 19
Port Richey, FL 33568
(813) 848-3844

American Type & Graphics
10076 Boca Entrada Boulevard
Boca Ratan, FL 33428
(305) 483-2600

Birch Marketing
2002 Scotland Drive
Clearwater, FL 33575
(813) 736-5533

Stan Bodner Advertising
7211 SW 62nd Avenue
Miami, FL 33143
(305) 667-2547

Howard Branston & Associates
1770 NW 187th Street
Miami, FL 33056
(305) 621-7047

The Bureau
2555 SE Bonita Street
Stuart, FL 33494
(305) 283-8850

Caribbean Advertising Group
100 NW 37th Avenue
Miami, FL 33125
(305) 643-1150

Communicomp
9748 Cedar Villas Boulevard
Plantation, FL 33324
(305) 473-2044

Customized Mailing Lists
1906 Field Road
Sarasota, FL 33583
(813) 921-6500

Dee Cee
6110 Gunn Highway
Tampa, FL 33688
(813) 961-9643

Direct Mail Expertise
4775 NW 150th Street
Hialeah, FL 33014
(305) 621-6043

Direct Response Marketing
11801 28th Street, N.
St. Petersburg, FL 33702
(813) 578-1985

Louis Entier Associates
1651 NW 34th Street
Miami, FL 33142
(305) 635-3737

Evans & Ciccarone
420 NW 42nd Avenue
Miami, FL 33126
(305) 445-1433

Federal Mailers
2701 E. Sunrise

Fort Lauderdale, FL 33304
(305) 561-9101

Floridata
7101 Biscayne Blvd.
Miami, FL 33138
(305) 751-5323

Fowler & Fowler
12405 River Road, SE
Fort Myers, FL 33905
(813) 694-8211

Susan Gilbert & Co., Advertising
1501 Verona Avenue
Miami, FL 33160
(305) 667-9386

Rene Gnam Consultation Corp.
Box 3877
Holiday, FL 33590
(813) 938-1556

Grif Creative
400 Madison Avenue
Old Town, FL 32680
(904) 542-7904

The Institute of Internal Auditors
249 Maitland Avenue
Altamonte Springs, FL 32701
(305) 830-7600

Bruce Kane & Associates
Box 21264
Tampa, FL 33622
(813) 986-2383

Sid Kleiner Music Enterprises
4701 25th Street, NW
Naples, FL 33964
(813) 455-2696

L & B Advertising Photography
4028 SE First Court
Cape Coral, FL 33910
(813) 542-4669

LJM Advertising
37 Tara Lakes Drive E.
Boynton Beach, FL 33436
(305) 736-1245

Mr. Mailer/Leads Plus
2471 John Young Parkway
Orlando, FL 32804
(305) 295-6767

The Mail Man
7475 W. 20th Avenue
Hialeah, FL 33014
(305) 558-7230

The Marketing Federation
7141 Gulf Boulevard
St. Petersburg Beach, FL 33706
(813) 367-4934

Mastermailer
1926 Hollywood Boulevard
Hollywood, FL 33020
(305) 921-0000

Media Motivations
3306 Landpiper Circle
Port St. Lucie, FL 33452

John Murchake & Associates
Box 83
Stuart, FL 33495
(305) 692-9105

National List Counsel
701 E. Altamonte Drive
Altamonte Springs, FL 32701
(305) 831-5478

National New Products
5449 Beneva Woods Way
Sarasota, FL 33583
(813) 921-7809

Page Marketing Services
319 NE Elmira Boulevard

Port Charlotte, FL 33952
(813) 627-3333

Jack Perez Advertising
342 SW Eighth Avenue
Miami, FL 33130
(305) 324-7443

Planned Promotions
3275 Riviera Drive
Coral Gables, FL 33134
(305) 445-7547

Professional Marketing Services
Box 530282
Miami, FL 33153
(305) 757-4843

Recreation World Services
Box 17148
Pensacola, FL 32522
(904) 478-4372

Response Group
20200 NE 10th Place
N. Miami Beach, FL 33160
(305) 652-4610

Showall Displays
5407-B Southern Comfort
Boulevard
Tampa, FL 33614
(813) 886-5692

Diane Sorelle Design
106 South Federal Highway
Pompano Beach, FL 33062
(305) 941-8035

Galen Stilson
Box 1075
Tarpon Springs, FL 34286
(813) 937-3480

Stone Brook Advertising Agency
100 S. Bumby Avenue

Orlando, FL 32803
(305) 894-8700

Stuffit
12450 Automobile Boulevard
Clearwater, FL 33520
(813) 576-7883

Sunbelt Marketing Services
12 S. Park Avenue
Apopka, FL 32704
(305) 886-5594

Andrew Svenson Co.
1950 Landings Boulevard
Sarasota, FL 33581
(813) 923-1465

Val-Pak Direct Marketing
Systems
4970 Park Street N.
St. Petersburg, FL 33709
(813) 541-2626

Wolf Productions
Box 25556
Tamarac, FL 33320
(305) 748-1286

GEORGIA

American Advertising
Distributors
6065 Roswell Street
Atlanta, GA 30328
(404) 255-4466

A.H. Anderson Associates
1465 Westwood Avenue, SW
Atlanta, GA 30310
(404) 752-9353

The Asian Group
570 Colonial Park Drive
Roswell, GA 30075
(404) 998-9900

The Benson Organization
4 Baywood Lane
Savannah, GA 31411
(917) 598-1051

Kent Buescher & Associates
1412 E. Park Avenue
Valdosta, GA 31601
(912) 244-5634

Caldwell List
2025 Peachtree Road, NE
Atlanta, GA 30309
(404) 351-7372

Can-Am Marketing
500 Northridge Road
Atlanta, GA 30356
(404) 394-3104

Communications Trends, Inc.
2045 Peachtree Road, NE
Atlanta, GA 30309
(404) 352-2200

The Deville Group
6540 Powers Ferry Road, NW
Atlanta, GA 30339
(404) 951-1146

Direct Marketing/R&D
97 Peachtree Road, NE
Atlanta, GA 30309
(404) 355-8061

Edgehouse & Zani
7076 Peachtree Industrial
Boulevard
Norcross, GA 30071
(404) 441-0220

Grizzard Advertising
1144 Mailing Avenue, SE
Atlanta, GA 30315
(404) 622-1501

Kaiser Kuhn Bennett
3400 Peachtree Road
Atlanta, GA 30326
(404) 233-5900

Austin P. Kelley
5901 Peachtree Dunwoody Road
Atlanta, GA 30328
(404) 396-6666

Kimberly-Clark Karolton
Envelope Div.
1400 Holcolm Bridge Road
Roswell, GA 30076
(404) 587-8736

Lanphear & Brettner
3E, 5675 Roswell Road, NE
Atlanta, GA 30342
(404) 255-4735

O'Pry/Bagwell
195 Newton Bridge Road
Athens, GA 30607
(404) 548-1260

Michael Penland Enterprises
4678 Mitchell Bridge Road, NE
Dalton, GA 30720
(404) 226-6657

Premier Forms & Graphics
125 Copeland Road
Atlanta, GA 30342
(404) 255-1986

Paul M. Reardon
3263 Rangers Gate Dive
Marietta, GA 30062
(404) 971-2375

Response Communications
5865 Lake Placid Drive
Atlanta, GA 30342
(404) 256-1500

RMV Enterprises
3131 Campbelltown Road, SW
Atlanta, GA 30311
(404) 349-5215

Symmes Systems
468 Armour Drive
Atlanta, GA 30306
(404) 876-7260

TM (Telemarketing
Communications Mgt)
468 Armour Drive, NE
Atlanta, GA 30324
(404) 876-7260

Umphenour & Martin, Inc.
2135 Cooledge Road
Tucker, GA 30084
(404) 939-6820

Emil J. Walcek Associates
2060 Peachtree Industrial Court
Atlanta, GA 30341
(404) 451-7737

Wemmers Communications
6 Piedmont Center
Atlanta, GA 30305
(404) 237-9222

HAWAII

Consumer Communications
Box 628
Koloa, HI 96756
(808) 742-6966

Pacific Marketing Group
1750 Kalakaua Avenue
Honolulu, HI 96826
(808) 945-2020

IDAHO

Aspenwood Advertising
1325 Schweitzer Basin Road
Sandpoint, ID 83864
(208) 263-1594

The Evergreen Associates
325 Park Drive, Box 1136
Coeur d'Alene, ID 83814
(208) 667-4542

Shiloh Advertising Agency
1245 Idaho Street
Lewiston, ID 83501
(208) 746-7435

ILLINOIS

Abarbanell & Associates
3950 N. Lake Shore Drive
Chicago, IL 60613
(312) 871-4388

Abelson-Taylor
35 N. Wacker Drive
Chicago, IL 60601
(312) 781-1700

Adler & Associates
28897 W. Main Street
Barrington, IL 60010
(312) 381-6770

Advanced Products
136 Pepperwood Drive
Bolingbrook, IL 60439
(312) 759-1418

Anderson Advertising Associates
151 N. Michigan Avenue
Chicago, IL 60602
(312) 565-6530

Apparel Communications
2500 Crawford Avenue
Evanston, IL 60201
(312) 492-1400

Armenio & Co.
5701 N. Sheridan Road
Chicago, IL 60660
(312) 989-7151

Noble Arnold & Associates
1501 Woodfield Road
Schaumburg, IL 60195
(312) 882-8808

Artist's Guild of Chicago
664 N. Michigan Avenue
Chicago, IL 60611
(312) 951-8252

Associated Marketing Group
11714 Grant Street
Lansing, IL 60438
(312) 474-2256

Association, Direct
436 Glendale Road
Glenview, IL 60025
(312) 724-9136

Automation Marketing
Consultants
1346 Cove Drive
Prospect Heights, IL 60070
(312) 541-8755

Ayer Direct
11 E. Wacker Drive
Chicago, IL 60601
(312) 645-8800

Baerson & Associates
2640 Golf Road
Glenview, IL 60025
(312) 724-6447

B.A.I. Data Processing & Eng'g
Rsrch
Box 609
Glen Ellyn, IL 60138
(312) 790-4080

Glen Bammann Communications
818 S. Second Street
DeKalb, IL 60115
(815) 756-6132

Irv Basevitz
307 N. Michigan Avenue
Chicago, IL 60601
(312) 641-7272

Basinger
1620 Central
Evanston, IL 60201
(312) 475-3525

Keith Bates & Associates
20 N. Wacker Drive
Chicago, IL 60606
(312) 263-5820

Behavioral Images
302 Leland
Bloomington, IL 61701
(309) 829-3997

Ronald A. Bernstein & Associates
310 W. Chicago Avenue
Chicago, IL 60610
(312) 440-3700

BES Designs
1602 Greenwood Cemetery Road
Danville, IL 61832
(217) 443-4619

Beta Communications Systems
41 Indian Hill Road
Winnetka, IL 60093
(312) 446-7056

Leo P. Bott, Jr. Advertising
111 E. Chestnut Street
Chicago, IL 60611
(312) 787-7890

Bozell & Jacobs Direct
625 N. Michigan Avenue
Chicago, IL 60611
(312) 988-2000

David L. Brody & Associates
6001 N. Clark Street
Chicago, IL 60660
(312) 761-2735

Samuel E. Brown Advertising
333 N. Michigan Avenue
Chicago, IL 60601
(312) 236-2423

Burton Advertising Agency
203 N. Wabash Avenue
Chicago, IL 60601
(312) 332-0187

Carlyle Marketing
5850 N. Lincoln Avenue
Chicago, IL 60659
(312) 271-2700

Century Consultants
Box 20854
Chicago, IL 60620
(312) 651-2212

CMF Communications
20 E. Jefferson Street
Naperville, IL 60540
(312) 369-8212

Chicago Direct Marketing Group
114 W. Illinois
Chicago, IL 60610
(312) 787-8435

Clark/Ladd Direct
211 W. Wacker Drive
Chicago, IL 60606
(312) 346-6897

Coe Marketing
520 N. Michigan Avenue
Chicago, IL 60611
(312) 644-0660

Combined Graphics
3239 W. Belmont
Chicago, IL 60618
(312) 267-8400

Communications Strategies
233 E. Ontario
Chicago, IL 60611
(312) 943-3061

Cooper & Cooper
436 Frontage Road
Northfield, IL 60093
(312) 446-1123

C.E. Cooper Studios
4503 N. Whipple Street
Chicago, IL 60625
(312) 539-2208

Cramer-Krasselt/Direct
225 N. Michigan Avenue
Chicago, IL 60601
(312) 977-9600

Creative Marketing Concepts
32 W. Garden
Palatine, IL 60067
(312) 577-1234

John Crowe Advertising Agency
1104 S. Second Street
Springfield, IL 62704
(217) 528-1076

CSR
21 W. Drummond
Glendale Heights, IL 60139
(312) 690-6536

Denton, Larson & Weckerly
1513 Pebblewood Drive
Sycamore, IL 60178
(815) 895-3611

Timothy E. Devereux &
Associates
735 S. Wesley
Oak Park, IL 60304
(312) 383-6256

Din & Dangrazio
415 N. Dearborn
Chicago, IL 60610
(312) 527-0870

Dixon Direct
3033 Ogden Avenue
Lisle, IL 60532
(312) 369-9561

Edward G. Dorn & Associates
1801 S. Hicks Road
Rolling Meadows, IL 60008
(312) 991-1270

Dundee Press/The Other Office
109 N. Second Street
W. Dundee, IL 60118
(312) 426-7110

Dynamic Press
307 S. Milwaukee
Wheeling, IL 60090
(312) 537-6300

FCB/Direct
401 N. Michigan Avenue
Chicago, IL 60611
(312) 467-9200

Feldman Associates
213 W. Institute Place
Chicago, IL 60610
(312) 649-6800

First National List Service
2265 W. Eastwood Street
Chicago, IL 60625
(312) 275-4422

Forbes & Co.
201 N. Wells
Chicago, IL 60606
(312) 346-2858

Franklin & Welker
203 N. Wabash, #1016
Chicago, IL 60601
(312) 726-4740

Fulfillment Awards
213 W. Institute Place
Chicago, IL 60610
(312) 649-0757

G-A-M Associates
616 Laramie
Wilmette, IL 60091
(312) 256-2016

Gartner & Associates
2 N. Riverside Plaza
Chicago, IL 60606
(312) 454-0282

George Printing
1500 N. Farnsworth Avenue
Aurora, IL 60507
(312) 820-1770

Godfrey Group
230 N. Michigan Avenue
Chicago, IL 60601
(312) 269-0088

Green Group
Box 1555
Morton Grove, IL 60053
(312) 965-3673

Grubb, Graham & Wilder
115 N. Neil Street, #415
Champaign, IL 61820
(217) 359-0624

Gruen & Sells
645 N. Michigan Avenue
Chicago, IL 60611
(312) 943-8789

GSP Marketing Services
156 N. Jefferson
Chicago, IL 60606
(312) 944-3000

Hahn, Crane & Associates,
Advertising
114 W. Illinois Street
Chicago, IL 60610
(312) 787-8435

H & R Advertising
910 N. Milwaukee Avenue
Wheeling, IL 60090
(312) 520-0030

Holden Copywriting Service
1628 Keeney Street
Evanston, IL 60202
(312) 491-1680

Hughes Communications
211 W. State Street
Rockford, IL 61105
(815) 963-7771

Tom Hundley & Associates
R2, Box 285, Walnut Hill Road
Danville, IL 61832
(217) 446-3257

Incentive Travel
213 W. Institute Place
Chicago, IL 60610
(312) 649-0073

Insurance Direct Marketing
Associates
114 W. Illinois
Chicago, IL 60610
(312) 787-8435

International Merchandise
213 W. Institute Place
Chicago, IL 60610
(312) 943-8827

Jacobs & Clevenger
612 N. Michigan Avenue
Chicago, IL 60611
(312) 944-2075

Jamieson Group
3648 Venard Road
Downers Grove, IL 60515
(312) 969-9235

Lauren R. Januz & Associates
26940 N. Longwood Road
Lake Forest, IL 60045
(312) 362-0016

Susan K. Jones & Associates
187 Ridge Avenue
Winnetka, IL 60093
(312) 446-1324

JSL
One Northfield Plaza
Northfield, IL 60093
(312) 446-2797

JSR Advertising
247 E. Ontario Street
Chicago, IL 60611
(312) 266-9266

Kable News
Kable Square
Mt. Morris, IL 61054
(815) 734-4151

Kandan Creative
822 W. Lill Avenue
Chicago, IL 60614
(312) 348-0224

Keroff & Rosenberg Advertising
444 N. Wabash Avenue
Chicago, IL 60611
(312) 321-9000

Kestenbaum & Co.
221 N. LaSalle Street
Chicago, IL 60601
(312) 782-1351

Knuth & Associates
865 Arthur Drive
Elgin, IL 60120
(312) 888-4532

Kobs & Brady Advertising
625 N. Michigan Avenue
Chicago, IL 60611
(312) 944-3500

Krebs-Dodson Advertising, Inc.
2625 Butterfield Road
Oak Brook, IL 60521
(312) 325-8010

Herbert Krug & Associates
500 Davis Center
Evanston, IL 60201
(312) 864-0550

Nick Kutzko, Consultant
17114 Grant Street
Lansing, IL 60438
(312) 474-2256

Walter Latham
2001 W. 21st Street

Broadview, IL 60153
(312) 345-8787

Laurence & Laurence
8745 Keeler
Skokie, IL 60076
(312) 675-7175

Le Fevre & Associates
5616 N. Broadway
Chicago, IL 60660
(312) 271-4910

Lerner Scott
1000 Skokie Boulevard
Wilmette, IL 60091
(312) 256-2940

LitCom/USA
425 N. Michigan Avenue
Chicago, IL 60611
(312) 245-0079

Ross Llewellyn
345 N. Canal
Chicago, IL 60606
(312) 648-1339

John T. Maguire
401 N. Prairie
Champaign, IL 61820
(217) 351-1161

Mailworks
230 N. Michigan Avenue
Chicago, IL 60601
(312) 263-0665

Mallof, Abruzino & Nash
Marketing
477 E. Butterfield Road
Lombard, IL 60148
(312) 964-7722

Mandabach & Simms
111 N. Canal

Chicago, IL 60606
(312) 902-1300

MARCOA Direct Advertising
10 S. Riverside Plaza
Chicago, IL 60606
(312) 454-0660

Mark & Associates
925 N. Milwaukee
Wheeling, IL 60090
(312) 520-4087

Marketing-Advertising-
Promotion
20685 N. Long Meadows Drive
Kildeer, IL 60047
(312) 438-5790

Marketing for Profit
Box 624
St. Charles, IL 60174
(312) 377-3321

The Marketing Group
3839 Louise Street
Skokie, IL 60076
(312) 929-1100

Marketing Logistics
175 Olde Half Day Road
Lincolnshire, IL 60069
(312) 634-4700

Marketing Support, Inc.
3 Illinois Center
Chicago, IL 60601
(312) 565-0044

K.L. Mathers & Associates
Route 3, Box 217
Momence, IL 60954
(815) 944-5385

Matrix
405 N. Wabash Avenue

Chicago, IL 60611
(312) 822-0935

Merchandising Dynamics
1002 N. Plum Grove Road
Schaumburg, IL 60195
(312) 885-4544

Arthur Meriwether
1529 Brook Drive
Downers Grove, IL 60515
(312) 495-0600

Howard H. Monk & Associates
706 N. Main Street
Rockford, IL 61103
(815) 964-4631

The Norm Nanstiel Studio
1480 Renaissance Drive
Park Ridge, IL 60060
(312) 827-8210

William J. Narup & Co.
1955 Raymond Drive
Northbrook, IL 60062
(312) 480-1903

E. Phelps Nichols & Associates
800 Roosevelt Road
Glen Ellyn, IL 60137
(312) 790-9677

Nobart
1133 S. Wabash Avenue
Chicago, IL 60605
(312) 427-9800

A. Dudley Olsen & Associates
Box 0
Wheaton, IL 60189
(312) 682-0211

Omni Enterprises
430 W. Roosevelt Road
Wheaton, IL 60187
(312) 653-8200

Omni Marketing
1 Oakbrook Terrace
Oakbrook Terrace, IL 60181
(312) 932-8400

Performance Direct Marketing
550 Frontage road
Northfield, IL 60093
(312) 441-5050

PGM
640 N. LaSalle Street
Chicago, IL 60610
(312) 337-7676

David S. Powers & Associates
237 White Fawn Trail
Downers Grove, IL 60516
(312) 852-2316

Precise Communications
233 E. Erie
Chicago, IL 60611
(312) 664-6247

Pro Tech Communications
294B Mallard Pt-LBS
Barrington, IL 60010
(312) 381-1221

Pulse Communications
2445 N. Sayre Avenue
Chicago, IL 60635
(312) 622-7066

Red Tiger Products
176 W. Adams
Chicago, IL 60603
(312) 782-8468

Response Graphics
1480 Renaissance Drive
Park Ridge, IL 60068
(312) 827-0316

Rhea & Kaiser Advertising
2625 Butterfield Road

Oak Brook, IL 60521
(312) 654-3344

Robbytype
2635 W. Peterson
Chicago, IL 60659
(312) 769-9098

Rodgers & Associates
2344 S. Sixth Street
Springfield, IL 62703
(217) 753-2721

Rubin Response Services
3315 Algonquin Road
Rolling Meadows, IL 60008
(312) 394-3400

Lew Sanders Advertising
One N. Wacker Drive
Chicago, IL 60606
(312) 726-8562

Schram Advertising
170 W. Washington Street
Chicago, IL 60602
(312) 346-8585

Norman Seligman
4030 Micheline Lane
Northbrook, IL 60062
(312) 498-2643

Henry Senne
233 E. Wacker Drive
Chicago, IL 60601
(312) 565-2820

Slauf, Manley & Associates
1000 Jorie Boulevard
Oak Brook, IL 60521
(312) 325-1455

Sleepy Hollow Art Studio
RR2, Box 422A
Dundee, IL 60118
(312) 428-2464

Paul V. Smith
203 N. Wabash Avenue
Chicago, IL 60601
(312) 372-1188

Starmark
706 N. Dearborn
Chicago, IL 60610
(312) 922-3388

Stokes Gray Communication
43 Chestnut Avenue
Westmont, IL 60559
(312) 578-4300

Sunman Direct
136 Glenview Road
Glenview, IL 60025
(312) 729-5477

TDM Advertising
1301 W. 22nd Street
Oak Brook, IL 60521
(312) 789-2880

Technology Management
Associates
150 N. Wacker Drive
Chicago, IL 60606
(312) 984-5055

Tech Writers
49-C Sherwood Terrace
Lake Bluff, IL 60044
(312) 368-8640

The Thompson Group
201 E. Ogden Avenue
Hinsdale, IL 60521
(312) 323-1090

William A. Throckmorton, Inc.
101 E. Ontario
Chicago, IL 60611
(312) 661-1330

Trnka Group
25 Middle Avenue
Aurora, IL 60506
(312) 897-0817

Wardrup, Murtaugh, Temple &
Frank
333 N. Michigan Avenue
Chicago, IL 60601
(312) 750-9200

W.C. Enterprises
Box 48865
Niles, IL 60648
(312) 427-1068

West & Zajac Advertising
20180 Governors Highway
Olympia Fields, IL 60461
(312) 481-1740

Westgate Graphic Design
1111 Westgate
Oak Park, IL 60301
(312) 848-8323

Bess Winaker Communications
919 N. Michigan Avenue
Chicago, IL 60611
(312) 751-0565

Ben Wood & Associates
511 W. Wesley Street
Wheaton, IL 60167
(312) 665-6633

Zivi, Broitman & Kopelman
180 N. Michigan Avenue
Chicago, IL 60601
(312) 580-0812

INDIANA

Adco International
1601 E. Main Street
Plainfield, IN 46168
(317) 839-3928

Advantage Advertising
6857 E. Marmont Court
Indianapolis, IN 46220
(317) 849-1983

All Media Communications
625 Cherry Street
Fort Wayne, IN 46808
(219) 424-5295

Copywriters International
601 S. 10th Street
Lafayette, IN 47905
(317) 742-7885

CRE
22 E. Washington
Indianapolis, IN 46204
(317) 631-0260

Creative Advertising
419 S. Fulton Avenue
Evansville, IN 47708
(812) 422-4104

Creative Concept
4810 Pleasant Valley Drive
West Lafayette, IN 47906
(317) 583-2353

Graphic Edition
207 Hulman Street
Terre Haute, IN 47802
(812) 232-2875

Holliday Advertising
7202 N. Shadeland Avenue
Indianapolis, IN 46250
(317) 849-6752

Lichtenberger Design Associates
1455 N. Pennsylvania
Indianapolis, IN 46202
(317) 634-5106

Media Mix Advertising
209 N. Eighth Street

Evansville, IN 47713
(812) 426-9000

Paradox Marketing
4 Chamness Avenue
Elwood, IN 46036
(317) 634-1915

Response Center
933 Western Drive
Indianapolis, IN 46241
(317) 244-7660

Tri Marketing
215 S. Second Street
Elkhart, IN 46515
(219) 294-7239

Triplex Marketing
7015 U.S. 24 E.
Huntington, IN 46750
(219) 456-7229

Michael C. Wales & Co.
211 W. Madison Street
South Bend, IN 46634
(219) 232-4200

IOWA

CMF&Z
600 East Court
Des Moines, IA 50306
(515) 246-3500

Concept II
408 Eighth Street
Camanche, IA 52730
(319) 259-8666

Direct Response Associates
308 Merle Hay Tower
Des Moines, IA 50310
(515) 276-7797

Erickson & Erickson
524 B Avenue, Box 813

Kalona, IA 52247
(319) 656-3685

JV Associates
827 Broad Street
Grinnel, IA 50112
(515) 236-6209

L.W. Ramsey Advertising
111 E. Third
Davenport, IA 52801
(319) 326-0157

Wilson Corgin & Associates
2302 W. First Street
Cedar Falls, IA 50613
(319) 277-3735

World Advertising Service System
408 Fourth Street
Camanche, IA 52730
(319) 259-8666

KANSAS

Central Graphics
248 Cleveland
Wichita, KA 67201
(316) 262-7273

GMC Photography
112 W. Sixth Street
Topeka, KS 66614
(913) 233-4948

Dave Majure/Direct Mktg
Consultant
5845 Horton
Shawnee Mission, KS 62020
(913) 722-1137

Marketaide
1300 E. Iron
Salina, KS 67402
(913) 825-7161

Marketing Communications
10605 W. 84th Terrace
Lenexa, KS 66124
(913) 492-1575

Professional Computer Systems
Box 981
Topeka, KS 66601
(913) 232-3892

River City Associates
Box 657
Wichita, KS 67201
(316) 262-3859

Savik Business Systems
123 W. Eighth Street
Lawrence, KS 66044
(913) 841-8649

J. Schmid & Associates
3209 W. 68th Street
Shawnee Mission, KS 66208
(913) 236-6669

Words & Data
4220 Johnson Drive
Shawnee Mission, KS 66207
(913) 722-6424

KENTUCKY

Photography by Wilkinson
114 Wood Drive
Glasgow, KY 42141
(502) 651-5451

LOUISIANA

Herbert S. Benjamin Associates
2736 Florida Street
Baton Rouge, LA 70821
(504) 387-0611

Carter Advertising
401 Market Street

Shreveport, LA 71101
(318) 227-1920

Cornay Printing
1737 Pine Street
New Orleans, LA 70118
(504) 865-9426

Ekat Advertising & Public
Relations
8 Chateau
Kenner, LA 70063
(504) 468-7961

The Foster Agency
409 Lee Avenue
Lafayette, LA 70502
(318) 235-1848

Hermann
Box 1696
Slidell, LA 70459
(504) 641-0226

Root & Associates
830 Main Street
Baton Rouge, LA 70821
(504) 344-3198

Ryan & Company
2056 Texas E.
Bossier City, LA 71111
(318) 747-5562

MAINE

Creative Advertising Agency
561 Elm Street
Biddeford, ME 04005
(207) 284-8325

Snow Pond Designs
Pond Road, RFD 1, Box 3838
Oakland, ME 04963
(207) 465-3212

MARYLAND

Absher Direct Marketing
1110 Fidler Lane
Silver Spring, MD 20910
(301) 565-0350

American Information Network
8201 Corporate Drive
Landover, MD 20785
(301) 459-2626

Arlen Communications
7315 Wisconsin Avenue
Bethesda, MD 20814
(301) 656-7940

Brown Direct
6935 Arlington Road
Bethesda, MD 20814
(301) 986-0510

Buyer Photo & Art Marketing
9912 Colorado Court
Damascus, MD 20872
(301) 353-5791

Computat
Box 245
Brunswick, MD 21716
(301) 834-6542

The Copy Shop
7508 N. Arbory Way
Laurel, MD 20707
(301) 498-8740

Cranberry Graphic Des. &
Advertising
5611 Oakmont Avenue
Bethesda, MD 20817
(301) 493-4321

Creative Direct Response
9418 Annapolis Road
Lanham, MD 20706
(301) 731-5922

Cultural Relations International
4139 Mountwood Road
Baltimore, MD 21229
(301) 947-1015

Direct Design
1124 Halesworth Drive
Potomac, MD 20854
(301) 294-3085

Direct Marketing Concepts &
Copy
8206 Kenfield Court
Bethesda, MD 20817
(301) 469-8506

Doner Direct
2305 N. Charles Street
Baltimore, MD 21218
(301) 338-1600

East Coast Advertising Agency
201 N. Philadelphia Avenue
Ocean City, MD 21842
(301) 289-3738

Jack Fauntleroy Associates
12908 Gaffney Road
Silver Spring, MD 20904
(301) 622-9333

Government Sales Assistance
640 Homer Street
Salisbury, MD 21801
(301) 543-8999

The Image Makers, Inc.
2 Blaketon Court
Upper Marlboro, MD 20772
(301) 249-3600

Raymond L. Jackson Consulting
108 N. Church Street
Snow Hill, MD 21863
(301) 632-2574

Robert Francis Jones & Associates
4117 Leland Street
Chevy Chase, MD 20815
(301) 986-1970

Kolker Associates
9478 Greco Garth
Columbia, MD 21045
(301) 596-1168

Marjorie Kravitz DM Copy
Specialist
7128 Wolftree Lane
Rockville, MD 20852
(301) 770-6680

Bernard F. Kroeger & Associates
576 Glenrock Drive
Frederick, MD 21701
(301) 695-7156

Richard Leahy
8630 Fenton Street
Silver Spring, MD 20910
(301) 565-9006

Marketing & Design
8950 Gouran Plaza
Columbia, MD 21045
(301) 964-2605

Maryland Academy Dramatic
Arts
7649 Old Georgetown Road
Bethesda, MD 20814
(301) 652-7999

C. Paul Mendez
2025 Randolph Road
Silver Spring, MD 20906
(301) 942-8469

Money Mailer of Maryland
1709 Reisterstown Road
Baltimore, MD 21208
(301) 653-0744

The Newington Group
5407 Newington Road
Bethesda, MD 20816
(301) 656-8745

Original Designs by Anna
4139 Mountwood Road
Baltimore, MD 21229
(301) 947-1015

Jim Otradovec & Associates
1-3 E. Franklin Street
Baltimore, MD 21202
(301) 539-3566

Parker Mailing Service
3800 West Street
Landover, MD 20785
(301) 772-2255

Lee Richardson
Box 1106
Columbia, MD 21044
(301) 596-4899

Richardson, Myers & Donofrio
120 Fayette Street
Baltimore, MD 21201
(301) 837-4966

RJ&A
Box 21150
Baltimore, MD 21228
(301) 465-8870

MASSACHUSETTS

Ad Mail B
357 Cottage Street
Springfield, MA 01104
(617) 732-3333

Ad Tech Studios
289 Main Street
Rutland, MA 01543
(617) 886-6320

Agawam Direct Marketing
51 Summer Street
Rowley, MA 01969
(617) 948-2717

Allied Advertising Agency
800 Statler Office Building
Boston, MA 02116
(617) 482-4100

American Fund Raising Services
600 Winter Street
Waltham, MA 02154
(617) 890-2870

Artel Communications
93 Grand Street
Worcester, MA 01602
(617) 752-5690

Atlantic Associates Advertising
525 Lowell Street
Peabody, MA 01960
(617) 535-3636

Ausmar Associates
18 Champion Street
Tewksbury, MA 01876
(617) 851-9545

Berenson, Isham & Partners
38 Chauncy Street
Boston, MA 02169
(617) 965-8810

Harold Cabot & Co.
10 High Street
Boston, MA 02110
(617) 426-7600

Cambridge Consulting Group
33 Bedford Street
Lexington, MA 02173
(617) 863-5140

M. Charting
21 Sherwood Drive

Belchertown, MA 01007
(413) 323-6445

Concord Mail Marketing
61 Domino Drive
Concord, MA 01742
(617) 369-1904

Continental Cablevision
Pilot House, Lewis Wharf
Boston, MA 02110
(617) 742-6140

Davis-Info-Net
3 Harrington Terrace
Cambridge, MA 02141
(617) 576-1269

Delta Marketing Group
59 Temple Place
Boston, MA 02111
(617) 542-6936

Dickinson Direct Response
67 Federal Avenue
Quincy, MA 02269
(617) 471-9222

Direct Channel
394 Lowell Street
Lexington, MA 02173
(617) 861-6299

Directech
1620 Massachusetts Avenue
Lexington, MA 02173
(617) 861-9797

Direct Marketing Concepts
266 Beacon Street
Boston, MA 02116
(617) 247-1100

Dolphin Associates
9 Acton Road
Chelmsford, MA 01824
(617) 256-2853

Dove Associates
31 Milk Street
Boston, MA 02109
(617) 542-5520

Elbert Advertising Agency
815 University Avenue
Norwood, MA 02062
(617) 769-7666

Faulkner Group
401 County Road
Monument Beach, MA 02553
(617) 759-4343

Foster & Associates
4 Bay View Avenue
Hingham, MA 02043
(617) 749-1599

Future Communications
89 Inman Street
Cambridge, MA 02139
(617) 876-9011

The Graphic I
23 Keystone Park
Lynn, MA 01902
(617) 593-0177

G/R Direct
100 Galen Street
Watertown, MA 02172
(617) 926-5030

Greystone Services
23 Greystone Park
Lynn, MA 01902
(617) 593-0177

Stephen Henry Associates
120 Crest Avenue
Winthrop, MA 02152
(617) 846-3091

Ingalls Associates
2 Copley Place

Boston, MA 02116
(617) 437-7000

Jacques Advertising Agency
222 Union Street
New Bedford, MA 02741
(617) 997-2868

Kenyon & Eckhardt/Cinammon Assoc.
One Boston Place, 11th Floor
Boston, MA 02108
(617) 367-7300

Jeffrey Laurie
79 Garden Street
Cambridge, MA 02138
(617) 459-2610

Lyons Advertising
One Lyons Way
Attleboro Falls, MA 02763
(617) 699-4451

Market Response International
Harbor View Lane
N. Chatham, MA 02650
(617) 945-4010

Maslow, Gold & Rothschild, Direct
1220 Statler Office Building
Boston, MA 02116
(617) 482-7700

MKE Enterprises
193 Haverhill Street
N. Reading, MA 01864
(617) 664-3877

M.L.C. Associates
118 Albemarle Road
Norwood, MA 02062
(617) 762-4144

Paul Mogan Associates
Prudential Center, Box 265

Boston, MA 02199
(617) 545-2945

New England Direct
130 Sugarloaf Street
S. Deerfield, MA 01373
(413) 665-8592

Niemira Direct Communications
Box 147
Boston, MA 02101
(617) 325-9565

PCA
427 Plain Street
Marshfield, MA 02050
(617) 834-7814

J.M. Perrone Direct Marketing
74 Pleasant Street
Weymouth, MA 02190
(617) 335-6541

Paul A. Pollock
245 Elm Street
Braintree, MA 02184
(617) 848-7883

Provandie & Chirug
10 Thatcher Street
Boston, MA 02113
(617) 523-2200

Quill Marketing Communications
425A Broadway
Everett, MA 02149
(617) 389-2251

Rego Design Studio
89 Norman Street
New Bedford, MA 02744
(617) 992-2586

Rockett & Associates
28 Elm Street

S. Deerfield, MA 01373
(617) 665-3615

RSVP Marketing
450 Plain Street
Marshfield, MA 02050
(617) 837-2804

S.A.M.
325 Maple Street
Lynn, MA 01904
(617) 595-8325

Taurus Marketing
51 Water Street
Newburyport, MA 01950
(617) 465-2855

TeamBoston
Box 1246
Brookline, MA 02146
(617) 232-0953

Brian Turley & Co.
61 Sheffield Road
Melrose, MA 02176
(617) 662-8538

Webb & Co.
839 Beacon Street
Boston, MA 02215
(617) 262-6980

George H. Wojtkiewicz Associates
One Gladiola Terrace
Mansfield, MA 02048
(617) 339-4796

Woolard Advertising
125 Newbury Street
Boston, MA 02116
(617) 536-6800

Word Works
70 Washington

Salem, MA 01970
(617) 266-0788

MICHIGAN

Advertisers Publishing
1717 S. State Street
Ann Arbor, MI 48104
(313) 665-6171

Advertising House
821 Greenwood Avenue
Jackson, MI 49204
(517) 787-4900

Samuel Breck
306 Westwood
Ann Arbor, MI 48103
(313) 668-7703

Brewer Associates
806 Oakwood
Dearborn, MI 48123
(313) 562-4800

CMS
Box 1224
E. Lansing, MI 48823
(517) 332-0615

Colding Diversified Associates
Box 1004
Taylor, MI 48180
(313) 292-1936

Continuity Programs
2740 Woodward Avenue
Bloomfield Hills, MI 48013
(313) 334-9624

Corporate Communications
2950 E. Jefferson Avenue
Detroit, MI 48220
(313) 259-3585

CTS Associates
1150 Griswold
Detroit, MI 48226
(313) 965-0575

The Designery
Box 2887
Kalamazoo, MI 49003
(616) 345-9235

Gielow Associates
847 Parchment SE
Grand Rapids, MI 49506
(616) 942-1220

Graphic Design
23844 Sherwood
Centerline, MI 48015
(313) 758-0840

Gray & Kilgore
3001 W. Big Beaver
Troy, MI 48084
(313) 649-4150

Group 243 Design
4251 Plymouth Road, Building 1
Ann Arbor, MI 48105
(313) 995-0243

The Idea Bank
28250 Southfield Road
Lathrup Village, MI 48076
(313) 569-4332

Keller & Moleski Associates, Inc.
259 E. Michigan
Kalamazoo, MI 49007
(616) 349-8141

Lawler Ballard Advertising
259 E. Michigan
Kalamazoo, MI 49007
(616) 344-5046

Leo Associates
3553 Burbank

Ann Arbor, MI 48105
(313) 761-4111

Ada Mark
6232 Scotthille SE
Grand Rapids, MI 49506
(616) 791-2124

Market Resource
200 Renaissance Center
Detroit, MI 48243
(313) 259-8079

Marketing Partners
420 Main Street
St. Joseph, MI 49085
(616) 983-0016

Master Advertising Agency
2012 Royal Boulevard
Berkley, MI 48072
(313) 545-6300

Joseph Peter Miller
13326 Champaign
Warren, MI 48089
(313) 756-8168

MIRA Research Center
1 MIRA Station, Box 23037
Lansing, MI 48909
(517) 337-1525

Patten
27255 Lahser Road, Box 2150
Southfield, MI 48037
(313) 353-4520

River Shore Distributing
Lake at Main Street, Box 338
Caledonia, MI 49316
(616) 891-9136

T.I. Group
803 N. Main Street
Ann Arbor, MI 48104
(313) 994-4028

Tyner Communications
340 Hamilton Row
Birmingham, MI 48011
(313) 258-9711

Wolf Detroit Envelope/Mktg
Group
725 S. Adams
Birmingham, MI 48011
(313) 258-5700

Young & Rubicam, Inc.
200 Renaissance Center
Detroit, MI 48243
(313) 446-8600

MINNESOTA

The Ad Co.
1010 S. Benton Drive
Sauk Rapids, MN 56379
(612) 255-1158

Adventures Advertising Service
112 N. Ninth Street
Oliva, MN 56277
(612) 523-1716

Arnold
10709 Wayzata Boulevard
Minnetonka, MN 55343
(612) 544-0477

Beco & Associates International
5709 Harriet Avenue S.
Minneapolis, MN 55419
(612) 861-6823

John Borden & Associates
2010 Marshall
St. Paul, MN 55104
(612) 644-3443

Campbell-Mithun Direct
Marketing
1000 Northstar Center

Minneapolis, MN 55402
(612) 347-1338

CML Marketing Services
15612 Highway 7
Minnetonka, MN 55345
(612) 933-3453

Colle & McVoy Direct
1550 E. 78th Street
Minneapolis, MN 55423
(612) 861-7181

Combined Marketing Group
4018 W. 65th Street
Minneapolis, MN 55435
(612) 929-6677

The Communications Group
227 Shelard Plaza
Minneapolis, MN 55426
(612) 544-2115

The Comp/Editors
2517 Bryant Avenue S.
Minneapolis, MN 55405
(612) 874-1931

Datamap
6874 Washington Avenue S.
Eden Prairie, MN 55344
(612) 941-0900

Direct Response
7815 Telegraph Road
Bloomington, MN 55438
(612) 881-3400

DRM North
15500 Wayzata Boulevard
Wayzata, MN 55391
(612) 475-4041

Drucker & Halloran
3308 Library Lane
Minneapolis, MN 55426
(612) 922-1396

Educational Media
Box 21311
Minneapolis, MN 55421
(612) 636-5098

Bill Fitzgerald & Associates
6601 Grand Avenue S.
Minneapolis, MN 55423
(612) 866-0095

International Research &
Evaluation
21098 IRE Control Center
Eagan, MN 55121
888-9635

Karau & Associates
33 10th Avenue S.
Hopkins, MN 55343
(612) 933-6126

Karron Associates
2880 Zanzibar Lane
Plymouth, MN 55447
(612) 559-1779

James M. Laing & Associates
440 Union Place
Chanhassen, MN 55331
(612) 474-1138

Marketing Promotion
781 Pelham Boulevard
St. Paul, MN 55114
(612) 642-1483

Mediawerks
1400 Homer Road, Mktg Resource
Ctr.
Winona, MN 55987
(507) 454-1400

Miller Meester Advertising
2001 Killebrew Drive
Minneapolis, MN 55420
(612) 854-8944

Morr Direct
1825 Chicago Avenue S.
Minneapolis, MN 55404
(612) 872-1616

MW&A
30 N. 31st Avenue
Minneapolis, MN 55411
(612) 522-3673

Peterson-Morris
666 Transfer Road
St. Paul, MN 55114
(612) 645-0581

Primarketing
5909 Whited Avenue, Box 84
Hopkins, MN 55343
(612) 934-8072

Putman & Wangen, Inc.
2216 Myers Road
Albert, MN 56007
(507) 373-8267

Response Marketing
7125 Shady Oak Road
Eden Prairie, MN 55344
(612) 941-2335

Spangler-Fischer Advertising
126 N. Third Street
Minneapolis, MN 55401
(612) 339-0549

Michael Wikman & Associates
30 N. 31st Avenue
Minneapolis, MN 55411
(612) 522-3673

MISSISSIPPI

Ad Lab
6020 Jefferson Street
Tupelo, MS 38802
(601) 842-1976

Bowen Advertising Services
Rt 3, Box 323
Oxford, MS 38655
(601) 234-2572

Direct Mail & Computer Services
459 Highway 51 S., Box 55772
Jackson, MS 39216
(601) 856-7811

MISSOURI

American Direct Marketing
Resources
1400 Chesterfield
Chesterfield, MO 63017
(314) 532-7703

Archer Products/Magnets by
Archer
6611 Clayton Road
St. Louis, MO 63117
(314) 862-6363

BHN Direct
910 N. 11th Street
St. Louis, MO 63101
(314) 241-2000

Clayton-Davis & Associates
8229 Maryland Avenue
St. Louis, MO 63105
(314) 862-7800

Direct Mail of America
230 S. Brentwood
St. Louis, MO 63103
(314) 436-1122

Eiffert Media Communications
1031 E. Battlefield, No. 223
Springfield, MO 65807
(417) 881-0836

George Johnson Advertising
763 New Ballas Road S.

St. Louis, MO 63141
(314) 569-3400

Lang & Smith Communications
Group
1177 Warson Road
St. Louis, MO 63011
(314) 997-6700

Marketing Support Service
2925 Mitchell
St. Joseph, MO 64507
(816) 279-5869

Lori McGuire
Route 1, Box 185
Elklis Prairie, MO 65444
(417) 967-2890

M.C. Ross & Co.
2440 Pershing Road
Kansas City, MO 64108
(816) 471-5700

Sher, Jongs, Shear Associates
204 W. Linwood Boulevard
Kansas City, MO 64111
(816) 561-1065

Shoss & Associates
1750 S. Brentwood Boulevard
St. Louis, MO 63144
(314) 961-7620

Supreme Addressing
8840 Pershall Road
Hazelwood, MO 63042
(314) 521-2302

Tech-Vest Resources
1946 Greenpoint Drive
St. Louis, MO 63122
(314) 965-0184

James Townes Freelance Cub-
Copy-Club
6740 Torlina Drive

St. Louis, MO 63134
(314) 521-1321

Walker Advertising
3501 Sterling Avenue
Independence, MO 64052
(816) 252-8772

Walkerworks Printing &
Advertising
3501 "H" Sterling
Independence, MO 64052
(816) 252-8772

Wetzel Advertising & Marketing
1918 Gallaher
St. Charles, MO 63301
(314) 946-0873

MONTANA

Alpine Advertising
2639 St. Johns Avenue
Billings, MT 59107
(406) 652-1630

J.F. Preste & Associates
2639 St. Johns Avenue
Billings, MT 59102
(406) 652-1630

NEBRASKA

Ayres & Associates
6800 Normal Boulevard
Lincoln, NE 68506
(402) 483-4761

The DMR Group/Direct Response
Mktg.
2432 S. 130th Circle
Omaha, NE 68144
(402) 330-1905

Graphic Artworks
5414½ NW Radial Highway

Omaha, NE 68104
(402) 553-2262

IGL Litho Graphics Marketing
4804 Superior, Box 5059
Lincoln, NE 68505
(402) 466-6019

Bailey Lewis & Associates
924 NBC
Lincoln, NE 68508
(402) 475-2800

Murphy & Co.
Box 188
Boys Town, NE 68010
(402) 333-5964

Professional Training & Mktg
Assoc.
Haymarket Square, 814 P Street
Lincoln, NE 68508
(402) 476-7678

Doug Wall Advertising
2212 N. 91st Plaza
Omaha, NE 68134
(402) 391-1718

William-Nell Associates
1316 Illinois, Box 782
Sideny, NE 69162
(402) 254-6019

NEW HAMPSHIRE

The Continental Group
RFD 1, Box 190
Laconia, NH 03246
(603) 528-3021

Continental Mail
RFD 1, Box 190
Laconia, NH 03246
(603) 528-0321

The EM Space
Route 109, Winter Harbor
Wolfeboro, NH 03894
(603) 569-4779

I.T. Graphics
120 Main Street
Nashua, NH 03060
(603) 889-8558

Guyre Associates
22 Haverhill Road
Windham, NH 03087
(603) 3333

Maxson Creative
RR2, Box 99C
Peterborough, NH 03458
(603) 563-8830

Tom Pelletier Direct Mail
Palmer Drive
Londonderry, NH 03053
(603) 434-7372

Sharon Group
Davis Hill Road
New London, NH 03257
(603) 763-2535

Thomas Stuart Brokers
44 Franklin Street
Nashua, NH 03061
(603) 880-2751

Thompson Telecomputer Adv. &
Mktg.
7-3 Strawberry Bank Road
Nashua, NH 03062
(603) 888-6426

Wheelock Associates
S. Main Street, Box A-186
Hanover, NH 03755
(603) 643-6763

NEW JERSEY

Sol Abrams Associates
331 Webster Drive
New Milford, NJ 07646
(201) 262-4111

Advantage
108 W. Franklin Avenue
Pennington, NJ 08534
(609) 737-2000

Advantage Advertising
42 Old Mill Drive
Denville, NJ 07834
(201) 366-7730

Advertising Services
48 Main Avenue
Passaic, NJ 07055
(201) 777-68000

A.H.P. Advertising
160 Amherst Street
E. Orange, NJ 07019
(201) 736-3979

Alpine Marketing Associates
21 Main Street
Sparta, NJ 07871
(201) 729-9000

American Advertising
Distributors
Box 108
Pine Brook, NJ 07058
(201) 227-4607

Ardrey Advertising
100 Menlo Park
Edison, NJ 08837
(201) 549-1300

Astro Publications
Box 3658
Princeton, NJ 08540
(609) 987-0440

Sol Blumenfeld Direct Mktg &
Adv.
407 Main Street
Metuchen, NJ 08840
(201) 494-1773

Bob Bly
174 Holland Avenue
New Milford, NJ 07646
(201) 599-2277

Book World Promotions
87-93 Christie Street
Newark, NJ 07105
(201) 589-7877

Brown Advertising
125 Drake Road
Somerset, NJ 08873
(201) 246-2550

Bullen & Associates
770 Anderson Avenue
Cliffside Park, NJ 07010
(201) 224-9773

Arthur E. Burdge & Associates
28 Walnut Drive
Spring Lake Heights, NJ 07762
(201) 449-2103

Business Cards Wholesale
Box 1231
Teaneck, NJ 07666
(201) 384-6644

Business-to-Business Direct Mail
1341 Hamburg Turnpike
Wayne, NJ 07470
(201) 696-7843

Capell & Associates
375 Bedford Road
Ridgewood, NJ 07450
(201) 652-7061

CM Industries
220 E. Maple Avenue
Merchantville, NJ 08109
(609) 665-6555

Conrad Direct
80 West Street
Englewood, NJ 07631
(201) 567-3203

Creatique
290 Jefferson Avenue
Cresskill, NJ 07626
(201) 567-0436

Creative Marketing Concepts
11 Coventry Court
Englishtown, NJ 07726
(201) 536-4360

C.U.E. Marketing Services
3 N. Mississippi Avenue
Atlantic City, NJ 08401
(609) 345-6636

John Demario Advertising
15 E. Church Street, Box 233
Absecon, NJ 08201
(609) 646-3647

Direct Marketing
75 S. Union Street, Box 309
Lambertville, NJ 08530
(609) 397-3500

Direct Marketing Consultants
705 Franklin Turnpike
Allendale, NJ 07401
(201) 327-9213

B.J. Ellis Associates
93 Standish Road
Hillsdale, NJ 07642
(201) 664-4600

Falcon Graphics
615 Central Avenue
Westfield, NJ 07090
(201) 232-1991

Tsy Ford Associates
Box 324
Ho-Ho-Kus, NJ 07432
(201) 445-8498

Garden State Marketing Services
55 Princeton Terrace
Oakland, NJ 07436
(201) 337-3888

Gravzy-Miller Advertising
2-14 Fair Lawn Avenue
Fair Lawn, NJ 07410
(201) 796-3967

Jerry Hahn & Associates
86 Davison Place
Englewood, NJ 07631
(201) 569-0792

House of Excellence
483 Park Street
Montclair, NJ 07043
(201) 783-5113

IFC Advertising
Box 264
Roseland, NJ 07068
(201) 992-0629

Industrial Telemarketing
Associates
221 Chestnut Street, Box 163
Roselle, NJ 07203
(201) 245-3822

Dan Ingraham & Associates
Vermont Avenue at Paddock Place
Toms River, NJ 08753
(201) 341-0200

E.J. Krane
Box 2245
Princeton, NJ 08540
(609) 896-1900

Samuel Krasney Associates
2204 Morris Avenue
Union, NJ 07083
(201) 883-0835

Kreie-ative Associates
98 Broad Street
Bloomfield, NJ 07003
(201) 429-9853

Lander Design
3 Calvin Place
Metuchen, NJ 08840
(201) 549-0777

Layland/Allen Associates
638 Teaneck Road
Teaneck, NJ 07666
(201) 836-7849

The Lowery Group
Box 613
Short Hills, NJ 07078
(201) 467-8844

Loyer Enterprises
3 Campus Court
Trenton, NJ 08638
(609) 882-1669

Christopher Magalos Marketing
Design
3308 Church Road
Cherry Hill, NJ 08002
(609) 667-7433

Roger Maler
100 Stierli Court, Box 435
Mt. Arlington, NJ 07856
(201) 770-1500

Maple Mailing Service
24 W. Nicholason
Audubon, NJ 08106
(609) 546-0303

Marketing Communications
Associates
42 Oakview Avenue
Maplewood, NJ 07040
(201) 763-3360

McKelvey Printing
Box 1231
Teaneck, NJ 07666
(201) 384-6644

Media Consultants
656 Ridge Road
Lyndhurst, NJ 07071
(201) 933-2015

The MHR Group
436 Ferry Street
Newark, NJ 07105
(201) 589-3966

Morvay Advertising Agency
31 S. Mountain Road
Millburn, NJ 07041
(201) 762-3331

Michael J. Motto Advertising
1011 Route 22
Mountainside, NJ 07092
(201) 232-9100

Dan Newman
57 Lakeview Avenue
Clifton, NJ 07011
(201) 340-1165

Patmark
307 Fern Drive
Atco, NJ 08004
(609) 778-9660

Phone Power Unlimited
91 Palmer Drive, Box 3034
Wayne, NJ 07470
(201) 956-1085

Pictorial Offset
110 Amor Avenue, Box 157
Carlstadt, NJ 07072
(201) 935-7100

Positive Advertising
2175 Hudson Terrace
Fort Lee, NJ 07024
(201) 592-8717

Practical Computer Solutions
76 Addison Drive
Short Hills, NJ 07078
(201) 467-4610

Ramm Advertising
14 Commerce Drive
Cranford, NJ 07016
(201) 276-9190

Murray Raphel/Advertising
Gordon's Alley
Atlantic City, NJ 08401
(609) 344-5000

Reichenstein Advertising Agency
187 Mill Lane
Mountainside, NJ 07092
(201) 232-3200

Rein Associates
301-31 Spring Street
Red Bank, NJ 07701
(201) 741-8111

Reply-O-Letter
524 Hamburg Turnpike
Wayne, NJ 07470
(201) 942-2000

Response Unlimited
7000 Boulevard E.
Guttenberg, NJ 07093
(201) 662-1196

RFM Associates
35 Atkins Avenue
Trenton, NJ 08610
(609) 586-5214

Nicholas A. Roes Associates
Box 205
Saddle River, NJ 07458
(201) 327-8486

Schilling Sons
576 Main Street
Chatham, NJ 07928
(201) 635-6090

Self-Paced Instructions
236 Route 9 S., Box 32
Howell, NJ 07731
(201) 740-7020

Show & Tell Communications
19 W: Park Avenue
Merchantville, NJ 08109
(609) 488-9093

SMS
83 Hanover Road
Minitola, NJ 08341
(609) 697-1257

The Spokesmen, Inc.
1782 Pacific Avenue
Teaneck, NJ 07666
(201) 833-8262

H. Alan Stein Associates
72 Dryden Road
Upper Montclair, NJ 07043
(201) 783-6839

30-30
Box 208
Beach Haven, NJ 08008
(609) 492-3213

TM Marketing
11 Atlantic Street
Hackensack, NJ 07601
(201) 342-6511

Larry Tucker
Englewood Cliffs, NJ 07632
(201) 569-8888

Vam Com
Box 600
Florham Park, NJ 07932
(201) 966-0080

Nik Vitulio Advertising Agency
427 Chestnut Street
Union, NJ 07083
(201) 688-8383

Watts & Pacquet Communication
225 Franklin Avenue
Midland Park, NJ 07342
(201) 652-7200

Weinrich Associates
915 Clifton Avenue
Clifton, NJ 07013
(201) 473-6643

Maurice J. Weiss
10 Eastbrook Drive
River Edge, NJ 07661
(201) 488-1484

Ben West Creative
Communications
19 Francis Road
E. Brunswick, NJ 08816
(201) 254-9260

Westerhoff & Associates
180 Wachtung Drive
Hawthorne, NJ 07506
(201) 427-4072

World Marketing Group
2 Stanley Street
Dumont, NJ 07628
(201) 385-5446

NEW MEXICO

Madexco
160 Washington SE
Albuquerque, NM 87108
(505) 265-3505

Armand G. Winfield
3 Siler Lane, Box 1296
Santa Fe, NM 87504
(505) 471-6944

Woodworker's Supply
5604 Alameda NE
Albuquerque, NM 87113
(505) 821-0500

NEW YORK

Acento Latino de Lourdes
Box 149
Yonkers, NY 10702
(914) 963-6295

Ackerman Advertising
55 Northern Boulevard
Greenvale, NY 11548
(516) 484-5150

The Ad Agency
251 W. 57th Street
New York, NY 10019
(212) 581-2000

Adcraft Media Services
Box 333

Commack, NY 11725
(212) 979-6888

Adelante Advertising
386 Park Avenue S.
New York, NY 10016
(212) 696-0855

Ad Hoc Marketing Resources
7103 FDR Station
New York, NY 10150
(212) 496-5906

Adovations
19 Brompton
Huntington, NY 11746
(516) 673-8741

Ahrend Associates
80 Fifth Avenue
New York, NY 10011
(212) 620-0015

Albert Frank-Guenther Law
71 Broadway
New York, NY 10016
(212) 248-5200

Alden Advertising Agency
535 Fifth Avenue
New York, NY 10017
(212) 867-6400

Alford & Partners
126-13 101st Avenue
Queens, NY 11419
(718) 847-5200

Allied Graphic Arts
1515 Broadway
New York, NY 10036
(212) 730-1414

A.M. Marketing
381 Park Avenue S.
New York, NY 10016
(212) 889-9411

America's Hobby Center
146 W. 22nd Street
New York, NY 10011
(212) 675-8922

Anselmo & Associates
45 Cedar Ridge Lane
Dix Hills, NY 11746
(516) 499-7131

Any List
10 Tumble Brook Court
Pleasantville, NY 10570
(914) 747-0546

Jerrold P. Applebaum
40-07 201st Street
Bayside, NY 11361
(718) 423-5052

Arbach
692 Jewett Avenue
State Island, NY 10314
(718) 720-6945

Arrow Direct Marketing
35-27 Vernon Boulevard
Long Island City, NY 11106
(718) 274-1900

Artdesign
324 E. Sixth Street
New York, NY 10003
(212) 228-6735

Artistic Greetings
409 William Street
Elmira, NY 14901
(607) 733-5541

B & J Direct
6 E. 43rd Street
New York, NY 10017
(212) 916-8500

BBDO Direct
385 Madison Avenue

New York, NY 10017
(212) 418-7200

Beekman & Packard
212 Kilburn Road
Garden City, NY 11530
(516) 248-1966

Benn & MacDonough
111 Broadway
New York, NY 10006
(212) 267-6900

Benton-Bowles
909 Third Avenue
New York, NY 10528
(212) 758-6200

Berman Consulting
14 Frederick Drive
Plainview, NY 11803
(516) 681-8792

Robert J. Berretone Associates
501 W. Commercial Street
E. Rochester, NY 14445
(716) 586-6510

Biomedical Enterprises
73 Dogwood Lane
Irvington-on-Hudson, NY 10533
(914) 591-7980

D.L. Blair
185 Great Neck Road
Great Neck, NY 11021
(516) 487-9200

John Blair Marketing
1290 Sixth Avenue
New York, NY 10104
(212) 603-6009

Bloom & Gelb
445 Park Avenue
New York, NY 10022
(212) 906-3887

Bolling Peterson Advertising
300 Theater Place
Buffalo, NY 14202
(716) 854-1473

Phil Bozzo Direct Response
156 Fifth Avenue
New York, NY 10010
(212) 206-0621

Warren Brath Associates
864 Willis Avenue
Albertson, NY 11507
(516) 746-1330

Monte Brick, Wordsmith
6 Inwood Place
Melville, NY 11747
(516) 549-9640

Brightspot Advertising
Moriches Road, Box 463
St. James, NY 11780
(516) 862-6200

Lawrence Butner Advertising
228 E. 45th Street
New York, NY 10017
(212) 682-3200

Campbell
1010 Turtle Street
Syracuse, NY 13208
(315) 471-1817

The Catskills Agency
Bridge Street, Box 246
Roxbury, NY 12474
(914) 586-2900

Certified Business Bureau
7603 Empire State Building
New York, NY 10118
(212) 246-7777

Chapman Direct Marketing
415 Madison Avenue

New York, NY 10017
(212) 758-8230

Communication Services
Associates
42-15 Crescent Street
Long Island City, NY 11101
(718) 729-6003

Communications Diversified
23 E. 22nd Street
New York, NY 10010
(212) 460-5700

Communications Plus
360 Park Avenue S.
New York, NY 10010
(212) 686-9570

Computer Marketing Services
2000 Winton Road S.
Rochester, NY 14692
(716) 272-2500

Comspec Corp.
200 Park Avenue
New York, NY 10017
(212) 986-2515

Conklin, Labs & Bebee
Box 4871
Syracuse, NY 13221
(315) 437-2591

Consoil Associates
5 Riverside Drive
New York, NY 10023
(212) 874-7362

Consolidated Marketing Services
Box 1361
New York, NY 10163
(212) 688-8797

Copy-That-Clix
Box 102, Lefferts Station

Brooklyn, NY 11225
(718) 756-1712

Alexander Courage Associates
25 E. Chestnut Street
Massapequa, NY 11758
(516) 541-5252

Dandelion Design & Marketing
McHenry Valley, Box 473-Z
Alfred, NY 14802
(607) 587-9558

D & O/Transnational
801 Second Avenue
New York, NY 10017
(212) 694-1411

Danel Manhattan
9 E. 75th Street
New York, NY 10021
(212) 288-9356

Delfino Marketing
Communications
401 Columbus Avenue
Valhalla, NY 10595
(914) 747-1400

Dependable Direct
20 Crossways Park N.
Woodbury, NY 11797
(516) 364-0100

Design & Creation
Box 873
New Paltz, NY 12561
(914) 255-0279

Design Synergy
50 Helendale Road
Rochester, NY 14609
(716) 288-8000

DFS Direct
405 Lexington Avenue

New York, NY 10174
(212) 878-3333

Dillon, Agnew & Marton
12 W. 18th Street
New York, NY 10011
(212) 255-6102

Direct Marketing Graphics
88 Purchase Street
Rye, NY 10580
(914) 967-8063

The Direct Marketing Group
477 Madison Avenue
New York, NY 10022
(212) 355-2530

Doremus Direct
120 Broadway
New York, NY 10271
(212) 964-0700

The DR Group
522 Fifth Avenue
New York, NY 10036
(212) 391-8600

Dun & Bradstreet International
99 Church Street
New York, NY 10007
(212) 285-7525

Dun's Marketing Services
1 Penn Plaza
New York, NY 10119
(212) 971-9288

Dwayne
176-60 Union Turnpike
Flushing, NY 11366
(718) 591-4747

E.B. Design
330 E. 39th Street
New York, NY 10016
(212) 682-9229

EBW Direct Marketing
136 Madison Avenue
New York, NY 10016
(212) 684-5220

Edigraph
45 Cantitoe Street, RFD 1
Katonah, NY 10536
(914) 232-3725

Ehrlich Group
515 E. 82nd Street
New York, NY 10028
(212) 879-9545

El Amigo Universal
72-22 Roosevelt Avenue
Jackson Heights, NY 11372
(718) 779-1177

The Emerson Marketing Agency
44 E. 29th Street
New York, NY 10016
(212) 213-0320

Emertex Marketing
444 Park Avenue S.
New York, NY 10016
(212) 685-3535

Empire Promotion Graphics
114 E. 32nd Street
New York, NY 10016
(212) 685-3264

ETC Communications Group
386 Park Avenue S.
New York, NY 10016
(212) 889-8777

Fairbanks Associates
199 Jericho Turnpike
Floral Park, NY 11001
(516) 328-3399

Feigen
261 E. 71st Street

New York, NY 10021
(212) 288-9260

Sam Feldman Associates
165 West End Avenue
New York, NY 10023
(212) 362-5033

Fenvessy & Schwab
645 Madison Avenue
New York, NY 10022
(212) 758-6800

Flex
150 Fifth Avenue
New York, NY 10011
(212) 741-8020

F.M. International
77 Bainbridge Street
Brooklyn, NY 11123
(718) 773-0127

Fox/MSSM Direct Response
555 Madison Avenue
New York, NY 10022
(212) 832-6963

FPS Associates
240 E. 82nd Street
New York, NY 10028
(212) 988-0725

Sheldon Fredericks Advertising
71 Vanderbilt Avenue
New York, NY 10017
(212) 867-0110

J.K. Fuchs & Associates
45 W. 34th Street
New York, NY 10001
(212) 239-4102

The Fulfillment House
74 State Street
Westbury, NY 11590
(516) 997-7500

Gabriel Graphics/GNB
Box 38, Madison Square Station
New York, NY 10010
(212) 254-8863

Gamut International Ltd.
121 W. Oak
Amityville, NY 11701
(516) 598-1411

Gardner Communications
71 Waterside Avenue
Northport, NY 11768
(516) 749-0449

Garson Associates
172 Babylon Turnpike
Merrick, NY 11566
(516) 868-9833

Gaylord Direct Marketing
1 Byrambrook Place
Armonk, NY 10504
(914) 273-2222

Lois K. Geller
8 Lotus Street
Cedarhurst, NY 11516
(516) 374-6031

Bernard W. Gelman
826 E. 14th Street
Brooklyn, NY 11230
(718) 434-6050

Richard C. Goldrosen
38 Sherman Street
Brooklyn, NY 11215
(718) 499-3446

Graphics International
555 Madison Avenue
New York, NY 10022
(212) 688-0564

Grey Direct
875 Third Avenue

New York, NY 10022
(212) 303-2300

Eugene A. Griffin
269-1-0 Grand Central Parkway
Floral Park, NY 11005
(718) 224-1643

Gordon W. Grossman
606 Douglas Road
Chappaqua, NY 10514
(914) 238-9387

M. Grumbacher
460 W. 34th Street
New York, NY 10001
(212) 279-6400

Guthrie & Proctor
160 Fifth Avenue
New York, NY 10010
(212) 645-2037

Wallace F. Hainline Associates
45 Kensico Drive
Mount Kisco, NY 10549
(914) 666-8070

Hansen, Nigro & Wulfhorst
205 Lexington Avenue
New York, NY 10016
(212) 889-1540

Harrison Associates
15 Oakland Avenue
Harrison, NY 10528
(914) 835-0900

Healy, Schutte, Northrup & Teel
One Lockwood
Pittsford, NY 14534
(716) 248-2460

Harry W. Hochman & Associates
120 E. 56th Street
New York, NY 10022
(212) 371-4932

House of Brick
6 Inwood Place
Melville, NY 11747
(516) 367-4678

Intermedia Communications
Box 199
Pleasantville, NY 10570
(914) 769-7671

International Associates
150 E. 35th Street
New York, NY 10016
(212) 213-8238

The International Conference
Group
326 Clermont Avenue
Brooklyn, NY 11205
(718) 855-2064

The Iverson-Norman Associates
5 S. Buckhout Street
Irvington, NY 10533
(914) 591-6505

Richard D. Jordan Creative
Services
67 S. State Road
Briarcliff Manor, NY 10510
(914) 762-0058

Mort Junger Advertising
211 E. 43rd Street
New York, NY 10017
(212) 867-1737

JWT Direct
420 Lexington Avenue
New York, NY 10017
(212) 210-8440

Harold Katz Advertising
150 Great Neck Road
Great Neck, NY 11021
(516) 466-8610

Ketchum Direct
1133 Avenue of the Americas
New York, NY 10036
(212) 536-8800

Keye Advertising
1782 Coney Island Avenue
Brooklyn, NY 11230
(718) 645-9006

Kirk/Marsland
Box 938, Ansonia Station
New York, NY 10023
(212) 874-4853

Klafter Marketing
45 North Station Plaza
Great Neck, NY 11021
(516) 466-8665

Graham Knowles Associates
139 Fulton Street
New York, NY 10038
(212) 513-1522

Walter Kryshak Design &
Illustration
Box 8089
Long Island City, NY 11101
(718) 937-9068

Laddin & Co.
2 Park Avenue
New York, NY 10016
(212) 532-4381

LaMonica Circulation
Management Svcs.
1450 Broadway
New York, NY 10018
(212) 869-1616

Landrau's Concepts
9 Morningside Avenue
Yonkers, NY 10702
(914) 963-6295

Russ Lapso & Associates
322 W. 48th Street
New York, NY 10036
(212) 397-3560

Lardas Advertising
Box 1440
New York, NY 10001
(212) 688-5199

Launey, Hachmann & Harris
292 Madison Avenue
New York, NY 10017
(212) 679-1702

Lawler Communications
212 N. Barry Avenue
Mamaroneck, NY 10543
(914) 698-6655

Lawrence Executive Search
32 Reni Road
Manhasset, NY 11030
(516) 627-5361

LC&S Direct
100 Cedar Street
Dobbs Ferry, NY 10522
(914) 693-2834

Leavitt Advertising
225 W. 34th Street
New York, NY 10022
(212) 244-4555

Lettergraphics
433 W. Onondaga Street
Syracuse, NY 13201
(315) 476-8328

Levit & Sherman Advertising
44 Park Avenue S.
New York, NY 10016
(212) 696-1200

Levy, Flaxman, Tremba Direct
104 Fifth Avenue

New York, NY 10011
(212) 620-3100

List Process
420 E. 79th Street
New York, NY 10021
(212) 517-8550

Lithographic Concepts in Color
Center Lane, Village Green
Levittown, NY 11756
(516) 796-5342

Lockhart & Pettus
212 Fifth Avenue
New York, NY 10010
(212) 725-2828

Logos Enterprise
395-17 N. South End Avenue
New York, NY 10280
(212) 938-7824

M2 Associates
58 E. 1st Street
New York, NY 10003
(212) 677-5601

The Mailbox
Box C
Merrick, NY 11566
(516) 379-4675

The Mailing Works
Box 828
Highland, NY 12528
(914) 691-8285

Mailographic
315 Hudson Street
New York, NY 10013
(212) 269-7777

Malverne Specialty
105-15 Metropolitan Avenue
Forest Hills, NY 11375
(718) 268-5277

Manhardt-Alexander
400 Creekside Drive
Getzville, NY 14068
(716) 691-5533

Marketing Communication
Services
4006 Highland Avenue
Brooklyn, NY 11224
(718) 372-8030

Marketing III
24 Stuart Road
Mahopac, NY 10541
(914) 628-8772

Marshall/Altman Advertising
111 Great Neck Road
Great Neck, NY 11021
(516) 829-4460

McAndrew Advertising
2125 St. Raymond Avenue
Bronx, NY 10462
(212) 892-8660

McCaffrey & McCall Direct
Marketing
575 Lexington Avenue
New York, NY 10022
(212) 593-0700

McCann Direct
485 Lexington Avenue
New York, NY 10017
(212) 286-0460

McCurley Marketing Services
22 E. 72nd Street
New York, NY 10021
(212) 744-1150

McKinney Marketing Group
345 E. 86th Street
New York, NY 10028
(212) 289-9125

Mediaplus
15 W. 44th Street
New York, NY 10036
(212) 840-2866

Mediaprint
38 W. 21st Street
New York, NY 10010
(212) 982-7777

Merit Advertising & Printing
Service
45 W. 34th Street
New York, NY 10001
(212) 564-0018

Mitelman & Associates
19 N. Broadway
Tarrytown, NY 10591
(914) 631-6333

MMI Direct
1841 Broadway
New York, NY 10023
(212) 581-4690

Moonlighters Anonymous
Advertising
5924 Liebig Avenue
Riverdale, NY 10471
(212) 543-1935

Kenneth Morris & Associates
14 Westview Avenue
Tuckahoe, NY 10707
(914) 793-1724

Muldoon Direct
70 W. 36th Street
New York, NY 10018
(212) 594-8900

Multi-Media Graphics & Design
149 Jericho Turnpike
Mineola, NY 11501
(516) 294-7884

Multimedia Promotions
45 Stephen Drive
Plainview, NY 11803
(516) 822-3825

National Expositions
14 W. 40th Street
New York, NY 10018
(212) 391-9111

National Religious Names
5 S. Buckhout Street
Irvington, NY 10533
(914) 591-6505

Dick Neff
114 E. 84th Street
New York, NY 10028
(212) 744-0011

Nostradamus Advertising
250 W. 57th Street
New York, NY 10107
(212) 581-1362

Nynex Business Information
Systems
210 Penn Plaza
New York, NY 10021
(212) 760-0770

Ogilvy & Mather Direct
450 Park Avenue S.
New York, NY 10016
(212) 340-3500

Ogilvy Mather & Partners, Inc.
380 Madison Avenue
New York, NY 10017
(212) 687-2510

Olivestone Publishing Services
6 W. 18th Street
New York, NY 10011
(212) 691-8420

P.R. Olmsted Associates
13 Spring Street
Cambridge, NY 12816
(518) 677-5560

Oram Group Marketing
275 Madison Avenue
New York, NY 10016
(212) 889-2244

Package Fulfillment Center
2105 Lakeland Avenue
Ronkonkoma, NY 11779
(516) 588-7520

B. Paolucci
39 Kane Avenue
Larchmont, NY 10538
(913) 834-9594

Sid Paterson Associates
97-45 Queens Boulevard
Rego Park, NY 11375
(718) 897-1234

Pearlman/Rowe/Kolomatsky, Inc.
250 W. 57th Street
New York, NY 10019
(212) 246-4555

PGD
513 SW Eighth Street
Syracuse, NY 13201
(315) 474-5311

Phillips, Miller, Speyer, Frost
121 W. Oak
Amityville, NY 11701
(516) 691-1911

Phoenix Direct Marketing
Box 188
Bronxville, NY 10708
(914) 961-8419

Milt Pierce & Associates
162 W. 54th Street

New York, NY 10019
(212) 246-2325

Pierce & Others/Video Imagery
227 Perry Avenue
Staten Island, NY 10314
(718) 761-5816

P-J Promotions
605 Third Avenue
New York, NY 10158
(212) 986-0221

Dean Powell Advertising
254 Park Avenue S.
New York, NY 10010
(212) 473-0192

J.W. Prendergast & Associates
605 Third Avenue
New York, NY 10158
(212) 687-8805

Qualified Lists
135 Bedford Road
Armonk, NY 10504
(914) 273-6700

Joseph H. Radder, Marketing
Counsel
20 Guilford Lane
Williamsville, NY 14221
(716) 688-8593

Robert Ralske Management
89 Fifth Avenue
New York, NY 10003
(212) 929-8888

Rapp & Collins
475 Park Avenue S.
New York, NY 10016
(212) 725-8100

Reid Resources
454 W. 23rd Street

New York, NY 10011
(212) 206-0035

Respond Direct Marketing
16 E. 32nd Street
New York, NY 10016
(212) 696-3960

Response Resources
120 E. 16th Street
New York, NY 10003
(212) 982-2531

Richard-Lewis
455 Central Park Avenue
Scarsdale, NY 10583
(914) 723-3020

Riffkin Direct
64 Appletree Lane
Roslyn Heights, NY 11577
(516) 621-1076

Rollins Burdick Hunter
605 Third Avenue
New York, NY 10158
(212) 661-9000

Sig Rosenblum
45 Breese Lane
Southampton, NY 11968
(516) 283-2284

Rosenfeld Sirowitz & Lawson Direct
111 Fifth Avenue
New York, NY 10038
(212) 505-0200

Rothschild Design
141 W. 36th Street
New York, NY 10018
(212) 736-0060

RR Management
1650 Broadway

New York, NY 10019
(212) 265-3366

R.T.F.T. Marketing Services
69-10 Yellowstone No. 617
Forest Hills, NY 11375
(718) 896-6485

Sawyer Direct
19 Gramercy Avenue
Rye, NY 10580
(914) 967-8014

Saxe Walsh
42 E. 75th Street
New York, NY 10021
(212) 570-9670

Scali, McCabe, Sloves Direct
800 Third Avenue
New York, NY 10022
(212) 421-2050

Nicholas T. Scheel
342 E. 53rd Street
New York, NY 10022
(212) 688-8797

Schein/Blattstein Advertising
420 Madison Avenue
New York, NY 10017
(212) 758-1555

Schiller Direct Response
6 W. 18th Street
New York, NY 10011
(212) 691-7111

Schneider & Associates
127 E. 59th Street
New York, NY 10022
(212) 421-1950

SET Marketing Communications
Box 1436 FDR Station
New York, NY 10050
(212) 888-7838

Rik Shafer & Associates
260 Main Street
Northport, NY 11768
(516) 754-1750

Gregory John Sheffield
Route 1, Box 37
Lockwood, NY 14859
(607) 598-2586

Ruth Koffler Sheldon & Associates
585 West End Avenue
New York, NY 10024
(212) 873-0496

Sheldon Fredericks Advertising
71 Vanderbilt Avenue
New York, NY 10169
(212) 867-0110

David Shepard Associates
2 Micole Court
Dix Hills, NY 11746
(516) 271-5567

Mike Siegelbaum
158 S. Buckhout Street
Irvington, NY 10533
(914) 591-8046

The Silbert Group
645 Madison Avenue
New York, NY 10022
(212) 308-5660

Richard Silverman
8333 Austin Street
Kew Gardens, NY 11415
(718) 441-5358

Jack Slater & Associates
326 First Street
Liverpool, NY 13088
(315) 457-8858

SMG Services
Box 119
Staten Island, NY 10314
(718) 697-5895

Smiley Promotion
26 Broadway
New York, NY 10004
(212) 809-1700

SNO Advertising
156 E. 51st Street
New York, NY 10021
(212) 888-1009

Solay/Hunt
28 W. 44th Street
New York, NY 10036
(212) 840-3313

Springer-Verlag New York
175 Fifth Avenue
New York, NY 10010
(212) 460-1600

Starcom
374 Pacific Street
Brooklyn, NY 11217
(718) 625-2424

Starmet Sales
174 Fifth Avenue
New York, NY 10010
(212) 807-6145

Steen Advertising
55 Atlantic Avenue
Lynbrook, NY 11563
(516) 593-3030

The Stenrich Group
160 Fifth Avenue
New York, NY 10021
(212) 255-7273

Strategic Services for Management

233 Kneeland Avenue
Yonkers, NY 10705
(914) 965-7552

Susser Letter Service
70-01 Queens Boulevard
Woodside, NY 11377
(718) 639-7500

Joan Throckmorton
1175 York Avenue
New York, NY 10021
(212) 308-6677

Thumb Print
44-09 Third Avenue
Sunnyside, NY 11354
(718) 786-6431

John Francis Tighe
72 W. 85th Street
New York, NY 10024
(212) 873-2520

Mark Titton Advertising
401 E. 81st Street
New York, NY 10028
(212) 794-2662

TLK Direct Marketing
605 Third Avenue
New York, NY 10158
(212) 972-9000

Tobol Group
260 Northern Boulevard
Great Neck, NY 11021
(516) 466-0414

Tolliver
123 E. 54th Street
New York, NY 10022
(212) 758-7344

Trade-Mark Business Barter Exchange
Box 175

Baldwin, NY 11510
(516) 599-7854

Tradition
414 E. 77th Street
New York, NY 11021
(212) 794-0144

Tricom Direct Mail Services
Box 625
Amawalk, NY 10501
(914) 962-5516

TV Design Group
11 E. 47th Street
New York, NY 10017
(212) 308-4778

TVL Media Associates
790 Allwyn Street
Baldwin, NY 11510
(516) 623-3434

21st Century Marketing
Box 9521
Farmingdale, NY 11735
(516) 293-8550

Tyler-Shaw
229 King Street
Chappaqua, NY 10514
(914) 238-8961

Ultimate Design
19 Wentworth Drive
Dix Hills, NY 11746
(516) 595-2140

Ultimo Advertising
370 E. 76th Street
New York, NY 10021
(212) 861-0322

USA Marketing
2182 Camp Avenue
Merrick, NY 11566
(516) 868-6893

Valenti Direct Response
1874 Pelham Parkway S.
New York, NY 10461
(212) 863-9619

Peter Vane Advertising
401 Park Avenue S.
New York, NY 10016
(212) 679-8260

The Frank Vos
475 Park Avenue S.
New York, NY 10016
(212) 684-7600

Weissberg Associates, Inc.
300 E. 42nd Street
New York, NY 10017
(212) 986-3611

Willen's Advertising Concepts
Box 1059
Riverdale, NY 10471
(212) 543-1935

Winchester
850 Seventh Avenue
New York, NY 10019
(212) 582-0895

Wolff Communications
75-05 35th Avenue
Jackson Heights, NY 11372
(718) 565-8059

NORTH CAROLINA

Cleland, Ward, Smith &
Associates
201 N. Broad Street
Winston-Salem, NC 27101
(919) 723-6070

Jackson & Associates
1323 Durwood Drive
Charlotte, NC 28204
(704) 333-1146

Marketing Resources
Box 10481
Greensboro, NC 27404
(919) 294-4822

McMillan & Moss
Box 1327
Chapel, Hill, NC 27514
(919) 732-7794

James C. Sarayiotes & Co.
11800 Black Horse Run
Raleigh, NC 27612
(919) 847-3032

Technique Marketing
Highway 64, Box 741
Hayesville, NC 28904
(704) 389-9211

Wellex
McLeansville Square, Box 128
McLeansville, NC 27301
(919) 698-0500

NORTH DAKOTA

Huseby Agency
206 Broadway
Fargo, ND 58107
(701) 235-0506

Response Advertising
718 First Avenue N.
Fargo, ND 58102
(701) 235-1101

OHIO

The Adman
1044 Bellefontaine Avenue
Lima, OH 45802
(419) 227-6407

Advertising Alternatives
Box 9358

Canton, OH 44711
(216) 499-2122

A.J. Enterprises
9844 N. Dixie Highway
Franklin, OH 45005
(513) 746-5221

Allen's
527 Cherry Street
Ashland, OH 44805
(419) 323-3915

The AV Group
514 E. Archwood
Akron, OH 44301
(216) 773-3143

Babcox Publications
11 S. Forge Street
Akron, OH 44304
(216) 535-6117

Richard L. Bencin & Associates
7922 Seth Paine Street
Brecksville, OH 44141
(216) 526-6726

Cincinnati Bell-Creative Services
201 E. Fourth Street
Cincinnati, OH 45201
(513) 397-2960

Creative 3
24700 Center Ridge Road
Westlake, OH 44145
(216) 835-1300

D & S Advertising
140 Park Avenue E.
Mansfield, OH 44902
(419) 524-4312

Direct Marketing Services
11288 Hanover Road
Cincinnati, OH 45240
(513) 851-2745

Dobie
6070 Royalton Road
N. Royalton, OH 44133
(216) 237-5466

Erlandson Industries
2508 N. Verity Parkway
Middletown, OH 45042
(513) 423-5008

Fahlgren & Swink
120 E. Fourth Street
Cincinnati, OH 45202
(513) 241-9200

Flourney & Gibbs
241 N. Superior Street
Toledo, OH 43604
(419) 244-5501

Douglas C. Grant, Lettersmith
3145 Arville Road
Bainbridge, OH 45612
(614) 493-2464

Graphic Service
1640 Mahoning Avenue
Youngstown, OH 44509
(216) 793-2046

Graphics International
20475 Bunker Hill Drive
Fairview Park, OH 44126
(216) 333-9988

Griswold
55 Public Square
Cleveland, OH 44113
(216) 696-3400

Huey Communications
38114 Third Street
Willoughby, OH 44094
(216) 951-2792

JDM Marketing
1201 30th Street NW

Canton, OH 44709
(216) 492-6525

Franklin Lavin & Associates
6428 Union Avenue
Alliance, OH 44601
(216) 821-4136

B.T. Lazarus & Co.
935 Schrock Road
Columbus, OH 43229
(614) 846-8424

Leff & Squicciarini Advertising &
PR
350 E. Broad Street
Columbus, OH 43215
(614) 228-4900

Roy J. Ljungren Associates
5297 Grantland Drive
Dayton, OH 45429
(513) 434-3996

Marketing Arts People
1662 Breese Road
Lima, OH 45802
(419) 227-7000

Marschalk Direct Marketing
601 Rockwell Avenue
Cleveland, OH 44114
(216) 687-8800

Martiny & Co.
2260 Francis Lane
Cincinnati, OH 45206
(513) 281-7545

McElroy & Associates Promotions
212 E. Third Street
Cincinnati, OH 45202
(513) 421-2555

Meldrum & Fewsmith, Inc.
1220 Huron Road

Cleveland, OH 44112
(216) 241-2141

Metrodyne
7375 Carmen NW
N. Canton, OH 44720
(216) 493-1734

Miami Valley Marketing Group
1250 W. Dorothy Lane
Dayton, OH 45409
(513) 299-1825

Mills Hall Walborn
29125 Chagrin Boulevard
Cleveland, OH 44122
(216) 464-7500

Norris & Co.
7710 Shawnee Run Drive
Cincinnati, OH 45243
(513) 561-5400

Over & Von Fischer
2228 Gilbert Avenue
Cincinnati, OH 45103
(513) 281-8899

Parhelion Direct
3636 Dayton Park Drive
Dayton, OH 45414
(513) 233-5120

Pendell & Associates
2622 Wayland Avenue
Dayton, OH 45420
(513) 254-4210

Penny/Ohlmann/Neiman
1605 N. Main Street
Dayton, OH 45405
(513) 278-0681

Pihera Advertising Associates
1605 Ambridge Road
Dayton, OH 45459
(513) 433-9814

Professional Marketing
Communications
38 S. Beckel Street
Dayton, OH 45403
(513) 228-0103

Ransom & Associates
4070 Nottinghill Gate Road
Columbus, OH 43220
(614) 451-6487

Roberts Printing
314 Chestnut Street
Ironton, OH 45638
(614) 843-5262

Robert A. Sherman & Associates
333 Harmon NW
Warren, OH 44483
(216) 394-2575

Sidney Printing Works
2611 Colerain Avenue
Cincinnati, OH 45614
(513) 542-4000

Jerry Schwartz Advertising
7326 Parkdale Avenue
Cincinnati, OH 45237
(513) 821-9906

Stan Speer Advertising
415 Pennsylvania
Marion, OH 43302
(614) 389-6440

Stark Graphics
22420 S. Woodland Road
Shaker Heights, OH 44122
(216) 751-7510

Leonard J. Stone & Associates
3645 Warrensville Road
Cleveland, OH 44122
(216) 283-8080

Team Associates
4823 Willocroft Drive
Willoughby, OH 44094
(216) 946-2528

Triad (Terry Roble Industrial Adv.)
124 N. Ontario Street
Toledo, OH 43624
(419) 241-5110

Worth Printing
1791D Rolling Hills Drive
Twinsburg, OH 44087
(216) 292-6111

Writing & Creative Services
230 Defiance Avenue
Findlay, OH 45839
(419) 424-0119

OREGON

Horticultural Photography
1810 NW Circle Place
Corvallis, OR 97330
(503) 758-1216

Michael Linden Agency
364 Hargadine
Ashland, OR 97520
(503) 488-2326

Terry Mandel Communications
5331 SW Macadam
Portland, OR 97201
(503) 228-9711

Arthur N. Orans
1810 NW Circle Place
Corvallis, OR 97330
(503) 758-0660

Young & Roehr
6415 SW Canyon Court
Portland, OR 97221
(503) 297-4501

PENNSYLVANIA

ADVO-System
367 S. Gulph Road
King of Prussia, PA 19046
(215) 768-0175

Shell Alpert Direct Marketing
444 Lakeview Court
Langhorne, PA 19047
(215) 752-3433

Anderson Direct Response
4252 Sunnyside Drive
Doylestown, PA 18901
(215) 794-5225

Barcla Direct Marketing
19 Oxford Drive
Langhorne, PA 19047
(215) 757-5785

Ted Barkus
225 S. 15th Street
Philadelphia, PA 19102
(215) 545-0616

Beaumont, Heller & Sperling
Sixth & Walnut Streets
Reading, PA 19603
(215) 375-4311

Braemar Advertising
Box 716
Warrington, PA 18976
(215) 343-9493

Peter Bressler Design
301 Cherry Street
Philadelphia, PA 19106
(215) 925-7100

J. Stewart Caverly
216 McLean Street
Wilkes Barre, PA 18702
(717) 822-8926

CIS of Pittsburgh
5919 Verona Road
Verona, PA 15147
(412) 793-6659

Communicate Direct
Box 1097
Media, PA 19063
(215) 565-6167

The Communications Center
Fox Pavilion, 413A
Jenkintown, PA 19046
(215) 576-5000

Communications Ink
810 Penn Avenue
Pittsburgh, PA 15222
(412) 263-2979

Copy Direct!
Fox Pavilion, 413A
Jenkintown, PA 19046
(215) 576-5000

Creative Marketing Associates
130 Seventh Street
Pittsburgh, PA 15222
(412) 355-0823

The Creative Shoppe
400 Stenton Avenue
Plymouth Meeting, PA 19462
(215) 828-4385

Demographics
3005 Brodhead Road
Bethlehem, PA 18017
(215) 861-0950

Devon Direct Marketing &
Advertising
Greentree Office Plaza
Malvern, PA 19355
(215) 644-0333

Direct Marketing Mgmt
Consultants
151 S. Warner Road
Wayne, PA 19087
(215) 964-9200

Direct Marketing Services
4321 W. Ridge Road
Erie, PA 16506
(814) 833-9652

Direct Response Advertising
1166 Dekalb Pike
Center Square, PA 19422
(215) 275-1901

Direct Response Broadcasting
Network
225 S. 15th Street
Philadelphia, PA 19102
(215) 735-7911

Direct Strategies
500 N. Gulph Road
King of Prussia, PA 19406
(215) 337-1928

Diversified Consultants
Box 3447
York, PA 17402
(717) 757-3647

D.B. Duff & Associates
239 Fort Pitt Boulevard
Pittsburgh, PA 15222
(412) 281-2150

Dunlap & Co.
622 Lancaster Avenue
Berwyn, PA 19312
(215) 296-2535

Egan Advertising
151 Warner Road
Wayne, PA 19087
(215) 964-9200

Elkman Advertising
150 Monument Road
Bala Cynwyd, PA 19004
(215) 835-2400

Fifer Advertising
3561 N. Providence Road
Newtown Square, PA 19073
(215) 353-3366

Donald F. Flathman, Writer
533 Twickenham Road
Glenside, PA 19038
(215) 886-0955

Goodway Marketing
930 Benjamin Fox Pavilion
Jenkintown, PA 19046
(215) 887-5700

Greenspoon Agency
300 Market Street
Kingston, PA 18704
(717) 287-8078

Hanover House Industries
340 Poplar Street
Hanover, PA 17331
(717) 637-6000

Hardy Business Service
Box 13
Zelionople, PA 16063
(412) 843-4219

Heisco
3522 Primrose Road
Philadelphia, PA 19114
(215) 637-2726

Helix Communications
Box 13400
Pittsburgh, PA 15243
(412) 344-0344

Help Business Services
417 Dartmouth Avenue

Swarthmore, PA 19081
(215) 544-9787

JRA Marketing Communications
1831 Chestnut Street
Philadelphia, PA 19103
(215) 567-4551

JVW Direct
142 Fernbrook Avenue
Wyncote, PA 19095
(215) 886-6832

Kemp Homestead
806 Union Cemetery Road
Greensburg, PA 15601
(412) 832-0420

Kensington Printing
1815 E. Wensley Street
Philadelphia, PA 19134
(215) 739-0221

Levy Advertising Enterprises
21 Sixth Street
Williamsport, PA 17701
(717) 322-2695

Liberty Marketing Associates
650 N. Cannon Avenue
Lansdale, PA 19446
(215) 855-7757

B.L. Lippincott Associates
25 N. Buck Lane
Haverford, PA 19041
(215) 649-6718

Mass Marketing Insurance Group
125 Graham Way
Devon, PA 19333
(215) 688-8454

Mattis Advertising
60 State Road
Media, PA 19063
(215) 565-2166

MBR Marketing
26 Evergreen Avenue
Moremenster, PA 19874
(215) 672-1054

Measured Marketing
222 W. Lancaster Avenue
Devon, PA 19333
(215) 688-8377

The Mecklerstone
112 N. 12th Street
Philadelphia, PA 19107
(215) 567-6575

Metropolitan Data Processing
Systems
325 S. 69th Street
Upper Darby, PA 19082
(215) 734-2393

Lawrence I. Miller & Associates
247 E. Chelsea Circle
Newtown Square, PA 19073
(215) 356-5069

Mitchell & Co.
Benson East, B-5
Jenkintown, PA 19046
(215) 572-7000

Charles Moore Associates
Box 6, Stump Road
Southampton, PA 18966
(215) 355-6084

Morton-Adler Associates
1208-1 Benson E.
Jenkintown, PA 19046
(215) 884-4272

MSA Advertising
260 S. 15th Street
Philadelphia, PA 19102
(215) 546-8000

National Mail/Marketing
97 Cedar Grove Road
Media, PA 19063
(215) 353-6733

NEFCO
836-40 Montgomery Avenue
Narberth, PA 19072
(215) 664-5505

Neibauer Press
20 Industrial Drive
Warminster, PA 18974
(215) 322-6200

Packman Marketing Associates
1918 Pine Street
Philadelphia, PA 19103
(215) 546-2311

Pal Associates
231 Redwood Road
King of Prussia, PA 19406
(215) 337-4787

Park Lane
516 Park Lane
Sewickley, PA 15143
(412) 741-6248

Peerless Paper Specialty
1013 N. York Road
Willow Grove, PA 19090
(215) 657-3460

George N. Pegula Agency
400 Lackawanna Avenue
Scranton, PA 18503
(717) 343-4745

Perceptive Marketing Agency
1920 Chestnut Street
Philadelphia, PA 19103
(215) 665-8736

Susan Perloff Public Relations
6389 Overbrook Avenue
Philadelphia, PA 19151
(215) 879-3101

W.S. Ponton
5149 Butler Street
Pittsburgh, PA 15201
(412) 782-2360

Price Graphic Design
400 Stenton Avenue
Plymouth Meeting, PA 19462
(215) 828-4385

E.J. Quigley Associates
701 Penrith Place
Gwynedd Valley, PA 19437
(215) 628-3037

Recon Publications
Box 14602
Philadelphia, PA 19134
(215) 843-4256

G.E. Richards Graphic Supplies
928 Links Avenue
Lanidsville, PA 17538
(717) 898-3151

Rittenhouse Marketing
Associates
1845 Walnut Street
Philadelphia, PA 19103
(215) 448-6090

Roberts & Rose Advertising
203 Fern Avenue
Willow Grove, PA 19090
(215) 659-8463

Rue Publications
Box 246
Philadelphia, PA 19105
(215) 238-0357

Sargeant House
1433 Johnny's Way
Westtown, PA 19395
(215) 399-0962

Helen Schonbrun
1325 Pine Street
Philadelphia, PA 19107
(215) 732-1463

Sidney Schreiber
215 S. Broad Street
Philadelphia, PA 19107
(215) 545-2223

Sea Voss
888 N. 25th Street
Philadelphia, PA 19130
(215) 236-7821

Smith & Co.
812 Country Lights Villas
Bensalem, PA 19020
(215) 757-0477

Robert Smith-Felver Associates
4497 Mechanicsville road
Doylestown, PA 18901
(215) 794-8937

Spiro & Associates
100 S. Broad Street
Philadelphia, PA 19124
(215) 923-5400

Stigelman Associates
114 Park Avenue
Swarthmore, PA 19081
(215) 328-0325

Thistlewood
2113 Pinto Road, Box 716
Warrington, PA 18976
(215) 343-9493

Topak Marketing
2225 Richmond Street
Philadelphia, PA 19125
(215) 739-3636

Trichon Communications
602 Washington Square
Philadelphia, PA 19106
(215) 923-7633

Sheldon Vale Associates
1120 First Eastern Bank Building
Wilkes Barre, PA 18701
(717) 825-6466

Writers: Free-Lance
12 Cavalier Drive
Ambler, PA 19002
(215) 646-7550

Xenvirons/Mediad
29 Poplar Street
Hatfield, PA 19440
(215) 368-8693

Rosemary Zemon Advertising
734 Homestead Road
Havertown, PA 19083
(215) 649-1917

RHODE ISLAND

Business Mailing Service
545 Pawtucket Avenue
Pawtucket, RI 02860
(401) 333-8717

H.B.M. Creamer
800 Turks Head Building
Providence, RI 02903
(401) 456-1500

Dial Media
Dial Media Building
40 Freeway Drive

Cranston, RI 02920
(401) 785-2600

Fern/Hanaway
270 Elmwood Avenue
Providence, RI 02907
(401) 421-7202

Graphic Productions
36 Boyle Avenue
Cumberland, RI 02864
(401) 769-5628

Halladay Advertising
76 Boyd Avenue
E. Providence, RI 02914
(401) 438-4300

SOUTH CAROLINA

Advertising Service Agency
24 Vendue Range
Charleston, SC 29401
(803) 577-7560

Biggs-Gilmore Advertising
508B Pineland Mall Office
Building
Hilton Head, SC 29928
(803) 681-3711

CommPlan Associates
30B Sugar Creek Villas
Greer, SC 29651
(803) 292-0503

Data Master Associates
1438 E. North Street
Greenville, SC 29607
(803) 271-8038

Henderson Direct
60 Pelham Pointe
Greenville, SC 29602
(803) 298-1650

Shorey & Associates
1617 E. North Street
Greenville, SC 29607
(803) 242-5407

Southern Marketing Services
Box 5220
Hilton Head, SC 29938
(803) 785-6655

SOUTH DAKOTA

Fred Courey & Associates,
Consultants
113 S. Poplar Street
Lennox, SD 57039
(605) 647-2235

Dakota Advertising
110 Capitol Street
Yankton, SD 57078
(605) 665-4451

TENNESSEE

Ad Satterwhite, Inc.
4004 Hillsboro Road
Nashville, TN 37215
(615) 383-2170

Advertising Concepts
50 Music Square W.
Nashville, TN 37203
(615) 320-5372

Rodney Baber & Co.
303 Madison Avenue
Memphis, TN 38103
(901) 525-6731

R. Benson
118 Saddletree Court
Hermitage, TN 37076
(615) 889-8260

Brumfield-Gallagher, Inc.
3401 West End Avenue
Nashville, TN 37203
(615) 385-1380

The College Press
5047 Industrial Drive
Collegedale, TN 37315
(615) 396-2164

Direct Video Marketing
Box 1248
Franklin, TN 37064
(615) 790-1005

Eric Ericson & Associates
1130 Eighth Avenue S.
Nashville, TN 37203
(615) 385-1050

Felknor Marketers
Route 4, Box 334, Palmer Drive
Lenoir City, TN 37771
(615) 986-0061

Gish, Sherwood & Friends
4301 Hillsboro Road
Nashville, TN 37215
(615) 292-2000

The Ron Hoffman Group
593 S. Cooper
Memphis, TN 38104
(901) 725-4971

John P. Lodsin & Associates
1600 Willoughby Road
Knoxville, TN 37928
(615) 573-3000

Miller Media
Box 400
Harrison, TN 37341
(615) 344-4444

W.B. Morris Publishing
2036 Woodcreek

Germantown, TN 38138
(901) 854-2283

Personal Expressions Advertising
164 Eighth Avenue N.
Nashville, TN 37203
(615) 254-8387

Rogers, Carroll & Quinn
2835 Hickory Valley Road
Chattanooga, TN 37422
(615) 894-8319

Salesleaders/Creative Marketing
4615 Delashmitt Road
Chattanooga, TN 37415
(615) 875-9226

TEXAS

Ad-Direct
3027 Routh Street
Dallas, TX 75201
(214) 745-8982

Alpha USA Direct Response
14800 Quorum Drive
Dallas, TX 72240
(214) 980-8838

American Standard, Inc.
102 Decker
Irvington, TX 75062
(214) 659-9292

Create-A-Craft
Box 330008
Fort Worth, TX 76163
(817) 292-1855

Custom Mailers
900 Cumberland
Odessa, TX 79761
(915) 332-9801

Creative Computer Services
10804 N. Stemmons

Dallas, TX 75220
(214) 358-4493

Creative Interventions
1939 Stadium Oaks, No. 210
Arlington, TX 76004
(817) 861-9191

Creative Printing & Mailing
10415 Perrin-Beitel Road
San Antonio, TX 78217
(512) 654-4777

The Dews Laboratories
813 Hood Road, Building 759
Mineral Wells, TX 76067
(817) 325-0771

Doron-Byrd & Associates
1213 Ridgecrest
Denton, TX 76203
(817) 566-1366

Fellers, Lacy & Gaddis
2211 S. IH 35
Austin, TX 78741
(512) 445-3492

Budd Gore
3202 W. Anderson Lane
Austin, TX 78766
(512) 454-2009

Insmark Systems
Box 28903
Dallas, TX 75228
(214) 270-6626

MacNabb Enterprises
104 Travis Lane
Hewitt, TX 76643
(817) 666-2166

Marketing Express
12770 Coit Road
Dallas, TX 75374
(214) 991-5263

Miracles
4106 Crestover Court
Arlington, TX 76010
(817) 429-0069

Moore Paper
100 Hogan, Box 805
Houston, TX 77009
(713) 228-9191

Overton Direct Marketing
11511 Katy Freeway
Houston, TX 77079
(713) 558-5333

Pan American Electronics
1117 Conway Avenue
Mission, TX 78572
(512) 581-2765

Rudolph J. Pazdernik &
Associates
15531 Kuykendahl
Houston, TX 77090
(713) 586-8270

Popejoy & Fischel Advertising
Agency
5151 Belt Line Road
Dallas, TX 75240
(214) 233-8461

Porter & Associates
3301 Golden Road
Tyler, TX 75701
(214) 597-0181

Richards Direct Marketing
7557 Rambler Road
Dallas, TX 75231
(214) 987-2700

Seib-Fred & Scott
2626 Cole Avenue
Dallas, TX 75248
(214) 871-1616

Select Marketing
7745 Chevy Chase Drive
Austin, TX 78752
(512) 450-0582

Southwest Marketing
415 Van Dyck
Temple, TX 76501
(817) 771-1601

John Walton Associates
14677 Midway Road
Dallas, TX 75224
(214) 392-9222

Yudell Communications
4801 Woodway
Houston, TX 77056
(713) 961-5830

UTAH

Communication Design
Associates
200 S. Orchard
N. Salt Lake City, UT 84054
(801) 298-1001

R.J. Spencer, Advertising
330 N. 970 E.
Logan, UT 84321
(801) 752-1309

VERMONT

Daniel Breckenridge Adv.
Services
RD#2
Middlebury, VT 05753
(802) 462-2382

Gene Cowell & Associates
Route 4, Box 58
Woodstock, VT 05091
(802) 457-3057

Hill Sullivan Brownell
Kingwood Park, Box 450
Randolph, VT 05060
(802) 728-9624

Mansfield Advertising Agency
9400 Shaw Mansion Road
Waterbury Center, VT 05677
(802) 244-7212

New England Marketing
Associates
31 Academy Street
Fair Haven, VT 05743
(802) 265-8820

Robert M. Sabloff
93 Barlow Road
Springfield, VT 05156
(802) 885-4632

VIRGINIA

Applied Marketing
1304 Vincent Place
McLean, VA 22101
(703) 821-0555

Associated Direct Marketing
Services
7777 Leesburg Pike
Falls Church, VA 22043
(703) 893-1442

Associated Marketing
9017 Bowlee Drive
Fairfax, VA 22031
(703) 280-4040

Better Business Communications
8300 Merrifield Avenue
Fairfax, VA 22031
(703) 849-8660

Brand Edmonds Associates
410 S. Jefferson Street

Roanoke, VA 24011
(703) 345-5403

Buterbaugh Partners
1624 Great Falls Street
McLean, VA 22101
(703) 356-7952

Denny Byrne
3005 Cedar Lane
Fairfax VA 22031
(703) 560-6953

The Cable Agency
301 Eastwood Circle
Virginia Beach, VA 23454
(804) 463-3845

CBC
13916 Sterlings Bridge Road
Midlothian, VA 23113
(804) 744-3866

Claritas
201 N. Union Street
Alexandria, VA 22314
(703) 683-8300

CLCo/5M List
2525 Wilson Boulevard
Arlington, VA 22201
(703) 528-6688

Communique
250 Jersey Avenue
Virginia Beach, VA 23462
(804) 499-3761

Steve Cram & Associates
8472 Tyco Road
Vienna, VA 22180
(703) 893-5440

The Creative Advantage
9401 Lee Highway
Fairfax, VA 22031
(703) 352-3444

DMP National
1800 Diagonal Road
Alexandria, VA 22314
(703) 548-2871

Downtown Press
Box 425
Harrisonburg, VA 22801
(703) 434-0807

Felvey & Associates
2701 Emerywood Parkway
Richmond, VA 23229
(804) 288-4582

Good Deeds & Co.
1506 Staples Mill Road
Richmond, VA 23230
(804) 355-1555

Group III Communications, Inc.
921 Crawford Parkway
Portsmouth, VA 23704
(804) 397-9148

H&H Direct
1402 Grandin Road
Roanoke, VA 24015
(703) 344-6825

HJV Direct
809 Brook Hill Circle
Richmond, VA 23227
(804) 266-2499

Hodges & Associates
1403 Pemberton Road
Richmond, VA 23233
(804) 740-7439

Holtje Associates
2560 Glengyle Drive
Vienna, VA 22180
(703) 281-9528

Information Marketing Services
2518 Swift Run Street

Vienna, VA 22180
(703) 560-0710

Lee Advertising Agency, Inc.
Middleburg, VA 22117
(703) 687-6343

Lewis Communications
Box 29865
Richmond, VA 23229
(804) 270-0867

The Linden Agency
1 Columbus Center
Virginia Beach, VA 23462
(804) 497-2533

MarkeTechs
115 Brand Road
Salem, VA 24156
(703) 389-2575

Media Mania Unlimited
Box 13993
Roanoke, VA 24013
(703) 985-5810

Name Exchange
7015 Old Keene Mill Road
Springfield, VA 22150
(703) 451-7814

Omega List
8330 Old Courthouse Road
Vienna, VA 22180
(703) 368-4042

Response Unlimited
505 Maple Avenue
Waynesboro, VA 22980
(703) 943-6721

Ryter Advertising
2754 Broad Bay Road
Virginia Beach, VA 23451
(804) 496-1900

Stackig, Sanderson & White
7860 Old Springhouse Road
McLean, VA 22102
(703) 734-3300

Ann Stone & Associates
108 N. Alfred Street
Alexandria, VA 22314
(703) 836-7717

Targeted Communications
6059 Arlington Boulevard
Falls Church, VA 22044
(703) 237-8533

21st Century Marketing
Box 9521
Alexandria, VA 22304
(703) 922-8843

Viguerie
7777 Leesburg Pike
Falls Church, VA 22043
(703) 356-0440

Watson & Hughey
320 King Street
Alexandria, VA 22214
(703) 549-8977

Yeaman & Associates
116 N. Third Street
Richmond, VA 2319
(804) 782-1911

WASHINGTON

Baron Communication Design
1226 Bay Street
Bellingham, WA 98225
(206) 671-8708

Jerry Buchanan Advertising
Agency
9107 NW 11th Avenue

Vancouver, WA 98668
(206) 699-4428

Business Communications
454 Court C
Tacoma, WA 98401
(206) 572-5232

Cone-Heiden
3441 Thorndyke Avenue W.
Seattle, WA 98119
(206) 282-9988

Creative Options
Box 1089
Woodinville, WA 98072
(206) 481-3638

CR Marketing
785 112th Street NE
Bellevue, WA 98009
(206) 454-2922

Bob C. Donegan Consulting
126 NE 62nd Street
Seattle, WA 98115
(206) 526-8203

Fowler Communications
1515 Metropolitan Park Building
Seattle, WA 98101
(206) 623-6663

Galen Design Associates
Box 147
Mount Vernon, WA 96273
(206) 424-1000

Management Engineering
Associates
21904 SE 42nd Street
Camas, WA 98607
(206) 834-3009

Marketry
1205 150th NE

Bellevue, WA 98007
(206) 644-4369

Pacific Communications
1801 E. Fourth
Olympia, WA 98507
(206) 754-7081

Seattle Printing & Graphics
2633 Eastlake Avenue E.
Seattle, WA 98102
(206) 382-6600

Uplifting Ideas Direct Marketing
Box 55747
Seattle, WA 98155
(206) 775-4255

Ron Wilbur Associates
1408 10th Place NE
Bellevue, WA 98007
(206) 641-8017

Z Design-Reliable Products
1118 SE Front Street
Winlock, WA 98596
(206) 785-3055

WEST VIRGINIA

Cornerstone Marketing Services
535 Lakewood Circle
Washington, WV 26181
(304) 863-6125

Lockney & Associates
1 Wildwood Drive
Parkersburg, WV 26102
(304) 863-8004

Management Dynamics
Route 1, Box 3
Burton, WV 26562
(304) 775-2928

WISCONSIN

Advertising Accounts
890 Elm Grove Road
Elm Grove, WI 53122
(414) 785-1416

Career Development Center
1515 Ball Street
Eau Claire, WI 54702
(715) 834-2771

Computer Innovations
3447 N. 47th Street
Milwaukee, WI 53216
(414) 444-8534

Engineering & Processes
12255 W. Ohio Avenue
Milwaukee, WI 53227
(414) 545-4030

Fox Hills Resort/Conference
Center
Box 129
Michicot, WI 54228
(414) 755-2376

Fuller Biety Connell, Inc.
600 E. Mason
Milwaukee, WI 53202
(414) 273-1793

Hamilton-Mueller Co.
225 E. Michigan
Milwaukee, WI 53202
(414) 272-5151

Kris Hokanson & Associates
13337 N. Lakewood
Mequon, WI 53213
(414) 258-9780

Hunter Business District
8793 N. Port Washington Road

Milwaukee, WI 53217
(414) 351-5850

Johnson Litho Graphics of
Eau Claire
2219 Galloway Street
Eau Claire, WI 54703
(715) 832-3211

K.R. & Associates
Box 17355
Glendale, WI 53217
(414) 438-0875

Madson & Madson
318 E. Deer Place
Milwaukee, WI 53207
(414) 744-9190

Marketing Group, Inc.
8909 N. Port Washington
Milwaukee, WI 53217
(414) 351-5723

McCarthy Marketing Group
867 Laura Street
Sun Prairie, WI 53590
(414) 837-8774

Patrick Murphy Advertising
Box 17421
Milwaukee, WI 53217
(414) 964-5989

Riordan Graphics
2827 N. Murray Street
Milwaukee, WI 53211
(414) 964-3937

Sunset Consulting Service
675 St. James Circle
Green Bay, WI 54301
(414) 468-14538

Thorman & Palmer Advertising
Cascade Street, Box 2

Osceola, WI 54020
(715) 294-2692

Uniplan
3907 N. Green Bay
Milwaukee, WI 53206
(414) 372-1500

Waldbillig & Besteman
6225 University Avenue
Madison, WI 53705
(608) 238-4767

White Pine
2700 Laura Lane
Middleton, WI 53562
(608) 836-4600

WYOMING

Target Direct Market
3845 Brookview
Caspar, WY 82604
(307) 237-5364

APPENDIX **B**

MAILING-LIST MANAGERS AND BROKERS

Many of the organizations listed in Appendix A offer list rental and marketing in addition to other services. The following, some of whom may have been included also in Appendix A, includes (1) many of the most prominent and/or largest organizations in mailing list management, rental, and related services; and (2) suppliers of highly specialized lists, not readily obtainable from other sources.

Advanced Management Systems
9255 Sunset Boulevard
Los Angeles, CA 90069
(213) 858-1520

American Bar Association
750 N. Lake Shore Drive
Chicago, IL 60611
(312) 988-5435

American Church Lists
1939 Stadium Oaks, No. 110
Arlington, TX 76004
(817) 261-6233

American Institute of Physics
335 E. 45th Street
New York, NY 10017
(212) 661-9404

American List Counsel
88 Orchard Road
Princeton, NJ 08540
(201) 874-4300

Ed Burnett Consultants
99 W. Sheffield Avenue
Englewood, NJ 07631
(201) 871-1100

CBS Magazines
1515 Broadway
New York, NY 10036
(212) 719-6677

Donnelley Mktg Information
Services
1351 Washington Boulevard

Stamford, CT 06902
(203) 965-5400

Dun & Bradstreet International
99 Church Street
New York, NY 10007
(212) 265-7525

Jammi Direct Marketing Services
2 Executive Drive
Fort Lee, NJ 07024
(201) 461-8868

List Services Corporation
890 Ethan Allen Highway
Ridgefield, CT 06877
(203) 438-0327

R.L. Polk & Co.
6400 Monroe Boulevard
Taylor, MI 48180
(313) 292-3200

W.S. Ponton
5149 Butler Street
Pittsburgh, PA 15201
(412) 782-2360

Qualified Lists Corporation
135 Bedford Road
Armonk, NY 10504
(914) 273-6700

Roman Managed Lists, Inc.
101 W. 31st Street
New York, NY 10001
(212) 695-3838

Standard Rate & Data Service
3004 Glenview Road
Wilmette, IL 60091
(312) 256-6067

Woodruff-Stevens & Associates
3435 Park Avenue S.
New York, NY 10016
(212) 685-4600

Alvin B. Zeller
475 Park Avenue S.
New York, NY 10016
(212) 223-0814

APPENDIX

DIRECT-MARKETING
ASSOCIATIONS

Association of Direct Marketing
Agencies
Kenyon & Eckhardt/Cinammon
Assoc.
One Boston Place
Boston, MA 02108
(617) 367-3005

Association of Independent Mail
ing Equipment Dealers
5310 Cleveland Avenue
Columbus, OH 43229
(614) 890-6211

Canadian Direct Marketing
Association
201 Consumers Road, Suite 205
Willowdale, ON M2J 4G8
Canada

Chicago Association of Direct
Marketing
221 N. LaSalle Street
Chicago, IL 60601
(312) 346-1600

Direct Mail Marketing
Association
1101 17th Street, NW, Suite 900
Washington, DC 20036
(202) 347-1222

Direct Marketing Association of
Detroit
806 Michigan Building
Detroit, MI 48226
(313) 961-9720

Direct Marketing Association of
North Texas
Box 711
Arlington, TX 76004
(817) 332-1161

Direct Marketing Association of
Orange County

Box 16473
Irvine, CA 92713
(714) 380-9100

Direct Marketing Club of St.
Louis
818 Olive Street
St. Louis, MO 63101
(314) 241-1445

Direct Marketing Association,
Inc.
6 E. 43rd Street
New York, NY 10017
(212) 689-4977

Direct Marketing Association of
Washington
655 15th Street, NW, Suite 300
Washington, DC 20005
(202) 347-6245

Direct Marketing Club of Southern California
5301 Laurel Canyon Blvd, Suite
219
North Hollywood, CA 91607

Direct Marketing Creative Guild,
Inc.
516 Fifth Avenue
New York, NY 10036
(212) 213-0320

Direct Marketing Credit Association
Prentice-Hall, Inc.
200 Old Tappan Road
Old Tappan, NJ 07675
(201) 767-5104

Direct Selling Association
1776 K Street, NW, Suite 600
Washington, DC 20006
(202) 293-5760

Florida Direct Marketing Association
Box 4550
S. Daytona, FL 32021
(904) 756-0060

Houston Direct Marketing Association
904 Hutchins
Houston, TX 77003

Hudson Valley Direct Marketing Association
220 Grace Church Street
Port Chester, NY 10573
(914) 937-5600

Kansas City Direct Marketing Association
Box 1133
Kansas City, MO 64141
(816) 931-0843

Mail Advertising Service Association International
7315 Wisconsin Avenue, Suite 440W
Bethesda, MD 20814
(301) 654-6272

Mail Advertising Service Association of New York
60 E. 42nd Street
New York, NY 10165
(212) 867-2785

Mailing List Users & Suppliers Association, Inc.
300 Bucklelew Avenue
Jamesburg, NJ 08831

Midwest Direct Marketing Association
Box 2353, Loop Station
Minneapolis, MN 55402
(612) 481-6301

National Mail Order Association
5818 Venice Boulevard
Los Angeles, CA 90019
(213) 934-7986

New England Mail Order Association
Duncraft
33 Fisherville Road
Peacock, NH 03303
(603) 224-0200

Northeast Ohio Direct Mail and Marketing Association
Statler Office Tower, Suite 303
Cleveland, OH 44115

Philadelphia Direct Marketing Association
198 Allendale Road
King of Prussia, PA 19406
(215) 337-0117

Phoenix Direct Marketing Club
Box 8756
Phoenix, AZ 85066
(602) 268-5237

Rocky Mountain Direct Marketing Association
Box 17874
Denver, CO 80217
(303) 399-0900

San Diego Direct Marketing Club
Box 1027
Solana Beach, CA 92075
(714) 268-5237

San Francisco Advertising Club
150 Post Street, Suite 325
San Francisco, CA 94108
(415) 986-3878

Seattle Direct Marketing Association
Box 85118

Seattle, WA 98145
(206) 453-8060

Southeast Direct Marketing Club
290 Interstate North, Suite 230-235
Atlanta, GA 30339
(404) 952-0220; 477-7797

Third Class Mail Association
1341 G Street, NW, Suite 500
Washington, DC 20005
(202) 347-0055

Western Fulfillment Management
Association
Box 4102
Los Angeles, CA 90028
(213) 657-5100

Women's Direct Response Group
of Chicago
2201 Bennet
Evanston, IL 60201
(312) 977-3600

INDEX